CONTROLLING COSTS: STRATEGIC ISSUES IN HEALTH CARE MANAGEMENT

T0231591

Controlling Costs: Strategic Issues in Health Care Management

Edited by
HUW T.O. DAVIES, MANOUCHE TAVAKOLI,
MO MALEK and AILEEN R. NEILSON
Department of Management, University of St Andrews,
Scotland

Routledge
Taylor & Francis Group
LONDON AND NEW YORK

First published 1999 by Ashgate Publishing

2 Park Square, Milton Park, Abingdon, Oxon OX14 4RN
711 Third Avenue, New York, NY 10017, USA

Routledge is an imprint of the Taylor & Francis Group, an informa business

First issued in paperback 2016

British Library Cataloguing in Publication Data
Controlling costs : strategic issues in health care
    management
    1.Medical care - Cost control - Congresses 2.Health
    services administration - Congresses 3.Medical economics
    Congresses 4.Medical care, Cost of - Congresses
    I.Davies, Huw T. O.
    362.1'0681

Library of Congress Catalog Card Number: 99-72983

ISBN 13: 978-0-7546-1110-3 (hbk)
ISBN 13: 978-1-138-26371-0 (pbk)

Contents

List of Figures

List of Tables

Acknowledgments

We wish to thank, first of all, participants in the Third International Conference on *Strategic Issues in Health Care Management* held at the University of St Andrews, Scotland in April 1998. Despite inclement weather, their unfailing good humour and intellectual engagement ensured a productive and enjoyable time for all. We are particularly grateful to the session chairs, manuscript reviewers and contributors for their efforts in shaping the material in this volume.

Appreciation is also due to our colleagues in the PharmacoEconomics Research Centre, Department of Management, and School of Social Sciences, at the University of St Andrews. We are likewise grateful for the excellent support provided by Reprographics, Printing, and Residential and Business Services at St Andrews. These capable and friendly people assisted in preparing conference materials and ensured the smooth running of the conference. Mehran Zabihollah, Elisabeth Brock, Andrew Falconer and Fiona Spencer-Nairn also contributed to the conference management, and we thank them for their assistance.

Ann Hargreaves, Gail Gillespie and Elizabeth Brodie deserve a special mention for their assistance with all the organizational aspects of the conference and the production of this text. Unsung but not unappreciated.

Pat FitzGerald, Anne Keirby and Kate Trew contributed great skill and considerable patience in the preparation and publication of the text, and we thank them.

Regrettably, none of the above can be held responsible for the final product: this lies solely with the editors and the contributing authors.

Finally, Huw Davies would like to express his sincere gratitude to The Commonwealth Fund of New York City who funded a sabbatical in the United States. This manuscript was finalized during that period.

Huw T.O. Davies
Manouche Tavakoli
Mo Malek
Aileen R. Neilson

Preface: Introducing the Issues

Introduction

The *Third International Conference* on *Strategic Issues in Health Care Management* took place in St Andrews in early April 1998. Delegates from over 20 countries heard almost 100 presentations on a diverse range of topics – from the big issues of national health systems reform, to the human problems of developing a patient-focused culture. The rain lashed down outside but nothing could dampen the enthusiasm of those tackling the perennial issues of managing quality and controlling costs in health services.

The result of those three days was not only new friends and expanding professional networks, but also two eclectic collections of papers on the twin themes of costs and quality. The papers in this volume, selected from over 80 original high quality submissions, reflect international effort in researching cost containment strategies and economic evaluations. Papers in a companion volume examine the progress made in managing quality, with a particular emphasis on the use of performance indicators (*Managing Quality: Strategic Issues in Health Care Management*, Ashgate, 1999).

Controlling Costs in a Changing World

Health systems around the world have seen unprecedented upheaval over the past decade. Many have been opened up to competitive forces in an attempt to cap costs. Thus cost-containment policies and the consequences of health systems reform are the theme of the opening section of the book.

First out is Alan Maynard with his usual trenchant look at the issues underlying health care reform in the UK. The thesis explored is that, notwithstanding the political spin, the latest reforms are not so much a reversal of the previous government's policies but more a gentle and none too well articulated development of them. In examining the UK reform proposals,

Maynard illustrates well the complex interconnectedness between our two key issues of quality and cost.

Maynard's paper is complemented by a full and fascinating account of the health care reform process in Turkey provided by Nesrin Çilingiroglu. Following this, Siobhan McClelland examines the patterns of service delivery in Wales in the wake of the UK NHS reforms. Her interesting results show that patterns of service delivery have remained fairly constant despite some changes in productivity. These findings are largely confirmed by Sheila Ellwood's paper on GP fund holders. Ellwood's study shows that delegating budgets has apparently had little measurable influence on the referral patterns of most fund holders. This same theme is the subject of the paper by Moira Fischbacher and Arthur Francis as they examine the extent to which GPs (family doctors) are behaving as economic and/or strategic actors within their purchasing role. This study also shows that none of the practices studied engaged in sophisticated contractual arrangements.

Within most health systems that use public money there needs to be well-established mechanisms by which funds are allocated to lower tiers. The objective of the paper by Xiao-Ming Huang et al. was to develop a needs-based resource-allocation formula which is more locally relevant and responsive than the (current UK) York formula. The authors believe that the pragmatic approach suggested goes some way to reducing biases arising from the interactions between age, general health and socioeconomic variables and they advocate its use at the local level.

The sheer range of issues raised by health sector reform is exciting but also somewhat daunting. Bart Criel et al. explore the impact of financial exclusion on health care utilization. This issue is gradually emerging in government policies around the world as they try to tackle inequalities of access and utilization in health care. Two decades of sometimes-crude reforms and a preoccupation with efficiency have brought about a backlash that needs to be addressed. This paper is a welcome contribution to that debate. The final paper in this section brings evidence from the Trent region (in the UK) for evaluating a mechanism for supporting purchasing decisions in acute specialities. Nick Payne et al. are critical of the quality of the information available to local health authorities which hampers the development of evidence based policies on new interventions. This is an appropriate point of departure from this section as we enter into the realm of economic evaluation.

Economic Evaluation and its Contribution to Controlling Costs

Since purchasers are mandated to buy cost-effective treatments for their patients, the role of economic evaluation would appear to be paramount. However, pursuit of cost-effective interventions may not necessarily lead to the adequate control of costs. Indeed, one may argue that cost-containment policies can be in conflict with the objectives of economic evaluation: during a period of technical innovation in health care, new technologies may prove to be highly expensive but nonetheless also cost-effective.

In the first paper of this section Ceri Phillips develops a framework for commissioning agencies to assess the clinical and economic impact of new preventative technologies and treatments. His examples of hip fracture and stroke prove interesting and informative. The subject of hip fracture recurs in the paper by Jan Jones and David Scott who evaluate the cost-effectiveness of alendronate for fracture prevention in postmenopausal women. The issue of cost-effectiveness of MRI in neurology is the subject of the paper by Michael Clark et al., which combines the assessment of findings from a literature review with some pertinent comments of the difficulties of assessing emergent and expensive new technologies. This theme of evaluating emergent technologies is picked up again in the next paper. Derek Cramp and colleagues use a 'systems modelling' approach to evaluate the role of telemedicine as part of new decision support systems.

The two remaining chapters in this section explore methodological issues. Elizabeth Brock and Mo Malek deal with the old dichotomy between process and outcome utility. The issues are looked at from an 'investment decision' point of view, where prevention and treatment strategies can be compared to each other taking into account valuations attached to loss of quality of life. After this, Manouche Tavakoli and colleagues explore the potential and problems in using decision analytic approaches to inform evidence-based treatment guidelines.

Looking Ahead

The final contribution by Charles Normand looks ahead at the challenges facing health care policy and management and draws on the joint themes of the two companion texts: *Managing Quality* (Ashgate, 1999) and *Controlling Costs*, discussed at the *Strategic Issues in Health Care Management* conference, St Andrews, 1998. Normand identifies a number of important questions where sharper thinking may aid progress: measuring and improving quality; public participation in health care decision-making; coping with an ageing population; using incentives; and facilitating patient choice. This chapter thus draws together a number of the themes that arise throughout the two companion texts, and provides a fitting conclusion to an eclectic collection.

Concluding Remarks

After a decade or more of international health care reform, one message more than any other is clear: there are no quick fixes. The size, complexity and diversity of the policy and managerial problems in health care will ensure that further careful study will always have the potential to bring new insight. We hope that the ideas contained in this volume (and its companion) will inform, stimulate and occasionally provoke. After that, we look forward to welcoming you to SIHCM 2000* (again in St Andrews) to assess progress on this agenda and to identify the challenges for the next millennium.

Huw T.O. Davies, Manouche Tavakoli
Mo Malek, Aileen R. Neilson
Department of Management, University of St Andrews

*   For further information on SIHCM 2000 please email SIHCM@st-and.ac.uk

SECTION 1
CONTROLLING COSTS IN A CHANGING WORLD

1 Regulating Health Care Markets

ALAN MAYNARD

York Health Policy Group, University of York

Successive governments' inclination to reform the UK National Health Service is a product of their frustration with its performance. In the 1980s the government broke an implicit contract with the medical profession whereby the latter was not questioned about clinical practice provided providers did not question funding. The prime minister, after initial flirtation with the privatization of the NHS, was persuaded that insurance promised cost inflation and continuing inefficiency. As a result she 'squeezed' public funding of the Service and demanded 'efficiency savings'.

The politics of the 1987 election involved damaging and embarrassing claims that funding parsimony led to children waiting unnecessarily for cardiac surgery. After re-election, the prime minister unilaterally, and to the surprise of her Cabinet, announced a review of the NHS. This review was conducted behind closed doors in Downing Street and resulted in the proposals for an 'internal market'. Essentially the government accepted the wisdom of tax financed, cash limited budgets and focused on supply side reform with the creation of a purchaser-provider split with contracting, 'autonomous' Trusts and innovation in primary care involving general practice fundholding and a new GP contract (Maynard and Bloor, 1996).

The Labour government elected in 1997 was pledged to abolish the 'divisive' internal market and replace competition with 'collaboration'. The thesis explored in this chapter is that these reforms are not a reversal of the Thatcher policies but a gentle and not too well articulated development of them. Thatcherism in the NHS lives although the language is 'spun' to create an image of radical change.

Controlling Costs: Strategic Issues in Health Care Management, H.T.O. Davies, M. Tavakoli, M. Malek, A. R. Neilson (eds), Ashgate Publishing Ltd, 1999.

3

The Hospital Sector

The Thatcher Inheritance

The Thatcher proposals were that hospitals would become autonomous Trusts with increased freedom to vary labour remuneration and be innovatory in 'reconfiguring' services. However, any market's behaviour is determined by the regulatory regime and the Conservative government quickly realized that a lack of regulation would be politically damaging. As a consequence, an elaborate system of controls was introduced. For instance, rather than permitting price competition which would have threatened the viability of some Trusts, prices were regulated and set equal to average cost with contracts between purchasers and providers which were not to be enforceable at law but were to be 'understandings' between the parties.

Purchasers, both health authorities and GP fundholders, were reluctant to switch contracts in part because their knowledge of process and outcome in service delivery was limited and costly to develop, and in part because such switches could threaten the viability of popular local services: Thus for many Trusts, it was not the purchasers who drove changes in service delivery (e.g. the rapid expansion of day care) but their own initiatives and central policies. However, at the margin, purchasers could and did influence service delivery, even if such changes varied enormously between localities due to the feebleness of some purchasers.

The Trusts developed their infrastructure with publicly funded capital. They were not, like their New Zealand counterparts, given access to capital markets and it was not until the last few years of the Conservative administration that the Private Finance Initiative was developed to give Trusts access to private finance. Interestingly, the Tory PFI included the possibility (never taken up) of putting clinical services out to contract if doctors agreed to it. (Labour's current version of PFI excludes such possibilities.)

Initially the private sector was very conservative in developing PFI initiatives because the costs of innovation were high due to complexity. The South Buckinghamshire PFI hospital project involved the negotiation of 147 separate contracts for financing and service provision. All contracts are defined and often set at high standards; standards which might not normally be met in the NHS. This has the advantage of potential high quality, and the disadvantage of increased cost and some inflexibility between contract periods. Thus a Trust faced by a cost crisis has to cut non-PFI services or, if fully PFI funded, it has difficulty achieving 'efficiency savings'.

The development of local pay bargaining was limited. Initially some Trusts (e.g. St James in Leeds) offered short-term local contracts but discovered, unsurprisingly, that there is a trade-off between tenure and pay levels. The reduced tenure inherent in short-term contracts led to high levels of pay. Experimentation with local pay bargaining was limited, unevaluated and apparently (as measured in abandonment of such measures) unsuccessful.

Thus, whilst the Thatcher reformers offered market potential, they delivered constrained trading freedoms to purchasers and providers and, as a consequence, limited change in the roles and practice of NHS hospitals. Many of the problems evident for decades remained; in particular variations in medical practice, lack of accountability and weak, but improving due to the Griffith reform, general management. The Tory reforms changed, to some extent, power relationships and began the process of developing accountability and it is debatable whether this was attributable primarily to managerial or market reforms, or both.

The Labour Proposals

Since the election of the Labour government in 1997, hospital Trusts continue to be able to access PFI funds, but there is increasing emphasis on publicly financed capital. However, Trust Boards have reverted to Whitley scales and national determination of wages. Due to government pressure, they now face a major 'quality' agenda.

In the White Paper there continues to be expression of concern about medical practice variations and the quality of care (Secretary of State, 1997). The government proposes to develop a system of clinical governance and make the Chief Executive of all hospitals responsible, not only for financial solvency but also for the quality of care provided.

This is a radical departure but lacks precision because of a failure to define 'quality'. Both the White Paper and the quality paper (Department of Health, 1998) use the terms 'quality' and 'excellence' generously. However, in neither paper are these terms defined in the text or in the glossary. Furthermore, the terms 'clinical effectiveness' and 'cost-effectiveness' are used interchangeably and ambiguously.

Thus in the quality paper (ibid.) clinical governance is defined as:

> a framework through which NHS organisations are accountable for continuously improving the quality of their services and safeguarding high standards of care by creating an environment in which excellence in clinical care can flourish.

This definition is particularly useless in terms of operationalizing clinical governance. Are we to require managers, clinical and non-clinical, to pursue clinical effectiveness (a form of evidence-based medicine) or cost-effectiveness (economics-based medicine)? The latter implies that the objective of the NHS is the maximization of health gains and is a major challenge to the individual ethic by which clinicians are trained and normally practise.

The development of clinical governance will require the funding of a considerable managerial and information capacity. The Thatcher government introduced clinical audit, funded it generously and allowed a degree of medical capture which ensured that it was wasteful and bored many participants. This investment 'conditioned' hospital clinicians for the task ahead, particularly that now envisaged by Labour.

The political pressure for greater accountability has been heightened by a series of medical 'scandals'. The most notorious of these involves the death of 29 children at the Bristol Royal Infirmary where the consultant has been 'struck off' the medical register for bad practice. The remarkable thing about this is not just the mortality rate, but the fact that this poor performance persisted for seven years, with GPs diverting patients out of those 'killing fields' to other Trusts, and no-one acted. Furthermore, a registrar in anaesthetics who attempted 'to blow the whistle' had his career diverted to Australia.

Hopefully, following the publicity and criticism of the profession, a culture of supportive reporting of such obviously bad practice will emerge. This should not, except in extremes, involve 'naming and shaming', but supportive collegial intervention to take inadequate practitioners out of the 'firing line' and retrain them. Where retraining is unproductive or inefficient, and job relocation (e.g. outpatients-only work) is unavailable, redundancy and retirement, without golden handshakes, will be appropriate.

Where the problem is not mortality or other grievous practice, but activity, there are nice management challenges. For instance, the number of cataract removals carried out per session (of three and half hours) per consultant ophthalmic surgeon averages about five in the NHS. Some do only three; others do nine: outcomes (e.g. complication rates) are often similar. The effect on waiting times of raising the mean from five to six, let alone seven would be considerable. But how can this be done? The challenge for managers is to control both activity and quality.

From the individual perspective of the clinician, quality is often seen as the delivery to the individual patient of those interventions which are appropriate and clinically effective. However, providing all the care which has a benefit (in terms of improving health status) has an obvious opportunity cost: treating one patient deprives another of care from which they can benefit.

A simple example illustrates the choice between clinical and cost-effectiveness criteria as the definition of quality.

a) For patients with condition A, there are two therapies:

X which produces five years of healthy life (or quality adjusted life years: 5 QALYs); and

Y which produces 10 years of healthy life (10 QALYs).

A clinician providing evidence- (clinical effectiveness-) based medicine (EBM) would select therapy Y.

b) However

if therapy X costs £300 and therapy Y costs £2,000, the average costs per QALY are £60 and £200 respectively. As therapy Y produces five more QALYs at an additional cost of £1,700, i.e. the incremental cost per QALY of therapy Y is £340,

a clinician providing economics-based medicine (where EBM is cost-effective care) would select therapy X.

Some clinicians argue that it is not their role to ration care but to provide all clinically effective care for their patient. Such an approach may be inefficient, deprive patients in the queue of care from which they can benefit more relative to cost, and is unethical.

In England, the government has decided to create new national bodies: the National Institute of Clinical Excellence (NICE) and the Commission for Health Improvement (CHImp). The role of the former is to create practice guidelines.

The role of the latter is to enforce these guidelines (CHImp is to ensure clinicians don't monkey about?). But will guidelines and enforcement be based on clinical or cost-effectiveness guidelines? If the goal is maximizing improvements in population health from a given budget, the answer must be economics-based medicine. However, the challenge of this for the doctor-patient relationship and the management of clinical practice is considerable (Maynard, 1997).

If NICE provides guidelines related to cost-effectiveness, the processes of rationing in the NHS will become more explicit. The previous Conservative government and the new Labour government deny the existence of rationing in the Service despite the fact that all practitioners in the Service practise it explicitly or implicitly every day. Rationing involves depriving a patient of care from which they can benefit and which they want (Maynard and Bloor, 1998).

Often patient access to services of proven cost-effectiveness (e.g. orthopaedic procedures and cataract removal) involves waits in the NHS. A more rational Service might redistribute resources from services of dubious efficiency (e.g. some cancer interventions) towards proven, cost-effective interventions. There are two major obstacles to the more efficient allocation of resources: the knowledge base and the management of the labour force, in particular clinicians.

Despite the creation of the Cochrane Collaboration and the systematic review of the evidence base, the enormity of the review task and the gross deficiencies in the knowledge base mean that there is no evidence, in terms of clinical and cost-effectiveness, for many interventions used routinely in the NHS and health care systems worldwide. The social culture of trust and delegation of responsibility to the profession to establish practice standards and monitor performance has been carried out carelessly.

Much of the investment in trials of technologies (probably 90 per cent of the total) is controlled by the producers of drugs and equipment. The regulatory requirements (e.g. the 1968 Medicines Act) require, for pharmaceuticals, the demonstration of safety, efficacy and quality. The trials which are carried out meet the minimal requirements of this legislation but fail to inform purchasers about relative effectiveness and cost-effectiveness.

Thus drug trials may demonstrate efficacy (i.e. the product affects patient health in the carefully controlled circumstances of a clinical trial) but do not inform users of their effectiveness (i.e. the product's effects in general use) or cost-effectiveness. One challenge for the Labour government is their developing NICE to produce guidelines based on cost-effectiveness and requiring manufacturers to inform NHS reimbursement decisions with trial and modelling data about the cost-effectiveness of their products (Maynard and Bloor, 1997).

With or without this requirement the challenge is to ensure that research and development investments, both public and private, are based on good science and appropriate practice. At present much of this scarce resource is wasted in bad trial design and poor reporting of results which may corrupt the evidence base (Freemantle and Maynard, 1994).

Even if R and D is better focused and more productive in terms of improving the evidence base and NICE begins the long, slow and expensive process of producing guidelines, will clinical practice change?

The remarkable independence of the medical profession has provided substantial advantages, in particular the continuation of usually good medical services in the face of continuous 'redisorganizations' of the NHS. However the costs of leaving the clinical 'black box' unopened and unexplored is now evident: the profession has not met adequately the standards expected by society. Crises in the efficiency of services (e.g. cervical screening and the Bristol case, where 29 young children died as a result of deficient cardiac surgery), unaccounted for variations in medical practice, and a refusal to be more open and accountable, have eroded trust, leading to often naïve press campaigns and political rhetoric advocating 'naming and shaming'.

These problems are accentuated by ancient processes of accreditation and perverse incentives. For instance, hospital consultants in service areas providing elective care (orthopaedics, general surgery, anaesthesia and ophthalmic surgery) have part-time NHS contracts and lucrative private practices which can double their modest public salaries (of about £60,000 per annum). Such incentive structures lead at the margins to abuse (neglect of publicly funded work) and the creation of NHS waiting lists to ensure a 'nice' volume of private work.

Whilst the Royal Colleges manage entry into clinical specialisms, indeed NHS consultant status is dependent on membership of the appropriate College, there is no policing of practice over the life cycle. This contrasts with other trades, e.g. airline pilots are tested every six months to ensure physical and mental health as well as technical competency. The Colleges encourage education over the 30 year career of the consultant but only in 1998 did a College finally announce its intention to review and reaccredit surgical practitioners. The other specialisms are yet to follow this example but the government is pressing hard for the development of reaccreditation by, for instance, encouraging the national regulator, the General Medical Council, to implement a system.

In addition to clinical governance and better use of clinical staff, which are logical developments of the Tory 'internal market' reform, the Labour government has retained much of what went before. Contracts have been translated into long-term agreements which, as Dawson and Goddard (1998) note, will be expensive and may produce benefits best pursued by other means. A national list of 'reference prices' for procedures has been published by the

NHS Executive. These show enormous variations in prices of procedures: but prices and real resource costs are very different measures. The benefits of managerial investigation of these differences is not readily apparent.

Overall, the Labour reforms of the NHS hospital are a mixture of the well-intentioned, the half-baked and the poorly conceived and articulated. The intent is clear and admirable: improving the efficiency of the NHS. However the element of 'overkill' is evident (i.e. everyone is required to do everything very quickly) and the costs and risks of this are considerable for government, providers and patients.

Primary Care

The Thatcher Inheritance

The Thatcher reforms were, in relation to primary care, incomplete and disjointed. General practice fundholding was introduced into the 1989 proposals as an afterthought rather than as a fundamental part of reforms which were primarily focused on hospital care. Separately the government addressed the deficiencies of the GP contract, radically reforming it in a way which was not thoroughly evidence-based.

The idea of giving service budgets to general practitioners so that they financed their own services and purchased care from others for their patients, was articulated and discussed by academics in the 1980s (e.g. Maynard, Marinker and Gray, 1986; Maynard, 1987; Bevan, Holland, Maynard and Mays, 1988). Whilst these academics had advocated the notion of GP budgets, now known as fundholding, they had emphasized the need to pilot and evaluate.

This emphasis was ignored by the politicians who implemented it rapidly by generous initial funding of practitioners prepared to volunteer for this radically innovatory policy. From 1991 general practice fundholding was developed quickly so that by 1997 over 50 per cent of the population were included. Given its voluntary basis, those who joined (and those who refused to join) were often atypical. The evaluation of the reform was poor and demonstrated that initial effects (e.g. reduced prescribing costs) were not sustained (Maynard and Bloor, 1996).

The government developed fundholding from initially limited secondary care budgets to all inclusive budgets in what was called total fundholding. Evaluation of this was again limited, being largely descriptive (LeGrand, Mays and Mulligan, 1998).

The purpose of fundholding was to provide incentives for GP purchasers to be economical in their use of secondary care services. This policy did not address the problem of efficiency of primary care services themselves. There was well chronicled evidence of practice variations in primary care in the 1980s and a recognition that the service was largely a 'black box' which was poorly chronicled in terms of costs and effectiveness. In part this deficiency was a product of the absence of a representative national data base and the problem that much performance measurement in this sector had to be focused on process and activity rather than patient outcome.

The Thatcher government response to these problems was the 1990 GP contract. This retained the independent contract (self-employed) status of GPs and addressed the perceived deficiency of general practice, of low activity rates, by introducing a larger element of fee per item of service into remuneration. As a result of graduate payments (graduated according to the extent of the relevant patient covered) vaccination, immunization and cervical cytology rates increased considerably. However some parts of the new contract were less effective: e.g. GP payments for minor surgery ('lumps and bumps') were introduced to reduce hospital activity, but there has been little effect on minor surgery in hospitals and increasing rates in general practice.

Thus the Conservatives introduced radical and fragmented policies in primary care which were poorly evaluated. Just prior to losing office, and with Labour support, they passed legislation to facilitate alteration in the GP contract enabling practitioners to be employees.

The Labour Proposals

Labour will replace GP fundholding, described by them as 'divisive', with Primary Care Groups (PCGs) from April 1999. PCGs are compulsory and a form of general practice fundholding. Groups of GPs covering approximately 100,000 are being compulsorily 'herded' into organization which will 'grow' over time from being advisory to Health Authorities (purchasers) to being independent Trusts which purchase all health care for their locality.

The medical profession's response to these plans and the compulsion involved was to endeavour to 'capture' them. Their success has been considerable as government has agreed to there being a GP chair and up to seven (out of 12) GP members. However the radical changes introduced into the new Labour system of budgets owned and managed by GPs have been that primary care budgets will, for the first time in 50 years, be cash limited and allocated on the basis of weighted capitation.

The hospital budget has been allocated on the basis of population weighted by 'need' for over 20 years. However the inequalities in the funding of primary care between and within localities have been ignored although they are considerable e.g. the south and west are well endowed (15 per cent above average) whilst inner cities and the north of England are relatively poorly funded. The timing and nature of this redistribution together with cash limits is a radical and novel challenge for the new PCG managers.

A large element of the expenditure of GPs is pharmaceuticals. The initial focus of the National Institute of Clinical Excellence (NICE) may be the production of guidelines, based hopefully on the cost-effectiveness criterion, for the use of drugs. If such guidelines are produced, how will they be managed?

One of the most detailed and unexploited databases in the NHS is that produced by the Pharmaceutical Pricing Authority (PPA). Every prescription written by a GP and dispensed by a pharmacist goes to the PPA, who reimburse the chemists for their work. What is needed is the addition of a patient identifier to each scrip, together with a diagnostic code box. Then, provided PPA was given adequate computing capacity, it would be possible to manage GP prescribing in great detail, e.g. compare actual prescribing with guidelines. These data would also provide detailed epidemiological data down to the level of postcode.

The reluctance of graduates to enter primary care has created a 'shortage' of practitioners. As ever, the word 'shortage' has to be used with caution as pay increases might increase both participation rates and retention in general practice. Also the scope for nurse-doctor substitution appears to be considerable: perhaps, with vigorous nurse substitution, GPs could manage 3,000 patients rather than the current list 'optimum' of 1,800. However, careful management of substitution is essential if cost-inflating service development is to be avoided (Richardson, Maynard, Callum and Kindig, 1998). The reluctance of the Labour government to explore these issues systematically has led to their deciding to increase the entry into medical school by 20 per cent (to 6,000 students) in the next five years. This is a very expensive choice.

The focus of the Labour government's policy, like that of the Conservatives, tends to be their development of fundholding with PCG purchasers. There continues to be inadequate focus on the efficiency of primary care *per se*. Whether cash limits and weighted capitation together with clinical governance can mitigate manifest inefficiencies in primary care, improvements will be complex to implement. Furthermore, it is likely that such changes will be costly. As Aneurin Bevan argued, doctors only understand messages written on a cheque (Klein and Maynard, 1998)!

Equity

Throughout the preceding discussion it has been assumed that the purpose of the Conservative and Labour reform plans has been to improve the efficiency of resource allocation. Is this the only policy objective? Resource allocation in the NHS exhibits clear cases of deliberately inefficient practice. For instance, society apparently wishes to treat many low birth weight babies inefficiently, i.e. it makes an equity choice to give up efficiency (and the health gains it produces) in order to facilitate the survival of the young.

Williams (1997) has articulated this argument more fully in terms of the 'fair innings'. He argues that the elderly, who have had a 'fair innings', might be denied efficient treatment in order to fund the inefficient treatment of the young, who may be chronically ill, who have not had a fair innings. Thus the notion of equity here is the equalization of opportunities for health over the life cycle: once born we should be given a 'fair innings'. The pursuit of such goals may have considerable opportunity costs and need careful evaluation and public discussion.

Pursuit of greater equity in health may best be pursued by investments in income redistribution, housing and education rather than in health care. The government places considerable emphasis on equity but has failed to articulate and cost appropriate policies. The Acheson report (Independent Inquiry into Inequalities in Health, 1998) is extraordinarily vague with 136 unprioritized and uncosted recommendations and represents a lost opportunity in terms of 'hooking' government to well devised policies to reduce ever widening inequalities in health.

Overview

Whilst the 'spin' placed on the Labour government's health care reform is formidable and seeks to present its policies as a radical departure from the Thatcher-Major policies, they are, in large part, a continuation and a logical development of what was begun in the last decade. Perhaps the most remarkable similarity is the cost of change. The Tories increased NHS spending considerably in the early 1990s to facilitate the sometimes wasteful development of their reforms. The Labour government has announced considerable funding increases following the Comprehensive Spending Review: the budget in England will rise by £8 billion over three years (not the £21 billion produced by double and triple counting for the media). Hopefully these funds will be used to improve the quantity and quality of patient care and not dissipated on ineffectual political 'wheezes' designed to produce transient headlines rather than significant service development (Maynard and Sheldon, 1997). As ever with the NHS, hope springs eternal that its manifest problems will be tackled systematically and in relation to the evidence base rather than in relation to what medical and other experts dream up in Whitehall village in order to create electoral support.

References

Bevan, G., Holland, W., Maynard, A. and Mays, N. (1998), 'Reforming UK Health Care to Improve Health', University of York Occasional Papers, Centre for Health Economics, University of York.

Bloor, K. and Maynard, A. (1997), 'Regulating the Pharmaceutical Industry', *British Medical Journal*, 315 (reply: *British Medical Journal*, 1998, 228).

Dawson, D. and Goddard, M. (1998), *Longer Term Agreements for Health Care Services: What will they achieve?*, University of York Occasional Papers, Centre for Health Economics, University of York.

Department of Health (1988), *A First Class Service*, London.

Freemantle, N. and Maynard, A. (1994), 'Something Rotten in the State of Clinical and Economic Evaluations' (editorial), *Health Economics*, 3, pp. 63–7.

Independent Inquiry into Inequalities in Health, chairman Sir Donald Acheson (1998), HMSO, London.

Klein, R. and Maynard, A. (1998), 'On the Way to Calvary', *British Medical Journal*, 7150, p. 5.

LeGrand, J., Mays, N. and Mulligan, J-A. (eds) (1998), *Learning from the NHS Internal Market: A review of the evidence*, King's Fund, London.

Maynard, A. (1987), 'Incentives for Cost-effective Physician Eehaviour', *Health Policy*, 7 (2), pp. 189–204.

Maynard, A. (1997), 'Evidence-based Medicine: An incomplete method for informing treatment choices', *Lancet*, 349, pp. 126–8.

Maynard, A. and Bloor, K. (1996), 'Introducing a Market to the United Kingdom National Health Service', *New England Journal of Medicine*, 334, 9, pp. 604–8.

Maynard, A. and Bloor, K. (1998), *Our Certain Fate: Rationing in health care*, Office of Health Economics, London.

Maynard, A. and Sheldon, T. (1997), 'Time to Turn the Tide', *Health Service Journal*, 25 September, pp. 24–8.

Maynard, A., Marinker, M. and Gray, D.P. (1986), 'Alternative Contracts: Are they viable?', *British Medical Journal*, 292, pp. 1438–40.

Richardson, G., Maynard, A., Cullum, N. and Kindig, D. (1998), 'Skill-mix Changes: Substitution or service development?', *Health Policy*, 45, pp. 119–32.

Secretary of State for Health (1997), *The New NHS: Modern, dependable*, Cmd 3807, HMSO.

Williams, A. (1997), 'Intergenerational Equity: An exploration of the 'fair innings' argument', *Health Economics*, Vol. 6, pp. 117–32.

2   The Need for Change: Health Reforms in Turkey

NESRIN E. ÇILINGIROGLU
Department of Public Health, School of Medicine, Hacettepe University, Ankara

Why Health Reforms are on the Agenda

In every country, the overriding goal of health policy, in its broadest sense, is to protect and improve the health status of the population. But despite the consensus on its importance, there are factors that can impede moves toward this objective. These factors are cost and efficiency in resource allocation and the politics of health care reform, as well as health systems themselves (WHO, 1993).

Although they have broadly similar objectives, health systems across countries diverge in terms of funding sources and allocation mechanisms, provider payment systems, service delivery mode, regulations, and the roles of the public and private sectors. In addition, the relative strength of the participants – consumers, different types of providers, insurers, or others – varies across countries and may influence how health care systems are structured.

The Current Health System in Turkey

Turkey's population was 64.3 million in 1997 with considerable geographical variations in standard of living: east and southeast regions are especially deprived compared to other parts of the country. The demographic profile is relatively young compared to other European countries: 31.2 per cent of the population aged under 15 and only 5.0 per cent aged 65 and over in 1997. The projections for 2025 are 22.9 per cent and 9.0 per cent respectively, showing

Controlling Costs: Strategic Issues in Health Care Management, H.T.O. Davies, M. Tavakoli, M. Malek, A. R. Neilson (eds), Ashgate Publishing Ltd, 1999.

an ageing population that will require different types of health services (Table 2.1).

Table 2.1   Some demographic, socioeconomic and health-related data in Turkey

Variable	Value
Total population – 1997 (millions)	64.3
Urban population – 1995 (%)	60.9
Rate of natural increase – 1997 (%)	1.7
Crude birth rate·– 1997 (%0)	21.6
Crude death rate – 1997 (%0)	6.6
Life expectancy at birth – 1997 (years)	68.4
Total fertility rate – 1997 (number of children)	2.48
Contraceptive use for currently married women:	
modern – 1993 (%)	34.5
traditional – 1993 (%)	28.1
Infant mortality rate – 1997 (%0)	40.0
Maternal mortality rate – 1995 (%000) (estimated)	100
Under-5 mortality – 1993 (%0)	60.9
12–23 months fully immunized – 1995 (%)	69.6
Adult literacy ratio – 1994 (%)	81.6
Per capita income – 1997 ($)	3,010
Real GDP per capita – 1995 (PPP $)	5,411
Human development index – 1994 (HDI) value	0.772
Health expenditure/GNP – 1996 (%)	5.0
Per capita physician contact rate – 1992	2.44

Sources: SIS, 1995; TTB, 1997.

The main features of the current health system can be summarized as (Çilingiroglu, 1995):

a) *organization*: the health care services in Turkey are provided mainly by the Ministry of Health (MoH), the Social Insurance Organisation (SSK), independent university hospitals, the Ministry of Defense (MoD), and private bodies such as physicians, dentists, pharmacists, nurses and other health care professionals. Other public and private hospitals also provide services, but their total capacity is low. The autonomy of the agencies that provide health care makes it difficult to ensure effective coordination and

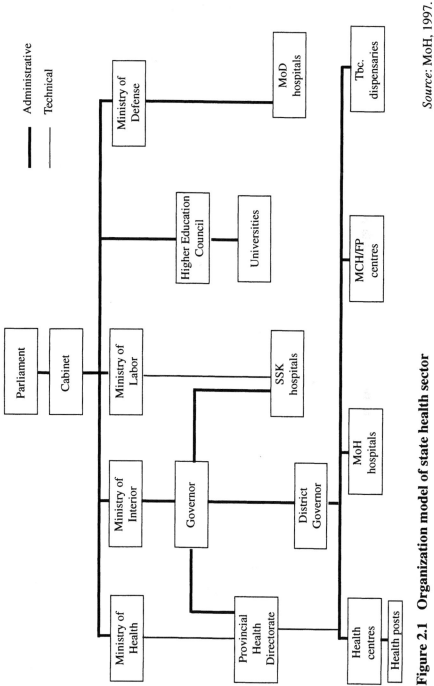

Figure 2.1 Organization model of state health sector

Source: MoH, 1997.

delivery of services (Figure 2.1). The MoH is the major provider of primary and secondary health care and the sole provider of preventive health services. At the central level, the MoH is responsible for the country's health policy and health services. At the provincial level, provincial health directorates accountable to the provincial governors administer health services provided by the MoH;

b) *planning, regulation and management*: parliament is the ultimate legislative body and regulates the health care sector. The two main bodies responsible for planning the services are the State Planning Organisation (SPO) and the MoH. The role of SPO is to define the macro policies regularly in 'Five Year Development Plans'. The MoH develops operational plans and implements the defined policies with an integrated model and provides primary, secondary and tertiary care (Table 2.2);

Table 2.2   Provision and financing of health services

Provision of Services	Sources of Funds
Public	*State budget through*
Ministry of Health	Ministry of Health
Social Insurance Organization	Higher Education Council – universities
University hospitals	Ministry of Defense
Municipalities	Other Public Sector Sources
State economic enterprises	
Ministry of Defense	*Compulsory Insurance*
Other Ministries	Social Insurance Organization
	Bag-Kur
	Government Employees Retirement Fund
Private	
Private hospitals	
Private physicians	*Private insurance funds*
Private pharmacists	
Private laboratories	*Out-of pocket payments (user charges)*
Philanthropic	

Source: Price Waterhouse, 1990.

c) *delivery*: since the law on Socialisation of Health Services was enacted in 1961, the government has been committed to a programme of nationwide provision of public health services with the main objectives of providing primary health care in rural areas and developing both preventive and curative services (Table 2.2);

d) *finance and expenditure*: the financing of health care is quite complex (Figure 2.2 and Tables 2.3–5) because of the large number of agencies involved in providing or financing health care services or both.

Table 2.3   Health expenditures in Turkey and OECD countries

Year	Public expenditures on health				Total expenditures on health					
	(million $) Turkey OECD		(%) of GDP Turkey OECD		(million $) Turkey OECD		(%) of GDP Turkey OECD		Value/Capita $ Turkey OECD	
1989	2,087.3	33,796.5	2.0	5.5	3,596.4	60,138.9	3.4	7.7	66.5	1,346.3
1991	3,644.4	43,363.6	2.4	6.0	5,796.0	74,857.4	3.8	8.2	97.8	1,690.5
1993	5,049.0	48,832.8	2.7	6.0	7,136.8	84,924.9	4.0	8.4	130.1	1,705.1

Source: OECD, 1995.

Table 2.4   Aggregate sources of funding for health services and expenditure in Turkey, 1993–95 (million $)

Sources of funds	1993	%	1994	%	1995	%
State budget	3,394	47.6	2,347	46.9	3,469	54.1
Insurance funds	1,472	20.6	1,159	23.1	1,168	18.2
User charges	2,271	31.8	1,503	30.0	1,770	27.6
Total	7,137	100.0	5,010	100.0	6,407	100.0

Source: PCU, 1997.

Table 2.5   Ministry of Health funding sources in Turkey, 1990–95 (%)

Fund sources	Years 1991	1993	1995	Average
State budget	83.0	84.0	70.0	80.0
Revolving funds	12.0	12.0	23.0	15.0
Special funds	5.0	4.0	3.0	5.0
Total	100.0	100.0	100.0	100.0

Source: PCU, 1997.

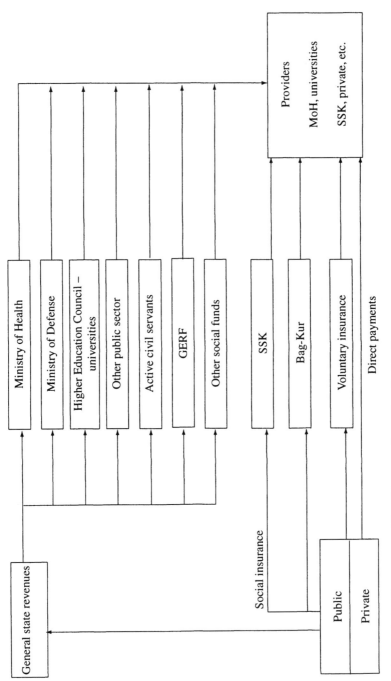

Figure 2.2   Structure of health care financing in Turkey

Source: PCU, 1997.

Rationale for Health Reforms in Turkey

Health services world wide are already major consumers of scarce national resources. In Turkey, total health care expenditure rose from 2.3 per cent of GNP in 1960s to 5.0 per cent in 1995, with 102.5 US$ per capita (PCU, 1997). In contrast, the MoH share of expenditure on health care has remained relatively constant at around 0.95 per cent of GNP in 1995 (MoH, 1997). However, demographic changes, more expensive disease patterns, changes in expectations of the people and, technological innovation and development are increasing pressure on health care resources.

Currently, Turkey cannot afford to satisfy all of the medical needs of its citizens, and, like other countries, is facing an increasing demand for limited resources. The government has demanded efficiency increases and value for money in the provision of health care services by the public sector, while the private sector has tried to achieve similar goals. The shortage of funds, instabilities in the quality of services and standards of the medical profession, low capacity utilization of resources despite their short supply and low efficiency, provided the main reasons for the rationale of health reform activities in Turkey.

On the other hand, the health indicators in Turkey are not satisfactory, given its level of socioeconomic development. The most common causes of mortality and morbidity are preventable and controllable especially for those less than five years old. Also, the demographic trend in Turkey implies the need for change in service planning and provision. The socialization of health services emphasized the rural services, as 70 per cent of population were rural in 1961, but currently the population is rapidly ageing and urbanizing. There are problems related to equity in the current health care system. Although all MoH services delivered in its institutions are subsidized to 60 per cent of the actual costs, only insured people are entitled to free access at the point of use. Equity problems occur in the utilization of health services, as well. For example, people living in urban settlements of western Turkey utilize health services more frequently compared with people living in rural areas in the eastern Turkey. Other problems with the current system can be summarized as follows.

Policy Development Problems

- There are no long-term, consistent, and stable health policies. Many institutions are involved with health policy.

- Insufficient support for policy development.
- There is a lack of qualified personnel for policy development.

Problems in the Delivery of Services

- Primary health care has not been sufficiently emphasized and this has made health services hospital-centred.
- The provision of care is inefficient owing to the lack of an effective referral system. As there is not enough incentive to use primary care, patients usually apply to the crowded outpatient clinics at hospitals, although almost 90 per cent of their problems could be solved at the primary level.
- The hospitals are managed and used inefficiently. In particular, the utilization of hospital beds is too low.
- Hospital management is very centralized, led by physicians, and there is a shortage of professional managers.
- Difficulty in access to hospital services in terms of geographic distance and service quality.

Problems in Financing

- The resources allocated to the health services are low compared with other countries. Total health care expenditure rose from 2.3 per cent of GNP in 1960s to 5.0 per cent in 1995, with 102.5 US$ per capita.
- Almost half of health expenditures are generated from out-of-pocket payments and are disbursed for services from private practice and for drugs.
- There is no adequate allocation for, or emphasis on, preventive and health promotion services.
- In the public sector, service providing and financing duties are usually provided within the same body, with no incentive for efficient and effective use of resources.
- A system based on subsidized services does not comply with social justice, and results with public subsidy to high income groups.
- As only 65 per cent of the population are covered by a social insurance scheme, there is unequal access to health services.

Problems in Human Resources

- There is no rational human resources plan based on epidemiological and demographic conditions and the utilization of services.

- The geographical distribution of health personnel is unbalanced.
- The functional mix of health personnel according to their specialty field is inappropriate.
- The basic training of health personnel does not meet the requirements of the health services, and the continuous training is inadequate and irregular.
- Health professionals have various occupational problems regarding the issues of employment, remuneration, and benefits. There is no incentive to improve performance.
- The legislation that defines the jobs and responsibilities of health care occupations is outdated and some existing occupations are not included.
- Specialist physicians have better status than general practitioners.

Management Problems

- The management of health services is very centralized.
- The central MoH organization is quite complicated and organized vertically, with some units responsible for certain types of services, some responsible for serving specific population groups, and some dealing with specific diseases. This results in coordination problems even among the divisions of the central MoH.
- The organizational structure at the local level does not comply with the administrative structure at the central level.
- There are few qualified managers and these are inappropriately recruited.
- Health management and decision making are not based on information.

Problems in Registration

- The current health legislation is quite old, reflecting the late 1920s and early 1930s.
- There are conflicts and duplications among the existing laws.
- Some of the laws are too detailed to keep pace with the changing needs.

Problems Related to Health Information

- There is a lack of information concerning health and health services, including epidemiological data and data on services and costs.
- There is no feedback system to control the data.
- The reliability, regularity, consistency and accuracy of the data are doubtful.

- Many of the data collected are not transformed into useable information. In some cases, different departments of MoH are collecting the same type of data, but they are not collated.

In view of these observations, awareness of the strong need for improvement in the health sector has pushed the government to look for alternative models. Therefore, the Ministry of Health started a comprehensive health reform project in 1990 in Turkey. This new reform process has been initiated in conformity with the country's and world's changing conditions and as an effort to improve the health status of the Turkish population. The project initiation was originally started as the 'Health Sector Master Plan Study' in 1989, but, throughout the process, it has evolved into the 'Turkish Health Reform Program'. The aim of the health reform is to make health care available to all citizens of Turkey in an efficient and equitable manner. The reform package was prepared by a group of multidisciplinary experts with backgrounds from health and non-health sectors. The initial implementation activities have already been initiated, and following the promulgation of the necessary legislation, the pilot implementation stage will be started. The MoH has undertaken many research projects, studies and workshops in the course of designing national health policies as well as health insurance, health enterprises and family practitioners system, which were expected to become fully operational by the year 2001.

The Proposed Health Reform Model

For the implementation of comprehensive reforms in the health system, there is a need for a long-term, consistent and stable inter-sectoral national health policy that will not be influenced by different government policies. The proposed health care reform adopts a problem-oriented approach, with the aim of improving health status and access to basic health services and reducing inequality. The objectives of reform in Turkey are to:

- improve the health status by covering the whole population under the social health insurance scheme;
- provide equity in health services and, efficiency in service provision;
- emphasize preventive services, health promotion and primary care;
- separate service purchaser and provider;
- establish competition between service providers;

- use appropriate technology;
- strengthen multi-sectoral cooperation for health services;
- collect effective, timely and accurate information to improve information-based decision-making;
- use appropriate human resources according to skill, duration, number and combination;
- delegate decision-making authority to the individual service units.

The reform programme consists of the following main headings: health financing reform; hospital and health enterprises' reform; family physician and primary care reform; health information systems; organization and management reform; and human resources reform.

Since the implementation of reforms requires changes in legislation, three major draft laws were prepared by the MoH Health Project Co-ordination Unit, with contributions from all interested parties and have been submitted to the parliament recently.

Characteristics of the Proposed Health Financing Reform in Turkey

The main problems related to present Turkish health care financing were summarized at the previous paragraphs. In Turkey, approximately 35 per cent of population are not entitled to formal social health security currently even though it is a constitutional right. The proposed health care financial model aims at providing social health security for this group of population as the first step. Therefore, the Health Financing Institution (HFI) will be established to cover the necessary finance and costs and expenses in order to ensure the health care services of those uninsured.

On the other hand, the financing of the health care services will be separated from the service provision. This separation is expected to promote efficiency in utilization of funds spent for health through cost consciousness and control of expenses from the insurance point of view, and promote quality by introducing competition in service provision. The HFI model will be based on the principles of social insurance. Membership will be compulsory to all Turkish citizens who are not covered by any scheme and the insured persons will pay premiums in order to benefit from the health services in the basic benefits stated by the draft law. The entire cost of health insurance benefits will be met by the premium income calculated on actuarial basis. However, the amount of premium to be paid by the insured persons liable to pay under this draft law will be determined according to the net aggregate monthly income of insured persons liable to pay and their dependants. The premium shares of insured persons unable to pay fully or partially will be subsidized by the transfers from the general state budget. Therefore, the state will be subsidizing needy individuals rather than the service. In addition, every insured person will benefit from the health benefit included in the *basic benefits package (BBP)* equally towards their health needs, regardless of the premium paid.

The ratio of gross state subvention to aggregate premium collection of HFI is estimated to be 49.6 per cent (Deeble, 1996). The additional financial burden will be undertaken by the state after the deduction of general state budget transfers for 'green card' implementation and personnel expenditures (the green card issued to poor Turkish citizens who lack the capacity to pay for health services, and their declared revenues are checked in detail). Public hospitals planned to be turned into '*autonomous health enterprises*'. The health expenditure realized according to the Social Assistance and Solidarity Encouragement Law will be approximately 10 per cent of the aggregate amount of premium collected by HFI. In attaining to the social objectives defined herein, HFI, attached to the MoH, autonomous in terms of finance and administration, will;

- make calculations relating to the amount of annual actuarial premium;
- prepare the content of the BBP to be submitted to MoH for approval;
- utilize the financial resources effectively;
- make contracts with provincial Health Directorates, private health insurance companies, other institutions and establishments and/or with service providers where deemed necessary in order to provide the benefits included in the BBP.

The *private health insurance companies* under contract will undertake important roles during the implementation of HFI model, such as providing the benefits within the scope of this law to insured persons registered by their party through the contracts realized with service providers. Additionally, they will be able to present their supplementary benefits packages to these individuals. Through cooperation between HFI and private insurance companies, the cost of health care services provided to insured persons and the insurance risk arising from the HFI scheme will be shared. Therefore, the efforts for minimizing the costs accordingly the actuarial premium will be exerted in the most rational manner, cooperatively. Moreover, common health insurance under public supervision will enhance the private insurance sector by improving insurance consciousness. The operation of the proposed model is presented as a flowchart in Figure 2.3.

In the transition period to the HFI, the 'green card' implementation has been started as a step toward ensuring equity in the distribution of state subsidies to needy citizens for health services The major problem in implementation arises during the determination of people's income levels. Various researches and examinations are expected to solve this and the results have been reflected to the proposed model and draft legislation.

In order to put forward the possible theoretical deficiencies of the model and take the necessary measures, pilot implementations will be conducted in four provinces. The spread of the scheme throughout the country will take six years after this process. The design of the HFI model has been revised during the last two years. The HFI is currently being analysed under a broader social insurance reform package.

After the realization of the initial aim of providing health insurance to 21.4 million people who were previously uncovered, the second phase will be the rationalization of the overall pension systems through separating health and pension plans of the existing social security schemes. Finally, in the third phase, transition to general health insurance through bringing social health plans under a single umbrella. At the beginning, HFI scheme will operate separately from the existing insurance schemes; the design will permit harmonization and integration of health insurance schemes in the long term in accordance with the implementation strategy stated above. But it should be noted that premium collection is going to be the major issue. Therefore, creating public consciousness through advocacy is an important issue, as are sustaining political stability of MoH, solving bureaucratic problems and sustaining political will of the parliamentarians.

As countries continue to experience pressure to contain costs and improve efficiency, they increasingly search for a 'middle way' to reform their health care systems – to combine the best aspects of market incentives with those of administrative hierarchies. All basic health care systems have weaknesses, whether the totally integrated system, in which insurers employ the physicians and own the hospitals or the non-integrated system, in which insurers reimburse independent health care providers at 'arm's length'. As a result, neither market systems nor administered systems can work perfectly. Countries searching for a 'middle way'– a change toward contract-based health systems that combine planning, regulation and markets – have given their efforts names such as managed competition, internal markets, planned markets and public competition (Jönsson, 1994; Mills and Gilson, 1988).

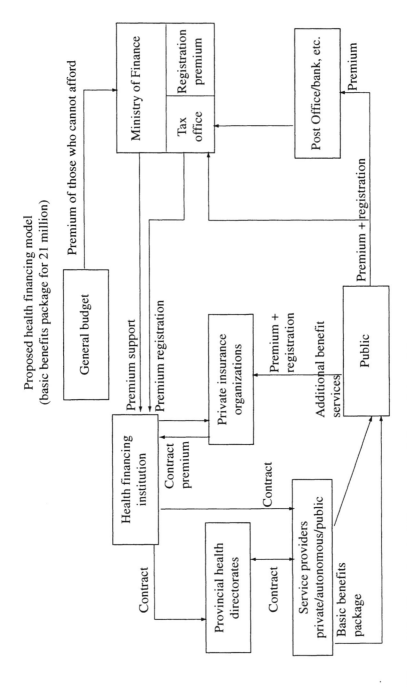

Figure 2.3 Flow chart of the proposed financial model

Source: PCU, 1997.

Clearly, Turkey's health care reforms will be the product of our social, cultural, political and economic environment. Health care reform is not an end in itself but rather a means to an end, although it is generally agreed that reforming the health care system is necessary according to the contemporary conditions. Therefore, the expected effects of the Turkish health care reform should be taken into account in the following way:

- *macroeconomic efficiency* (management of health care costs so that they do not exceed an acceptable share of national resources). This issue is very important in Turkey, due to the very limited resources with competing goals in the development process. And as it is known, 'more' does not always mean, 'better'. However, it seems as if general tax revenue will be the main source for public finance. But low tax ratios, high inflation and skewed income distribution can be a handicap for managing the health care costs. On the other hand, the health sector does not exist in isolation and it will be exposed to the effects of the other sectors, as well as the whole system. Therefore, without making the necessary arrangements, especially in the whole public system, the expected effects of the health reform could be undermined;

- *microeconomic efficiency* (identification and utilization of that mix of services that achieves desired objectives and the production and delivery of the optimal mix of appropriate services at least cost). This issue is also very important in Turkey, since private provision with public financing is quite common and many transactions rely more on administrative procedures than on competitive purchasing of services;

- *equity* (access to an appropriate minimum level of care and limitations on payments for health care that threatens income adequacy). Most of the developing countries like Turkey are in a special situation since they suffer wide discrepancies in terms of socioeconomic, health level and geographical status. For instance, in Turkey, 35 per cent of the population has no formal health insurance, and it is estimated that approximately 10–14 per cent of the total population lives under the subsistence level. Therefore, practice can temper the theory in policy-making and the realities both of scarce resources and of unequal distribution (of income and ill health) must be recognized. On the other hand, at a lower level, the allocation of services is likely to be left largely in the hands of health professionals. There will persist some non-price impediments to access that make complete equality hard to achieve;

- *choice* (greater discretion for consumers and appropriate autonomy for providers). Although this issue is strongly emphasized in the reform package, financial measures are not clear enough. Demand for health care is mixed but suggests that, especially for low income groups, demand is elastic with respect to price, falling as price increases and resulting in significant shifts in the use of alternative providers. Even though the premiums will totally subsidize low-income groups, availability and accessibility of the services will be more important than the monetary cost. Also, there is a risk in terms of favouring curative expenditures with the new reforms.

It is important to recognize that financing problems are not simply health sector problems, but often reflect economy-wide difficulties. As a result, the staff dealing with the health care reforms in general, and reform in the finance system in particular, must answer the following questions.

- What kind of factors explain success or failure in improving health system performance, while containing total expenditure in a country like Turkey with dual structure?
- With respect to total cost, 'how much is enough' and how is it decided?
- Are explicit priorities becoming a key feature of reform in health financing? If so, how are such priorities determined? Do the results of this approach differ from rationing services by other means?
- Can internal markets (competition) effectively integrate the quality and price concerns of society?
- While satisfactory payment systems may come in many forms, should they include both budget caps (i.e., global budgets, hospital budgets, capitation fees) and incentives for better performance at lower cost? Is it possible to identify an optimal reimbursement system?
- Does the whole system have enough capacity to tolerate the radical path of total redesign of system financing and delivery? (There is a risk of facing difficulties in obtaining approval for such dramatic changes.)
- How are trade-offs between efficacy of medical interventions and financing constraints determined? How can the quality of care be protected or enhanced?
- What progress has been achieved in measuring outcomes and, in particular, will there be advances in methods to assess medical technology?
- Finally, what successful innovations in the Turkish health system reform merit special consideration for adoption in other countries?

Countries should recognize that a wide variety of policy instruments is available to improve the financing and organization of health systems, each of which is likely to have some good and some bad consequences (WHO, 1993). The government's role in policy-making regulation and information gathering and dissemination is now more critical than ever. The government is also essential for preventive services. Such functions will not be fulfilled without the active participation of the government; in the enthusiasm for new market-oriented arrangements it is important not to lose sight of these core roles.[1]

Note

1   The author would like to thank to Dr. Haluk Özsarı, Vice-Under Secretary and the Director of Project Coordination Unit of the Ministry of Health, Turkey.

References

Çilingiroglu, N. (1995), 'Health Economics' in M. Bertan and Ç. Güler (eds), *Basic Principles of Public Health*, Güneş Kitabevi, Ankara (in Turkish).

Deeble, J. (1996), 'Health Financing Policy Options Study', *Journal of Treasury*, Special Issue, August, pp. 75–84.

Health Project Co-ordination Unit (1997), *Health Sector Reforms in Turkey*, Ministry of Health, Barok Matbaacilik, Ankara.

Jönsson, B. (1994), 'Making sense of health care reform', paper presented at the High Level Conference on Health Care Reform, DEELSA/ELSA/HR(94)8, OECD, November, Paris.

Mills, A. and Gilson, L. (1988), *Health Economics for Developing Countries*, EPC Publication No. 17, London.

Ministry of Health (1997), *Country Health Report*, Health Project General Coordination Unit, Ankara.

Organization of Economic Cooperation and Development (1995), *Health Data*, OECD, Paris.

Price Waterhouse (1990), *Health Sector Master Plan Study*, Price Waterhouse/Ankon, State Planning Organization, Ankara.

State Institute of Statistics (1996), *Statistical Yearbook of Turkey*, Prime Ministry Publication, Ankara.

Turkish Medical Association (1997), *Health Statistics of Turkey*, Ankara (in Turkish).

World Health Organization (1993), 'Evaluation of Recent Changes in the Financing of Health Services', report of a WHO Study Group, *WHO Technical Report Series*, 829, World Health Organization, Geneva, Switzerland.

3 Changing Patterns of Service Delivery in NHS Wales

SIOBHAN E. McCLELLAND
School of Health Science, University of Wales Swansea

Introduction

The reports of the death of the internal market in the UK may be exaggerated with the evolutionary approach towards integrated care proposed within the new White Papers (DoH 1997; NHS Wales). Nonetheless, the time is ripe to explore the impact of the market, even in its highly managed form, on the ways in which services have been delivered. Moreover, this aids an understanding of the factors which shape both decision-making and change within the National Health Service, shedding light not only on market mechanisms but on the factors which shape changing patterns of service delivery within the NHS. This chapter explores how and why patterns of service delivery have changed, using the principality of Wales as a case study, and focuses particularly on the role of Health Authorities as the potential strategic drivers for change.

The introduction of the internal market within the NHS in the UK, together with market-based reforms in other countries, constitute familiar territory. The introduction of a purchaser/provider split was intended to emulate the workings of the market, with Health Authorities (HAs) and GP fundholders acting as purchasers of care responsible for assessing health needs of their populations and NHS Trusts (together with a small contribution from the private and not for profit sector) providing community, secondary and a limited range of primary health care services (Walsh, 1995).

The objectives of the introduction of the internal market were both explicit, as outlined both in *Working for Patients* (DoH, 1989) and the subsequent National Health Service and Community Care Act (1990), and implicit. Along

Controlling Costs: Strategic Issues in Health Care Management, H.T.O. Davies, M. Tavakoli, M. Malek, A. R. Neilson (eds), Ashgate Publishing Ltd, 1999.

with reforms in health care in other countries, the changes in the UK sought to:

* contain costs;
* raise standards;
* increase efficiency (Ham, 1997).

As the changes to the NHS were implemented, it also became clear that the internal market was perceived as a mechanism by which patterns of service delivery could be changed and the role of Health Authorities as purchasers of care gained greater emphasis (Mawhinney and Nichol, 1993).

The NHS in Wales

Whilst health care in the United Kingdom is considered primarily to form part of what is termed a National Health Service, many studies focus on the English part of the NHS. Somewhat different structural and policy making arrangements exist in the other parts of the United Kingdom, that is Northern Ireland, Scotland and Wales. Whilst Wales is often perceived to form an adjunct of the English health service it retains its own policy making body in the Welsh Office, with its own Secretary of State responsible to parliament (Levitt and Wall, 1992). Devolution through the Welsh Assembly seems likely to alter further the balance of policy making power (Welsh Office, 1997; NHS Wales, 1998).

In contrast to England, Wales did not have a regional tier, with the responsibilities of Regional Health Authorities (RHAs) being taken by both the Welsh Office and the District Health Authorities (DHAs), which meant that DHAs in Wales, prior to the reforms, exercised a wider range of powers than their English counterparts. Whilst RHAs waned within England in the period following the 1990 legislation, the enhanced role of Welsh DHAs might have facilitated a slightly speedier move to purchaser status than English DHAs. However, in both countries the role of DHAs as decision-makers has been hampered by an early lack of clarity regarding the purchasing or commissioning role and both concurrent and subsequent major organizational upheaval from the early days of shedding responsibilities for directly managed units to mergers into unified Health Authorities, comprising both DHAs and Family Health Services Authorities (FHSAs) over larger geographical areas. The role of Health Authorities has also been further complicated by the presence of another purchaser of health care – the GP fundholder.

The Study

This study explores the role of Welsh DHAs in changing patterns of service delivery within the National Health Service. Specifically it poses the following two questions: how far have patterns of service delivery changed? What factors have shaped and driven change (or continuity)?

Until April 1996 Wales had nine DHAs, subsequently reorganized into five Health Authorities, including the DHAs and the Family Health Service Authorities. The study primarily focuses on a detailed documentary analysis of the purchasing plans, intentions and other reports produced by the Health Authorities from 1992 to 1997. The analysis of the documents, both published and unpublished, is supplemented by interviews with key stakeholders within the NHS in Wales.

The study seeks to establish general themes in relation to the two key objectives which emerged both across the Welsh Health Authorities and over time. It is intended that these themes should provide some understanding of the general drivers of policy formulation that emerged across Wales over the period since the introduction of the internal market. The study focuses on the role of the Health Authorities alone, given their scope for strategic change, and given the relatively slow and limited development of GP fundholding within the principality.

There are significant and perhaps unexpected difficulties in establishing answers to the first question – how far have patterns of service delivery changed? Much of this must be attributed to a lack of detailed data regarding resource allocation and volume levels particularly across specialties. Although the contract, the mechanism which brought both purchaser and provider together, might be expected to assist in this analysis, an examination of the contracts produced across Wales failed to elicit any more specialized data, and this is supported by more detailed studies (Jost et al., 1995).

However, whilst it is difficult to provide more detailed information, particularly at the micro level, the study does suggest that, broadly, patterns of service delivery have remained constant since the introduction of the internal market. This suggests that patterns of care remain very similar to those prior to the reforms and in particular that this is likely to replicate a model of care predominantly located in the acute hospital sector. However, important themes emerge which in part explain this continuity of service patterns and the relevance of market mechanisms.

The role of the internal market in driving change receives little attention in either the documents or the interviews. What does emerge strongly is the impact of central policy directives primarily generated by the Welsh Office. Whilst to some extent this reflects a requirement to publicly be seen to be committed to these directives there is no doubt that some, in particular the Patient's Charter, have substantive impact on the way in which services are delivered.

Health Gain

In the early years of the reforms the notion of health gain as articulated by the *Strategic Intent and Direction (SID) for Wales* plays an important role in at least shaping the language of Health Authorities. Sloganized as: 'to improve the health of the people of Wales to take them into the 21st Century with a level of health to compare with the best in Europe' (Welsh Health Planning Forum, 1989) with the *Health of the Nation* (DoH, 1992) following in its path.

However, there is limited evidence to suggest that SID significantly changed anything other than the language of health care delivery in Wales. It certainly offers a method for justifying developments, and, to a lesser extent, disinvestments, but whether this is still the same developmental wolf in the new sheep's clothing of health gain is open for debate. In part this may be attributed to the development of SID prior to the 1990 NHS/Community Care Act together with other changes including the 1990 GP contract, the Patient's Charter and the reorganization of the Health Authorities. This is identified and further analysed by the National Audit Office Report (1996) which concluded that whilst SID did create a climate conducive to change its impact on service delivery has so far been marginal.

The role of SID in shaping the language of future developments is taken in the later years by the new mantra of clinical effectiveness symbolically renamed 'clinical excellence' by the new government (DoH, 1997). However, if clinical effectiveness is to permeate the NHS further than linguistically, then attention needs to be paid to the example of SID and those factors which will facilitate change, if indeed the rational world of clinical effectiveness can ever in fact be achieved. Secretaries of States' priorities, as articulated through the two *Caring for the Future* documents, also play a part in shaping the policy language of Health Authorities. However, more specific policy documents appear to play a particular role in shaping services including documents on palliative care, mental health, mental handicap, elderly care and continuing care.

Most notable in its influence is the Calman/Hine Cancer Report, which has tangible recommendations and results, for example, in one Health Authority's developing specialist cancer units in each of its three district general hospitals. It is interesting to speculate why this report would have such influence and explanations may lie in the convergence of its message with the identification of cancer as an area of investment within SID and governmental prioritization, together with clear targets and attached funding, a model with some parallels in other studies (Bennett, 1994).

The Patient's Charter

Of greatest significance in influencing patterns of care lies another directive which may be seen to have its roots in consumerist notions of health care (Powell, 1997) – the Patient's Charter (DoH, 1991). The significance of the Charter grows over the course of the study both in changes in volume of care and in precluding other developments. This is clearly an area shaped by national requirements and nationally-formulated performance targets which become increasingly stringent and complex.

In 1992 the 'Waiting Times Initiative' emerges, through which specific waiting times are calculated in respect of the DHA's overall position. By 1995 the requirements of the Patient's Charter are general across all Health Authorities, and in 1996 the move towards total waiting times, whereby the combined out- and inpatient/day case waiting time will be no more than 12 months for all specialities as part of 'National and Local Charter Standards', continues to consume much of the attention and resources of the Health Authorities.

The achievement of waiting times is clearly a core priority for Health Authorities and, moreover, there are clearly stated resource implications in reaching waiting time targets. Specifically, the achievement of the targets requires Health Authorities to invest both recurring and non-recurring monies. Much reference is made to the important role of non-recurring monies provided centrally from the Welsh Office to achieve the targets. Inevitably this effects the development of other services, with some Health Authorities clearly stating that, as a result of allocation of resources to achieve the targets, a lack of development funds are available for other work. As one newly-configured HA states: 'Achieving Patient's Charter standards will be a major demand upon the financial resources of the new authority'.

The achievement of Patient's Charter targets also requires increases in productivity and this may occur within a resource-neutral context. However, it is contentious whether total waiting times and their achievement are congruent with the more symbolic intentions of health gain. In a bold statement in 1992 one Health Authority clarifies the dilemma:

> if the service is to be responsive to the public's demands then we must direct resources to reducing waiting lists and hence waiting times. However, it must be appreciated that this is not necessarily the same as meeting health gain targets and health needs.

Doing Things Differently – Alternative Methods of Service Delivery

One area in which some changes in service delivery can be established lies within the methods by which services are provided although it must be recognized that primarily this is a reprovision of services. A number of mechanisms for alternative provision of service emerged across the Health Authorities.

Day cases: the need to undertake more day case work, both to replace and as an addition to inpatient work, emerges across the HAs over the years and can clearly be linked back to centrally derived and administered productivity targets, which require that day cases form a specific percentage of inpatient and day case work as identified in the performance document *Agenda for Action*. For some HAs, the growth in day case work is explicitly linked to developments in minimally invasive surgery.

Locally-based services: the provision of more locally-based diagnostic and outpatient services represents a shift in methods of provision primarily linked to issues of accessibility, with one Health Authority clearly stating that 10 per cent of all outpatient consultations will take place outside the main DGH sites.

Open access: in part, perhaps as a response to the requirements of GP fundholders, attention is paid to the provision of a greater number of open access services, including physiotherapy, pathology, radiology and less often endoscopy, dietetics, chiropody and occupational therapy.

The development of the latter two areas is linked to another important shibboleth – the need to move towards primary care services or, as one HA terms it, the need to acquire a 'primary care perspective'. Again there is little evidence to support a view that this is translated into reality in terms of cost and volume, but it plays another important symbolic role and one which is enhanced by the new White Papers.

Alternative ways of providing services also provided one of the few examples of the role of the market in changing service patterns. In a managed market in which the contract is, at least in theory, the key mechanism by which purchasers can affect change, there is relatively little discussion of termination of contracts or of moving contracts from provider to provider, which indicates that the notion of a 'steady state' continues beyond central government requirements, although it is officially resurrected when the new five health authorities are created in 1996. Over the period under study, two Health Authorities shifted relatively small contracts primarily in order to repatriate work and provide services more locally. The specialty of rheumatology does emerge, however, across a number of Health Authorities as having been subjected to the limited workings of the market, with contracts being removed from Trusts, in one case as the result of a market testing exercise.

Changing Volumes and Cost Containment

Another area in which some changes can be observed is in volume, although from the outset it must be stated that this tends to be 'more of the same', with additional volume in the same areas of service. This is clearly linked to the requirements of the Patient's Charter, the pressures of rising emergency admissions and the requirements to make continuing improvements in productivity.

Most HAs across the majority of years studied demonstrated an increase in productivity using the familiar, although often not helpful, currency of in patients/day cases, new outpatients and total outpatients. There is little indication of case mix, although one HA states that 'historical case mix levels will be maintained'.

The financial constraints facing the Health Authorities emerge as an unsurprisingly dominant theme across all the HAs and consistently over time, although there is some evidence of cumulative financial pressures resulting from what one interviewee termed the 'pressure cooker' of the NHS. This is caused by the combination of emergency admissions, waiting times targets and requirements to achieve year-on-year cost improvement and efficiency savings (King's Fund, 1997). Thus the traditional ways in which the NHS could 'let off steam', for example by increasing waiting lists or closing facilities, become less and less available.

A number of Health Authorities clearly stated that there is little additional funding for developments, with funding predominantly committed to existing services, and that any further monies will need to be released from efficiency savings. Where development monies are released or generated, these form a relatively small proportion of the HAs overall budget and in any one year do not exceed £2 million.

Welsh Office guidance on the development of strategic plans states that they should be 'revenue neutral'. Therefore the only significant recurring funding available for new investment has to be generated by reducing the costs of existing services. This is combined with the requirement to achieve cost efficiency savings and productivity gains from providers through the contracting process, including hypothecated amounts for savings from management. These targets are again centrally derived and administered by the Welsh Office, although the Health Authorities may act primarily as the conduit for passing these pressures onto providers. In one year targets are set for reducing management, administration and clerical costs (5 per cent); to reach efficiency targets (3 per cent); cash-releasing cost improvement programmes (1.8 per cent) and productivity improvement (3.2 per cent). Whilst these figures are taken from one year, the year-on year-pressure to make these savings leads one Health Authority to state in its purchasing plan: 'The Authority recognises that a continuing requirement for Cost Improvement Programmes is not sustainable in the medium to longer term'.

The pressures on Health Authorities, and subsequently on providers, are further exacerbated by the increase in emergency admissions, an area which has received much attention (Jones, 1997). The rise in emergency admissions impacts both on the ability to achieve Patient's Charter targets and on the financial and service flexibility of the Health Authorities.

Disinvestments and Developments

Whilst it can be seen that the bulk of service delivery remains constant, with existing patterns replicated, there are some examples of developments and disinvestments in services, primarily operating on the margins of service delivery, although occupying a disproportionate amount of attention from the Health Authorities and perhaps also, as in the case of disinvestments, from commentators.

There is some agreement across Health Authorities in identifying a range of services which will no longer be routinely provided. The usual suspects include tattoo removal, sterilization reversal, gender reassignment, liposuction, aesthetic facial surgery, pinnaplasty, cosmetic mastopexy, cosmetic breast augmentation, cosmetic rhinoplasty, blepharoplasty, removal of varicose veins, for cosmetic reasons and abdominoplectomy.

The purpose, presumably, of identifying disinvestments is to free up monies to be invested elsewhere. For the majority of HAs, however, the monies to be released are not made explicit nor, indeed, is information regarding the volume of these services. It is difficult to establish, therefore, how many of these procedures were undertaken in previous years and how much they cost, which may lead to conclusions that decisions regarding disinvestment in these areas owe more to making a statement than actually achieving any savings. However, the area of rationing or prioritizing seems set to be one of the major challenges of the next few years (Ham, 1997). Gradually, however, the emphasis in disinvestment has moved to those services not considered clinically effective. It is interesting to note the high levels of convergence in a number of the themes under discussion amongst HAs and the relatively limited role of local considerations. Areas for investigation under this possibly new language for rationing included ENT operations performed on children, including glue ear and grommets, tonsillectomy and myringotomy, assisted reproduction, varicose veins, renal dialysis, prostrate operations for benign conditions and D&Cs for women under the age of 40.

The area of service developments where new forms of service delivery emerge also occurred primarily on the margins. As has been seen, a significant shift in patterns of service delivery has not occurred, for example into primary or community care, with resources remaining committed to historic patterns of service delivery. The majority of developments proposed and achieved by the HAs are minor in terms of revenue allocation. Revenue-based developments offer one of the few examples of highly localized changes. However, they can loosely be grouped around client groups and health gain areas derived from SID and include:

Health promotion – whilst the theme of health promotion is common amongst HAs, the actual developments differ in their detail from one to another, although not surprisingly an emphasis on reducing smoking appears common. The resource implications are again more difficult to draw out; although a number of programmes are costed and quantified and represent a relatively small part of the HA resources, nevertheless it is hard to establish the base line of existing services. Tellingly, one HA makes an attempt to identify a proportion of its budget for health promotion purposes and thus hypothecates 0.6 per cent of its revenue allocation.

Cardiovascular disease – including diagnostic and rehabilitation services.

Cancers – with an emphasis on the Calman/Hine Report.

Oral health – including the need to 'develop an effective response to the crisis in dental services'.

Maternal and child welfare – with some convergence on the development of genetic counselling services and 'integrated children's services'.

Pain, discomfort and disability – including the development of assessment and rehabilitation centres together with pain relief clinics and services.

Mental health – linked to All Wales Strategy and the provision of care in the community. A number of Health Authorities also emphasize the development of medium secure provision.

Conclusions

The findings of the study indicate that, whilst there is some evidence to indicate a change in productivity, patterns of service delivery have remained fairly constant, with change occurring primarily on the margins of delivery and resource allocation. Market mechanisms appear to have had a very limited impact on shaping policy decisions, with centrally-derived directives playing a very much more significant role. The triple pressures of the Patient's Charter, a rise in emergency admissions and the ever-increasing requirement to meet cost improvement and cost efficiency targets have further constrained changing services. Whilst this study focuses on Wales, the findings accord with views on changes within the NHS where the language of the market is matched by increasing central control over key policy objectives (Ham, 1997). It is interesting to speculate whether the announcement of £21b for the UK Health Service over the next three years (Butler, 1998) will impact on patterns of service delivery, although the current and continued emphasis on waiting lists seems likely to reinforce the status quo. It is important, therefore, to draw on the experience of the 1990s, which offers important lessons if the new vision of a primary care led NHS providing services based on the principles of clinical excellence is to be anything more than symbolic.[1]

Note

1   I would like to acknowledge the help of Professor Peter Spurgeon, Health Services Management Centre, University of Birmingham.

References

Bennett, C. and Ferlie, E. (1994), *Managing Crisis and Change in Health Care*, Open University Press, Buckingham.

Butler, P. (1998), 'Reality Cheque', *The Health Service Journal*, Vol. 108, No. 5614, pp. 10–11.

Department of Health (1989), *Working for Patients*, HMSO, London.

Department of Health (1990), *The National Health Service and Community Care Act*, HMSO, London.

Department of Health (1991), *The Patient's Charter*, HMSO, London.

Department of Health (1997), *The New NHS: Modern, Dependable*, HMSO, London.

Ham, C. (1997), 'Foreign Policies', *The Health Service Journal*, Vol. 107, No. 5555, pp. 24–7.

Jones, R. (1997), 'Admissions of Difficulty', *The Health Service Journal*, Vol. 107, No. 5546, pp. 28–31.

Jost, T., Hughes, D., McHale, J. and Griffiths, L. (1995), 'The British Health Care Reforms, the American Health Care Revolution and Purchaser/Provider Contracts', *Journal of Health Politics, Policy and Law*, Vol. 20, No. 4, pp. 885–908.

King's Fund Institute (1997), *Health Care UK 1996/97*, King's Fund Publishing, London.

Levitt, R. and Wall, A. (1992), *The Reorganised National Health Service*, Chapman and Hall, London.

National Audit Office (1996), *Improving Health in Wales*, HMSO, London.

NHS Wales (1998), *NHS Wales Putting Patients First*, HMSO, London.

Mawhinney, B. and Nichol, D. (1993), *Purchasing for Health*, NHSME.

Walsh, K. (1995), *Public Services and Market Mechanisms*, Macmillan, London.

Welsh Health Planning Forum (1989), *Strategic Intent and Direction for Wales*, HMSO, London.

Welsh Office (1997), *A Voice for Wales*, HMSO, London.

4 GP Fundholder Admissions and the New NHS

SHEILA ELLWOOD

Aston Business School, Aston University

In the NHS White Paper, *The New NHS*, the government proposes replacing the GP fundholding scheme with Primary Care Groups (Department of Health, 1997). A recently completed research project (Ellwood, 1997) sponsored by the Chartered Institute of Management Accountants examined how GP fundholders have used their delegated budgets to purchase hospital care for their patients in the NHS internal market. The main findings of this study are set out below and the implications for 'the new NHS' examined.

The GP Fundholding Scheme and the Research Design

GP fundholding, introduced in April 1991 by the NHS and Community Care Act 1990, was a fundamental part of the Conservative government's NHS internal market.

> The Government believes that this reform [GP fundholding] will deliver better care for patients, shorter waiting times, and better value for money (*Working for Patients*, 1989, paragraph 6.2).

By April 1996, nearly one in three (almost 3,000) practices was fundholding; 41 per cent of patients in England and Wales were registered with a fundholding practice; and, fundholders spent up to 14 per cent of hospital and community health service spending (Audit Commission, 1995). The research project provides a longitudinal study of the effect of GP fundholding on NHS and private admissions from 35 GPFHs in the West Midlands. GP practices are relatively small organizations and have the potential to respond

Controlling Costs: Strategic Issues in Health Care Management, H.T.O. Davies, M. Tavakoli, M. Malek, A. R. Neilson (eds), Ashgate Publishing Ltd, 1999.

rapidly to market signals such as price and waiting time. If GP fundholding was to achieve its prescribed aim of value for money, then, given the wide variation in referral patterns apparent before the introduction of the market, it could be expected that:

- admissions for planned operation/procedures would fall once initial backlogs for treatment had been removed;
- patients would be referred to alternative providers (NHS or private sector) which offered better value for money with possibly increased distance travelled;
- GPFHs would balance price with other service information (waiting times, service quality, etc.) in order to achieve better service provision for their patients.

GPFH reports of hospital admissions were matched with regional data on published prices and waiting time. For each GPFH in the study, the admissions for GPFH planned operations/procedures by provider (hospital), published price, distance and waiting time were held in the research database. The estimated spend on admissions for GPFH operations or procedures in West Midlands NHS hospitals by the 35 GPFHs over the fundholding years to 31 March 1995 was £43m covering over 70,000 operations or procedures. Changes in referral patterns were identified and the consequences in relation to distance, price and waiting time to be examined. In order to both validate the data and identify the reasons for the perceived changes, interviews were undertaken. The lead GP in each fundholding practice (and frequently the fundholding manager) was provided with an analysis of the practice's admissions and interviewed regarding the reasons for any identified changes or lack of change following the introduction of fundholding. The impact of service quality on the referral decision was also discussed. Thirty-two lead GPs were interviewed, two fundholding managers were interviewed in the absence of the lead GP. One GPFH did not take part in the interview stage. Thirty-three lead GPs ranked the relative importance of price, location, waiting time and service quality on referral decisions.

It was not possible to compare fundholding with non-fundholding GPs because similar information was not available at practice level for non-fundholding GPs and hospital information by GP was poor. As the Audit Commission (1996) points out, such comparisons would anyway be flawed as fundholding was initially restricted to comparatively large practices which opted to become part of the scheme, they are self-selected and have more of the features associated with high standards and better quality. It has been argued that in the first two years of fundholding, only the most well-organized, larger practices in affluent areas were eligible to take advantage of the generous development money on offer (King's Fund Institute, 1989; Glennerster et al., 1992; Ham, 1993). The GP practices in the study range in size of patient list from 7,600 to 19,000.

Previous Research on GP Fundholding

There have been several studies of a largely qualitative nature documenting the process of setting up fundholding and the perceptions of GPs involved concerning the effects it has had on the service (Table 4.1). Duckworth et al. (1992) claim the aim for such studies is 'to capture the experience through the eyes of the participants'. These qualitative studies have covered first wave fundholders in the West Midlands; three regions of southeast England (Corney, 1994); SE Thames region (Glynn et al., 1992) and the northern region (Newton et al., 1993). More recently, Llewellyn and Grant (1996) reported on six case studies within Grampian, Lothian and Tayside, and Glennerster et al. (1996) have examined the experiences of fundholding and non-fundholding GP practices in the areas of four health commissions. Individual fundholders have frequently published their reflections on the experience (Bain, 1991 and 1992; Wisely 1993). However, in the main, such studies do not provide information on whether GPs' perceptions matched reality. There are individual reflections from non-fundholding GPs to counter the main claims of GPFHs, e.g. Eve and Hodgkin (1991).

One study tested specific hypotheses regarding outpatient referral behaviour (Coulter and Bradlow, 1993). The study compared 10 first wave fundholding practices in the Oxford region with seven controls (non-fundholders). The hypotheses were: fundholders would be less restricted than non-fundholders to refer outside district boundaries; referrals from fundholders would decline; and referrals from privately insured individuals would increase. The evidence ran contrary to all three hypothesis, but the study only looked at the first year of fundholding when NHS policy adopted by the Oxford region was to maintain 'a steady state'. The findings do, however, illustrate some discrepancy between GP perceptions and reality. It is therefore important to base GP research on quantitative data as well as on qualitative data.

There have been no longitudinal studies following specific GPFHs through the fundholding years and, prior to the Audit Commission's dissemination of its survey work in 1995 and 1996, no large scale studies of GP fundholding.

Table 4.1   Research on GP fundholding

Researchers	Region	Study period	No. of fundholders	No. of non-fundholders	Data collected
Duckworth, Day and Klein, 1992	West Midlands	1st wave, Nov. '91–Jan. '92	All 26 in region	0	Qualitative experience of fundholders and interviews with related managers
Glennerster et al., 1992	3 regions in SE England	Prelim. year from Jan. 1990, 1st wave onwards	10	0	Mainly qualitative, fundholders and some related managers
Glynn et al., 1992	SE Thames (Kent FHSA)	During 1st fundholding year	8 first wave or prospective second wave		Questionnaire and interviews Largely qualitative data
Corney, 1994	SE Thames	1st wave	All 15 in region	0	Qualitative; fundholders
Newton et al., 1993	Northern	1st wave, March–July 1992	10 of 28 in region	0	Qualitative perceptions; GPs and practice managers
Coulter and Bradlow, 1993	Oxford	Prelim year (Oct. '90), 1st wave April 1991 onwards	10	7	Qualitative and quantitative on referral and prescribing rates, facilities. Also practice managers
Howie et al., 1992, 1993	Grampian, Tayside	'Pre-shadow', 'shadow', real funds	6	6	Qualitative and quantitative; GPs, practice managers, consultants and patients
Llewellyn and Grant, 1996	Grampian, Lothian, Tayside	The 1995 contracting round	6	3 not disseminated	Qualitative perceptions; GPs and practice managers
Glennerster et al., 1996	2 regions in SE England		8	8 plus 16 involved in non-FH purchasing schemes	Qualitative perceptions of GPs and managers
Audit Commission, 1995, 1996	All England and Wales	National questionnaire survey of fund and practice managers with 65% to 79% response rates from GPFH waves 1–4. Analysis of financial returns (preliminary results and audited accounts). Survey by auditors during audit of 1993/94 accounts			

The Referral Decision

GPFHs have the freedom to consider not only whether to refer, but to whom at which hospital. Prior to the introduction of fundholding, wide variations in referral rates to hospital existed (Wilkin and Dornan, 1990; Roland, 1988; Crombie and Fleming, 1988). Stewart and Donaldson (1991) showed that, for minor day case surgery at least, distance of travel is not a critical factor for patients or GPs in determining where to refer and that waiting time is the most important factor. However, this view is contradicted by Mahon et al. (1994), who, in a study of 449 GPs, found that the influences on the referral decision for planned surgery in 1991 were in order of importance: proximity and convenience; knowledge of the consultant; the general standard of clinical care; the patient's own preferences; and previous attendance at the hospital. Twenty-seven per cent of GPs did not mention waiting times as being influential. This research study examines how GPs *have* changed their referral patterns since they became fundholders and sets the discussion of the referral decision in that context. Even though referral choices may always have been available before the NHS internal market (though arguably not available to non-fundholding GPs in the market), the introduction of the market makes such choices explicit and backed-up by the power to commit funds. GP fundholding introduces price as a new factor in the referral decision and increasing patient awareness and consumerism in health care may have heightened regard for waiting times and service quality.

Earlier studies of NHS pricing, e.g. Ellwood (1996a), had shown that price signals had generally failed to encourage efficient operation of the NHS market. Two impediments cited by Ellwood were the inadequate definition of services (i.e. the lack of homogeneous product groupings) making reliable price comparisons difficult and the noncompetitive nature of the NHS market with few buyers and sellers. The market for planned operations from GPFH budgets, however, did not suffer from these two impediments: the planned operations had been closely defined on a standard basis for pricing purposes since the inception of the market and there were often several purchasers (GPFHs) and sellers (NHS trusts, health authority managed hospitals and private hospitals) of planned operations.

The Influence of GP Fundholding on Activity Levels and Referral Patterns

Increased Activity

Concerns that GPFHs would cut services in order to make savings appear unfounded. The database showed large increases in the number of admissions for planned operations and procedures since the introduction of fundholding. The first wave fundholders had a 35 per cent increase in activity in 1994/95 compared with 1991/92 (the first year of fundholding); second wave fundholders had a 14 per cent increase in activity in 1994/95 compared with 1992/93. The increases above the reference period for budget setting were even more dramatic, but it was generally accepted that the activity data prior to fundholding was severely deficient. Despite the large increase in activity, the increase in estimated spend on planned operations or procedures is 18 per cent and 3 per cent for first and second wave fundholders respectively. Use of day case provision increased markedly: this is not a direct consequence of GP fundholding, but many GP fundholders used the 'leverage' of GP fundholding to encourage use of day case surgery. GPFHs were able to buy activity more cheaply as the proportion of day cases increased. The comparatively low increase in spend in relation to activity could also be due to falling prices and/ or a change in case mix, i.e. buying proportionately more of the cheaper procedures (see below). The changes in the volume of activity, percentage of day case provision and total financial value are shown for the 16 first wave fundholders in Figure 4.1.

Over 100 different operations or procedures were included in the GP fundholding scheme, but only 16 accounted for either 2 per cent of activity or spend. Endoscopy (a keyhole investigation) accounted for 13 per cent of activity, but consumed less than 6 per cent of spend, whilst arthroplasty (replacement hips, knees etc.) accounted for less than 3 per cent of activity but consumed over 14 per cent of spend. The database enabled changes in referrals for individual procedures to be analysed. Although the picture is generally one of increasing activity and greater use of day case provision, trends vary by individual procedure.

The number of investigative procedures increased rapidly (for example, endoscopies increased by 52 per cent over the four years) while changing clinical practice has reduced activity in some areas, for example, the number of tonsillectomies had fallen since 1993/94.

The estimated spend on some procedures had declined despite increasing

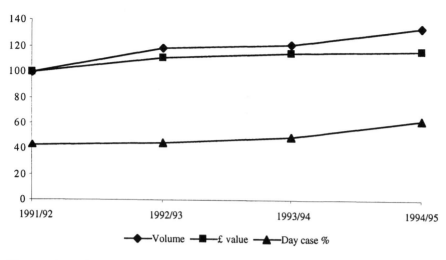

Figure 4.1   Changes in the volume of activity (admissions); day case % and financial value

activity. For example, cataract surgery purchased through contracts with NHS hospitals increased during the fundholding years (41 per cent between 1991/ 92 and 1994/95), but spending on cataract surgery did not increase proportionately due in part to a large shift to day case surgery. Discerning the specific effects of fundholding is particularly difficult, but the data shows, on the whole, large increases in activity following fundholding and no indication of reductions in activity on individual procedures due to fundholding.

Distance Travelled for NHS Admissions

Stewart and Donaldson (1991) found that, for minor day case surgery at least, distance of travel is not a crucial factor for patients or GPs in determining where to refer. However in this study the vast majority of patients were treated a short distance from their GP practice, Table 4.2. Ten out of 35 fundholders sent 98 per cent or more of their patients to the nearest hospital. If GPFHs are unwilling to increase the distance travelled by their patients, many providers may be in a monopoly position. Studies of the existence of hospital monopoly power in the West Midlands suggest that between a quarter to a third of hospitals are in a monopoly position for general surgery (Appleby et al., 1994; Robinson, 1991).

The average distance travelled by patients of fundholding doctors has not increased markedly since the introduction of fundholding. GPFHs have

Table 4.2   NHS admissions within 15 km of the GPFH practice

% of NHS admissions within 15km	Number of GPFHs
95% and above	14
85–94%	10
0–84%	8
No hospital within 15 km	3

continued to send the vast majority of their patients to the local hospital. However, there were a small number of noticeable shifts particularly where GPFHs had alternative hospitals within a short distance. Greater change is also apparent when examining admissions for specific procedures. Patients were more likely to be referred to more distant hospitals for investigative procedures such as endoscopies and where long NHS waits are common, e.g. cataract operations and replacement hip operations. In the interviews with the lead GPs it was found that attitudes to travel appeared to depend on patients' age and social class in addition to the proximity of health care providers.

Private Health Care

Although few shifts between NHS providers occurred, private health care was used by 32 of the 35 GPFHs and accounted for 4 per cent of planned operations or procedures. Price had rarely been a prime factor in decisions to use the private sector; most private care is more expensive. However, the procedure provided most by the private sector, vasectomies, is partly due to cheaper prices – 'Once the decision had been made to use the private sector for vasectomies, then price became a factor'.

Private provision was used for 40 per cent of vasectomies and was commonly used for lithotripsy, cataract operations, replacement hips/knees and a number of ENT procedures.

All but three of the 35 GPFHs had purchased private inpatient or day case treatment, but extensive use of private health care was limited to a small number of GPFHs. Seven GPFHs paid for more than 5 per cent of admissions to be undertaken privately.

Two GPFHs paid for private treatment for over 30 per cent of their hospital admissions covering a wide range of procedures in both 1993/94 and 1994/ 95. Both GPFHs were located near a large NHS hospital which had excellent facilities. Waiting list problems were stated by both GPFHs as the reasons for the use of private provision. On the whole, long NHS waits provided the impetus for using private provision, but for some treatments the private sector was seen as good value and a quality service provider (e.g. vasectomies) and in some instances the procedure could only be obtained outside the NHS (e.g. laser skin treatments). Private provision also tended to be used more extensively when alternative NHS providers were a considerable distance from the GPFH practice (Table 4.3).

Table 4.3   GPFHs with more than 5% of admissions purchased privately from the fund

GPFH	Distance to NHS providers km		% of 1994/95 admissions provided by private sector
	Nearest	**Next**	
H3	1	12	5
H4	1	38	9
S2	6	28	41
S3	1	23	31
H11	14	38	6
H12	5	16	20 *
S13	10	18	5

*   The procedures were largely minor, e.g. skin biopsies, and therefore the cost was much less than 5 per cent of GPFH spend on planned operations/procedures.

Potential Savings From Changing Referral Patterns

The potential savings from changing referral patterns were high (Table 4.4). In 1994/95 each GPFH, excluding two Staffordshire GPFHs which sent a large proportion of fundholding procedures privately (see below), could theoretically have saved over £100,000 on their NHS admissions by referring to NHS providers with the lowest published prices in the West Midlands. All could have saved over 40 per cent of their estimated spend and the total saving for all 35 GPFHs could have been over £6.6m. The estimates assume the use of day case surgery for all procedures where day case treatment is commonly available, this would not always be appropriate. The implications for distance travelled were often high for GPFHs a long distance from the conurbation, but most could have achieved sizeable savings without excessive travel implications and wait times frequently appeared comparable or shorter.

Despite the potential for large budget savings, GPFHs seldom referred to alternative providers because of lower prices. Price was ranked least important

Table 4.4 GPFH potential savings from shifting referral patterns

	1994/95			1991/92
GPFH [1]	Estimated spend [2]	Potential saving [3]		Potential saving
	£000	*£000*	*%*	*£000*
H1	432	209	48	156
H2	475	241	51	203
H3	392	202	51	235
H4	317	179	57	164
H5	380	180	47	205
H6	265	134	50	92
H7	492	254	52	269
S1	360	179	50	113
S2	180	90	50	147
S3	142	76	53	119
S4	408	216	53	128
S5	362	179	49	160
S6	314	155	49	122
S7	583	306	52	202
SA1	486	274	56	150
SA2	332	196	59	116
SO1	244	127	52	97
SO2	375	207	55	85
SO3	253	156	62	102
H11	269	154	57	Not applicable – second wave fundholders
H12	416	212	51	
H13	297	170	57	
H14	407	237	58	
H15	508	272	54	
H16	258	147	57	
S11	490	249	51	
S12	259	131	50	
S13	258	118	46	
SA11	390	229	59	
SA12	347	194	56	
SA13	257	115	45	
SO11	430	217	50	
SO12	236	122	52	
SO13	390	206	53	
SO14	600	296	49	

Notes

1 H1–H7 first wave fundholders, H11-H16 second wave fundholders, in Hereford-Worcester; S1–S7 first wave fundholders; S11–S13 second wave fundholders, in Staffordshire; SA1 and SA2 first wave fundholders; SA11–SA13 second wave fundholders, in Sandwell; SO1–SO3 first wave fundholders; SO11–SO14 second wave fundholders, in Solihull.

2 At published prices.

3 Based on published prices and use of day case provision where day case treatment is commonly available.

by 20 of the 32 GPFHs ranking the influences of location, price, waiting time and service quality; of the remainder, nine GPFHs ranked price as third and three placed price as the second most important influence after quality.

When interviewed, the lead GPs highlighted a number of factors impeding the influence of published prices.

1   *Destabilizing effect on local providers*

The GPFHs were keen to maintain their local services. This was particularly true of GPFHs outside the Birmingham conurbation.

It is the practice's intention to remain loyal to local hospitals and 'use the big stick' to improve services.

Our primary aim is to protect local services unless no improvement occurred within a reasonable period of intense negotiations.

2   *The lack of need to be receptive to price*

All the 35 GPFHs had cumulative underspends on their budget (for all fundholding services i.e. including outpatient services; drugs etc.). The average annual underspend per GPFH was £120,000 in 1991/92 and £68,000 in 1994/95; although some GPFHs had overspent in 1994/95 all the GPFHs had cumulative savings. The budget setting process of funding GPFHs according to local provider prices and the general fall in prices due to the shift to day case provision had supplied GPFHs with comfortable financial positions. Many GPs pointed out the lack of financial pressure; especially in the early years of fundholding 'there was no need to shop around for the best price'.

3   *Inconsistent published prices and the need to look at the total package of care*

The cheapest provider varies by specific procedure and over time (Ellwood, 1996b). GPFHs identified difficulties in trying to make efficient choices between providers. It is not easy to assess the cheapest provider, the total cost for a patient is made up of inpatient or day case admission plus outpatient attendances. Prices for outpatient attendances vary by provider as do the number of attendances per new outpatient.

4   *Building discounted prices into contracts*

The majority of GPFHs by 1994/95 had contracts which were set at a fairly low activity level and above which attractive discounts on published prices were received. Discounts of up to 50 per cent once thresholds were reached were common. Contracts with attractive price discounts at the margin discourage GPFHs from responding to published price lists. If GPFHs refer only a small number of patients to a provider they have no leverage for obtaining either discounted prices or relatively quick treatment.

5   *Patient expectations*

Patients expect to be treated locally. This was cited frequently when there was only one local provider, but some practices within the West Midlands conurbation, particularly Black Country practices, were also surprisingly parochial.

6   *Administrative arrangements and the late publication of prices*

Some GPs pointed out that the prices from providers other than their current main suppliers were frequently not available when contracts were being placed and previous prices are not always a good guide to future prices. Additional work would also result from dealing with a greater number of providers.

7   *Knowledge of local consultants*

The GPs expressed reservations about the principle of referring according to price signals.

> It would be wrong to refer on price, the cheapest may lead to disaster. I would not be happy sending to an unknown consultant.

Consequently, prices have rarely caused shifts in services, but if waiting times or service quality is unsatisfactory then price is considered when evaluating alternatives. Instances were found of where, once a decision had been made to consider services elsewhere, price became a factor. There were also indications that the increased financial pressure was beginning restrict GPFH activity, for example, GPFHs curtailing admissions in order to stay within the budget:

> November last year we added a rider to all our referral letters saying that we
> would not be able to fund unless it was an emergency inpatient or day treatment
> to anybody who was referred for an outpatient opinion from 1st November and
> we said we would pay for it after 1st April. ... we said that if they did treat
> without seeking our approval we would not pay for it.

As yet, where financial pressures have applied, GPFHs have acted like
their health authority counterparts and curtailed admissions rather than
shifted their suppliers in response to price signals.

Waiting Time

Patients had experienced shorter waits for hospital treatment since the
introduction of fundholding. Although waiting time provided the main impetus
for private provision and some wider NHS referrals, on the whole very few
shifts in service location had occurred. Many GPFHs had been able to gain
preferential waits for their patients through contract arrangements with existing
providers and/or the introduction of in-house outpatient clinics.

> We have not had a problem with waiting times, our in-house clinics [in all the
> main specialties] reduce the outpatient wait to two weeks. In fact we have had
> a problem with short waits last year.

In-house outpatient clinics gave GPFHs firm control over waiting time
and cost incidence.

> We can manage waits by holding clinics in-house, if you do not hold the clinic
> the wait is automatically extended. In 1995/96 we were short of money so no
> in-house clinics were held after Christmas.

Service Quality Issues

Service quality was regarded as the prime influence on the referral choice.
Service quality was ranked by 24 out of 32 GPFHs as the most important
influence on their referral decision. The knowledge of service quality was
often measured in terms of previous experience of patient outcomes (Table
4.5).

Table 4.5   Aspects of service quality

Service quality	Average rank	No. of GPFHs* ranking First (=first)	Last (=last)
Previous experience of outcomes	2.2	8 (7)	0
Reputation of consultant	2.5	8 (6)	0
Communication between consultant and GP	3.6	3 (1)	0
Courtesy of consultant to patients	4.6	0	0
Attitude of consultant to GP	5.1	(1)	0
Communications between hospital and GP	5.8	0	0
Reputation of hospital	6.1	0	4
Physical environment	7.3	0	8 (2)
Attitude of hospital management	7.8	0	11 (1)

*   32 GPFHs ranked the aspects of service quality.

This measure inevitably reinforces existing referral patterns unless service quality is unacceptable. Although the GPs claimed almost invariably that service quality was the main determinant in the referral decision of which hospital and/ or consultant. The GPs were much more likely to know and trust their local consultants. Tradition and past experience of health care providers were major factors in the GP referral decision and, particularly where local hospitals were threatened, GPs sought to protect their traditional service providers. Referrals to more distant hospitals were considered only when local provision was unsatisfactory and instigating change locally had failed.

The Perceived Benefits of GP Fundholding

All but one of the 35 lead GPs were pro-fundholding and felt it had provided considerable benefits despite the evidence from the study which showed they continued to refer the vast majority of their patients to a small number of nearby hospitals. GPFHs were more concerned with building relations and improving current service provision than taking advantage of lower prices from alternative providers. GPFHs had been empowered by fundholding and although large variations in their referral patterns had not occurred, 'holding the purse strings' had enabled them to influence service provision considerably. The GPs in the study pointed out the following improvements.

Direct improvements for GPFH patients:

- provision of in-house services, numerous outpatient clinics and therapy services had been developed since the introduction of fundholding;
- the building of primary care teams and facilities (savings from fundholder budgets often provided the stepping stone);
- reduction in waiting times for inpatient treatment and rapid access to outpatient services;
- the flexibility to use private health care;
- improved accommodation and equipment resulting from fundholder savings;
- improved communications between hospital clinicians and management with the GPs.

Service improvements for all local patients:

- provision of services locally, e.g. at local community hospitals;
- input into the development of treatment protocols and service planning;
- greater day case provision;
- more direct access services.

The GPs frequently saw fundholding as providing 'the big stick' to force change and felt there had been 'a sea change' in attitudes. Communication between the GPFHs, the clinicians and hospital management had improved considerably. Budget holding was regarded as crucial to their power and influence, but the GPs also saw fundholding as a means to protect their autonomy to refer where they wished. Virtually all the GPs saw the main disadvantages of fundholding as the time and effort necessary to operate the arrangements and the associated bureaucracy. Some GPs also pointed to a deterioration in the personal relationships with consultants. One second wave fundholding practice close to the centre of Birmingham had lost enthusiasm for the scheme completely; saw little advantage other than some personal benefit to the practice (extended premises, refurbishment and equipment); and regarded the scheme as divisive and causing two tiers. Although several total (or prospective total) purchasing pilot practices were included in the study there was generally little support for the extension of fundholding and concern was expressed about the increasing complexity that had occurred ('it is no longer *fun*holding'). Two GPs expressed the view that the benefits of fundholding could have been achieved by covering a smaller range of services and that some budgets had been devolved unnecessarily. Over 20 per cent of the GPFHs had moved to local commissioning arrangements whereby contracts were negotiated jointly. Most GPs felt the introduction of local commissioning diminished their power but also their workload.

The New NHS and Primary Care Groups

The White Paper proposed the move from GP fundholding to primary care groups (PCGs) from April 1999 with no new admissions to the fundholding scheme in the meantime. New unified budgets for PCGs covering hospital and community services, GP prescribing and the general practice infrastructure are to be established. These PCGs are to evolve from existing local groups and will typically cover 100,000 population and have a right to participate in the strategy and planning of health services (DoH, 1997).

It has been argued that involving GPs in purchasing decisions provided the main benefits rather than their holding of budgets; through the information they add to the process gains can be made without the power of 'the purse strings' (Ham, 1994; Graffy and Williams, 1994; Medical Practitioners' Union, 1995). The replacement of GPFHs with PCGs covering all GPs aims to provide the benefits of fundholding without overt two tierism and less bureaucracy. The GPFHs in the study were sceptical of whether GP commissioning groups could achieve appropriate responses from NHS providers, the threat of taking services elsewhere was seen as crucial even though GPFHs rarely carried out the shift. This problem is likely to be exacerbated by the move to more long term contractual arrangements set out in the White Paper. Glennerster et al. (1996) had also found that many of the GPs who had hoped to achieve change through the agency of health commissions working on their behalf had been disappointed. Although, on the evidence of this study, the effect of fundholding on referral patterns was small, the power which GP fundholding gave GPs to influence how care was provided (locally or elsewhere) was valued greatly. It is important that GPs' ability to influence service provision is protected within the new PCGs. On the other hand, there was little evidence of strategic planning by GPs or other entrepreneurial action.

Conclusion

The introduction of GP fundholding gave GPs an unprecedented involvement in the wider NHS and helped them resolve historic problems in their relationship with providers. However, the evidence from this study has shown that delegated budgets had little influence of on the referral patterns of most GPFHs. Admissions for planned operations did not fall under fundholding: on the contrary, the increases were dramatic. Patients were rarely referred to alternative providers. Where referral patterns did change the reason was seldom price-related. Distance travelled for most planned operations did not increase and the vast majority of referrals continued to be made to the nearest hospital. Private provision was used for a small percentage of referrals and tended to be concentrated on a small number of procedures. Although fundholding forced service providers to respond to GP demands in terms of service quality and waiting times and it expanded the scope of local primary care and encouraged innovation it is difficult to identify and quantify the extent to which such developments would have occurred without fundholding and whether they were cost effective. The Audit Commission (1996) questioned whether the benefits justified the cost of the system administratively – in the first five years of the scheme, fundholders received £232m to cover staff, computing and equipment costs of managing fundholding equivalent to about 4 per cent of their budgets.

In the search for greater equality and reduced bureaucracy, the government proposes integrating GPs into new PCGs. The evidence from this survey would support the move to budgeting and contracting for larger groups and for more than one year. However, even though GPFHs rarely took the ultimate step of referring patients away from their traditional health care providers, there is a danger that under the new arrangements GP power to improve local services will be considerably less than under fundholding.

References

Appleby, J., Smith, P., Renade, W., Little, V. and Robinson, R. (1994), 'Monitoring Managed Competition' in R. Robinson and J. Le Grand (eds), *Evaluating the NHS Reforms*, King's Fund Institute, Policy Journals, Berks.

Audit Commission (1995), *Briefing on GP Fundholding*, HMSO, London.

Audit Commission (1996), *What the Doctor Ordered*, HMSO, London.

Bain, J. (1991), 'A Step into the Unknown', *British Medical Journal*, Vol. 302, pp. 771–3.

Bain, J. (1992), 'Budgetholding in Calverton: one year on', *British Medical Journal*, Vol. 304, pp. 971–3.

Corney, R. (1994), 'General Practice Fundholding in SE Thames RHA: The Experience of First Wave Fundholders', *British Journal of General Practice*, Vol. 44, No. 378, pp. 34–7.

Coulter, A. and Bradlow, J. (1993), 'Effect of NHS Reforms on General Practitioners' Referral Patterns', *British Medical Journal*, Vol. 306, pp. 433–7.

Crombie, D.L. and Flemming, D.M. (1988), 'General Practitioner Referrals to Hospital: the Financial Implications of Variability', *Health Trends*, Vol. 20, pp. 53–6.

Department of Health (1989), *Working for Patients*, HMSO, London.

Department of Health (1997), *The New NHS: Modern, Dependable*, HMSO, London.

Duckworth, J., Day, P. and Klein, R. (1992), *The First Wave: A Study of Fundholding in General Practice in the West Midlands*, Centre for the Analysis of Social Policy, University of Bath.

Ellwood, S. (1996a), 'Pricing Services in the UK National Health Service', *Financial Accountability and Management*, Vol. 12, No. 4, pp. 281–301.

Ellwood, S. (1996b), *Cost-based Pricing in the NHS Internal Market*, CIMA, London.

Ellwood, S. (1997), *The Response of Fundholding Doctors to the Market*, CIMA, London.

Eve, R. and Hodgkin, P. (1991), 'In Praise of Non-fundholding Practices', *British Medical Journal*, Vol. 303, pp. 167–8.

Glennerster, H., Cohen, A. and Bovell, V. (1996), 'Alternatives to Fundholding', *Discussion Paper 123*, Welfare State Programme, London School of Economics.

Glennerster, H., Matsaganis, M. and Owens, P. (1992), 'A Foothold for Fundholding', *Research Report No. 12*, King's Fund Institute, Policy Journals, Berks.

Glynn, J.J., Michael, P. and Perkins, D.A. (1992), 'GP Practice Budgets: An Evaluation of Financial Risks and Rewards', *Financial Accountability and Management*, Vol. 8 (2), pp. 149–61.

Graffy, J.P. and Williams, J. (1994), 'Purchasing for All: An Alternative to Fundholding', *British Medical Journal*, Vol. 308, pp. 391–4.

Ham, C. (1993), 'How go the NHS Reforms?', *British Medical Journal*, Vol. 306, pp. 77–8.

Ham, C. (1994), Thinking Globally Acting Locally', *Health Services Journal*, 13 January, pp. 27–8.

HFMA (1997), *Multifunds*, HFMA (West Midlands) research report.

Howie, J., Heaney, D. and Maxwell, R. (1992), 'The Scottish General Practice Shadow Fundholding Project: First Results', *Health Bulletin*, 51, pp. 94–105.

King's Fund Institute (1989), 'Managed Competition: A new approach to Healthcare in Britain', *Briefing Paper 9*, King's Fund Institute.

Llewellyn, S. and Grant, J. (1996), 'The Impact of Fundholding on Primary Healthcare: Accounts from Scottish GPs', *Financial Accountability and Management*, Vol. 12 (2), pp. 125–40.

Mahon, A., Wilkin, D. and Whitehouse, C. (1994), 'Choice of Hospital for Elective Surgery Referrals: GPs' and Patients' views' in R. Robinson and J. Le Grand (eds), *Evaluating the NHS Reforms*, King's Fund Institute, Policy Journals, Berks.

Medical Practitioners' Union (1995), *Towards Primary Care Commissioning: An Agenda for an incoming Labour Government*, London, MPU/ MSU.

Newton, J., Fraser, M., Robinson, J. and Wainwright, D. (1993), 'Fundholding in the Northern Region: The First Year', *British Medical Journal*, Vol. 306, pp. 375–8.

Robinson, R. (1991), 'Who's playing Monopoly?', *Health Service Journal*, 28 March, pp. 20–2.

Roland, M. (1988), 'General Practitioner Referral Rates', *British Medical Journal*, Vol. 297, pp. 437–8.

Stewart, M. and Donaldson, L.J. (1991), 'Travelling for Earlier Surgical Treatment: The patient's view', *British Journal of General Practice*, Vol. 41, pp. 508–9.

Wilkin, D. and Dornan, C. (1990), *General Practitioner Referrals to Hospital*, Manchester Centre for Primary Care Research, University of Manchester.

Wisely, I. (1993), 'GP Fundholding: Experience in Grampian', *British Medical Journal*, Vol. 306, pp. 695–7.

5   Relationships in Health Care Commissioning: A Case Study of Glasgow

MOIRA FISCHBACHER[1] AND ARTHUR FRANCIS[2]

1   Department of Management Studies, University of Glasgow Business School
2   University of Bradford Management Centre

Introduction

Since the 1990 NHS reforms there have been many and varied developments within health care purchasing and commissioning (Carruthers et al., 1995). One such development, commissioning, is a multi-agency, multi-level process, dependent upon a network of relationships between health boards, Trusts, GPs, social work agencies, the general public, Local Health Councils and many other stakeholders in the public, voluntary and private sector. It follows, therefore, that the implementation of the commissioning arrangements was highly dependent upon the goals, objectives, behaviour and philosophies of these stakeholders.

The publication in December 1997 of the Scottish White Paper for health, *Designed to Care* (Scottish Office Department of Health, 1997), brought an end to the NHS market in favour of a new structure based on service planning and design within a framework of collaborative relationships between primary care, trusts and health boards.

This paper draws on empirical data from a study of GP purchasing in Glasgow to consider the relationships between GPs and Trusts and the relationships between GP practices that have developed in recent years under the market mechanism. The data are used to shed light on how relationships might be characterized under the new arrangements contained within current health policy.

Controlling Costs: Strategic Issues in Health Care Management, H.T.O. Davies, M. Tavakoli, M. Malek, A. R. Neilson (eds), Ashgate Publishing Ltd, 1999.

Managing Quality and Controlling Cost

The 1990 health reforms (Department of Health, 1989) were a response to a political dilemma about how to constrain the continually rising costs of the NHS (Teeling Smith, 1986; Glennerster, 1995). Competition between Trust hospitals was to be stimulated by encouraging fundholding GPs and Health Authorities/Health Boards to exercise discretion over their purchases thereafter removing contracts from hospitals who were inefficient and delivering unsatisfactory quality of care. Many questions were raised as to the suitability of the market arrangements. Some drew attention to the structural deficiencies of the market (see, for example, Le Grand and Bartlett, 1993; Propper, 1993; Bartlett et al., 1994), questioning the extent to which buyers had sufficient power, access to information and adequate incentives to perform their new role. Others focused on the economic (Matsaganis and Glennerster, 1994; Bachmann and Bevan, 1996) and organizational (Glennerster et al., 1994; D'Souza, 1995) aspects of the scheme. Further issues raised related to whether or not GPs and indeed HAs had the appropriate skills for purchasing (Bowie and Harris, 1994) and the extent to which purchasing strategies were fragmented across geographical areas (Hudson, 1995).

Competition is now formally being replaced by a vision in which 'a partnership approach based on co-operation, not competition, is the way ahead' (Scottish Office Department of Health, 1997; see also Department of Health, 1997). However, the government cannot afford to underplay the need for efficient health services and their emphasis on quality and cost effectiveness is clear in the current White Paper:

> We must root out inefficient and ineffective clinical procedures, subject new drugs and therapies to painstaking analysis in terms of their clinical and cost-effectiveness, eliminate inefficiencies that result from bureaucracy and address the differences in the availability of health care which re-enforce inequalities (Scottish Office Department of Health, 1997, p. 1; see also pp. 4, 6–7, 17, 20, 28).

GP Behaviour – Evidence from the Past, Implications for the Future

By reviewing how GPs have responded to the market reforms, some comment can be made about the likely direction and success of the NHS under new policy arrangements. This is hampered, though, by the lack of empirical evidence about the 1990 reforms. Research evidence during the last few years has been said to be inconclusive (Robinson, 1996). The specific impact of the fundholding scheme is unclear (Coulter, 1995; Gosden, Torgerson, and Maynard, 1997) and research has been limited in scope. Gosden and Torgeson (1997) reviewed the published quantitative fundholding studies and noted that only prescribing and referral behaviour had been considered. There is some evidence that GPs have responded to financial incentives as far as improving levels of generic and efficient prescribing but these improvements have not always continued and levels have often come back in line with those of non-fundholders (Whynes, Heron, and Avery, 1997). Studies of referral patterns have shown that hospital referrals have not decreased under the fundholding scheme but in places have increased (Coulter and Bradlow, 1993; Ellwood, 1996, 1998; Gosden and Torgerson, 1997). The Audit Commission review (1996) found that there was very little evidence of fundholders moving their purchasing contracts and seeking to stimulate efficiency, and the transactions costs of the scheme were thought to be high (see also Ham, 1994; Benton, 1995). What the scheme had yielded, however, was improved communications between primary and secondary care clinicians, and improvements in lowering prescribing budgets.

Commissioning has gained increasing support in recent years. It is argued to bring together the skills of general practice and public health (Alderslade and Hunter, 1994), to maximize the benefits of cooperation rather than competition whilst maintaining the purchaser provider split (Deakin and Walsh, 1996), to reduce fragmentation of strategy within a geographical area and to involve many relevant organizations in a way which suits the particular locality in which it operates (Shapiro, Smith, and Walsh, 1996). There is now a mosaic of different arrangements. Commissioning has been strongly promoted by the National Association of Commissioning GPs, who welcome the current health reforms and advocate that commissioning involves GPs in a strategic decision making without the bureaucracy and financial responsibilities contained within the internal market and fundholding scheme. It is not promised to be an easy solution, though (Wainwright, 1996).

Greater Glasgow Health Board – A Case Study

Greater Glasgow Health Board (GGHB) is an area about which little is known in relation to fundholding and purchasing/commissioning, unlike Grampian, Lothian and Tayside, which are recognized as being active in terms of fundholding (Llewellyn and Grant, 1996; Lapsley, Llewellyn, and Grant, 1997). GGHB's commissioning arrangement is based on three sectors, each with a commissioning team bringing together experts in epidemiology, finance, general practice, health promotion, contracting and information management.

This research explored the extent to which Glasgow GPs were behaving as strategic and/or economic actors within their purchasing role. The methodology drew upon semi-structured interviews and non-participant observation conducted between September 1996 and February 1998. The findings presented here are based on 24 interviews with GPs (fundholding – standard, community (PCP) – and non-fundholding), practice managers, HA and Scottish Office officials. Interview discussions focused on the degree of buyer power which fundholders had, GPs' concerns about the efficiency of secondary care provision, the extent to which fundholders were moving their contracts and the reasons behind their referral decisions. Also discussed were the views GPs held of one another, the nature of their relationship with their provider(s) and the role they believed they ought to play as fundholders and non-fundholders in the future purchasing/commissioning of services.

Nine participant observation episodes were also undertaken. The settings observed included a half day meeting of GP practices who were collaborating and coordinating their purchasing negotiations, clinical meetings between groups of GP practices and four NHS Trusts and one contracting meeting.

The research findings have three foci; the GPs' views of the Trusts; the GPs views of other GP practices and; the GPs' views of their own practice.

GPs and NHS Trusts: A Multiplex Relationship

GPs and NHS Trusts were found to be engaged in a multiplex relationship. Although termed in general to be a purchasing relationship, the relationship also involved mutual education, the formation of partnerships and the design of services (see Figure 5.1).

Education

Partnerships

Designing services

Purchasing

Figure 5.1   GPs and NHS Trusts – a multiplix relationship

During the interviews, GPs (fundholding and non-fundholding) placed a great deal of importance on the relationship that they had with their provider, particularly their local provider. This did not alter even where practices experienced difficulties in communicating and working with their main provider:

> *Interviewer*: When you took up your fundholding status and began negotiating contracts, what was the reaction from the Trust?
> *GP*: Oh, they were quite enthusiastic and quite positive until we started to try and change anything then they were extremely negative and obstructive. Trying to get to the clinicians has proved very difficult ... We can't get them to talk to us. They won't come to meetings, they won't give us any data. They elucidate tons of problems but they won't share with us what the problems are. They say they're terribly underfunded, give us the evidence and we'll fight your case, they never give us any evidence ...
> *Interviewer*: Would you prefer to keep a good relationship with the Trust and support them, do you see that as part of your role?
> *GP*: Yes. Very essential I think, yes. It's very important ... (GP, GPFH).

Purchasing

There was little evidence of practices moving their contracts. Two practices who had, did so only after considerable negotiations over what they considered to be excessive waiting times. The removal of their contract was thought to be a temporary measure, a signal of their dissatisfaction with the quality of service. Both had taken their contracts to the private sector despite a principled stance that they would always 'stick with the NHS' and fully intended to return to the original provider when the situation had improved:

> We're still not sending any patients there, ... even although we've given a lot of money for it ... to try and improve it. We believe a step forward has been made, but it's not the way we'd like it so we're continuing to go to the private sector, reluctantly ... We were willing, if the NHS can match a private hospital in speed and money, every single time we'll go to the NHS. Our ethos is stick with the NHS, support the local hospital, but if we think they're being unreasonable look elsewhere and use that as a stick to beat the local hospital to try and change their attitude ... we're very happy to work with them to give them *years* to change the way they do things if it's not what we believe is the best clinical practice (Fund manager, GPFH).

During purchasing meetings, GPs raised subjects which were of concern to them, e.g., waiting times and the quality and timeliness of discharge letters. These were issues which were addressed in the contracting relationship. In addition, where services had been improved, the Trusts took the opportunity to emphasize this point and to market themselves to secure current contracts and to win back any which had been lost.

Education

Mutual education was a core component of the relationship between practices and hospitals. There was a coming together of two different worlds with both parties seeking to explain 'how things are done' in their respective environment. One hospital consultant said that hospital consultants 'haven't a clue what goes on out there [in general practice]' because whilst GPs have spent time working in hospital during their early medical training years, hospital consultants do not spend time working in general practice so it is unknown territory. GPs also noted that hospital practice, drugs and surgical procedures, etc., are changing continually and they cannot keep track of them. GPs wanted more training from hospital consultants to help make appropriate referrals based on current, not former knowledge and practice. In one hospital some joint and soft tissue injection training had been given to GPs so that they could deal with more conditions in the primary care setting.

Partnerships

Seeking collaboration in service developments, research and funding was another characteristic of this relationship. Practices devoted large sums of money (taken from practice savings) towards developments in hospital services funding members of staff and/or specific pieces of equipment. The transfer of funds also flowed the other way though. In one area, purchasing had developed to a point where some practices did not really want very much more from their providers but were looking to develop primary care:

> ... I think the provider and ourselves have accepted that and therefore our negotiation with them is very much aimed at trying to release some resource that can come into primary care rather than us giving them extra finance for services they've already got ... We contract with a block contract with a discount of 4 per cent and the Trust and ourselves agree that that's for primary care development and that allows the GPs to provider for follow-up of patients, more diabetic services, psychology and other things. So we ring-fenced the

amount we spend with our local provider, get a discount of 4 per cent which we put into primary care one way or another and therefore we've achieved that (GP, GPFH).

Whilst it is commonplace to hear of GPs writing quality standards into contracts to ensure that discharge letters are received within a particular time period, etc., it is less common to hear of the reverse, i.e., GPs being penalized for poor quality referral letters. A partnership arose when hospital consultants complained that while they were penalized for not providing adequate and timely discharge information, they had to put up with inadequate referral information on a regular basis. When this was raised it was the GPs who responded by suggesting that GPs be penalized if this was the case and that provision should be made in the contract for such pecuniary measures.

Designing Services

Much discussion took place around the design of new services, or the reconfiguration of existing procedures. For example, in order to do more in primary care, GPs in one area requested protocols for diagnosing certain ENT conditions themselves thereafter referring only those which would need surgery. This was something which was discussed with the ENT surgeon who, rather sceptically, agreed to construct a protocol. Elsewhere, practices had collaborated with the Trust to set up a specimen collection and mail delivery service. Specimens were collected twice-daily by the hospital from the practice and two-way mail exchanges took place simultaneously. This meant that results were also returned more quickly. Other developments included open/direct access chest pain clinics, CAT scanning, X-ray and upper GI-endoscopy and so forth. A number of innovations were noted to have been stimulated and have been written up elsewhere (Fischbacher and Francis, 1998).

When asked whether he thought himself to be involved in designing services, one GP who was involved in HB commissioning and PCP fundholding said: 'Oh yes. We are looking at templates for the haematology service. *Like flowcharts of what will happen?* Yes and the kind of service specification for what we'd expect to happen. We're working with the consultants to do that' (GP, PCP fundholder and locality purchasing adviser).

GPs' Views of Other Practices; Collaboration in Purchasing

There was much evidence of collaboration between practices. This was particularly the case with three practices who were involved in a Total Purchasing pilot. Collaboration varied in its intensity but was characterized by informality and a lack of any apparent competition between the practices despite the emphasis within the 1990 Contract and Working for Patients, which sought to encourage practices to compete for patients in the area. In one area of the city (Area A), a large group of 10 practices collaborated on a regular basis to deal with two of the city's acute providers. They received an overall group discount for services and apportioned it between them according to who purchased the largest proportion of the services covered in the contract. This worked well up to a point but the provider was beginning to express concerns about the size of the group and stressed that it would not include in the discount, practices who purchased less than 50 per cent of their services there. The practices within the group all had their own contracts with providers but openly shared information on the quality, quantity and price of the services they were buying. They agreed among themselves on courses for action in dealing with, e.g., long waiting times, suggestions for new services, etc.

In other areas of the city, the nature of collaboration differed. Collaboration in Area B differed in that the practices met together with the Trust but not outwith GP-Trust meetings as was the case in Area A. Again, each practice had its own contract but they sought to agree service provision, referral procedures, etc. within their locality. They had stimulated certain service developments to benefit fundholding and non-fundholding practices in the area. In Area C, however, collaboration was in a more embryonic form. Practices were beginning to collaborate because of difficulties with their local service provision (they could not engage in discussion with hospital clinicians) and were hoping to work together towards some solution.

In Areas A and B there were practices who had removed contracts from their main provider when others in the group had not. GPs did not always agree on the best way forward but because they had their own budgets they had the autonomy to take the action they considered best for the practice. For example, in Area A, two practices who collaborated extensively, disagreed on the quality of clinical outcome from one provider (a private sector source). One practice had moved to the private sector provider but the others in the group remained with the NHS provider. The disagreement between the GPs prevailed despite efforts by both parties to change one another's views.

GPs' Views of their Own Practice

GPs and practice/fund managers were asked why they had decided to become (or not to become) fundholders. The reasons offered for becoming a fundholding practice covered a range from financial incentives (the opportunity to make savings, improved computing facilities, management costs, etc.) to the opportunity to improve services to patients. One common reason was that it gave them more control:

> ... just to have a little bit more control over how the practice was running and what we could do for our patients. That kind of sums it up (GP, PCP fundholder).

> From a professional point of view it's being in control of your own working environment ... to contribute to the decision making process both internally and externally (GP, GPFH).

After the 1990 reforms there was much talk about power, and the changing power balance between GPs and hospital clinicians now that GPs held the purse strings (Glennerster et al., 1994), but power was mentioned in only one interview in this study. Control over money, staff and decision making, in other words, professional autonomy, was however, highly valued by GPs. Professional autonomy enables them to collaborate whilst safeguarding the ability to take their own independent action when they feel it is necessary. Some spoke of the need to be free from 'constant interference' by the health board and the ability to replace staff when they needed to. Others mentioned that they could secure staff within the practice who the Trust had been all to quick to send elsewhere.

Towards a Collaborative Framework

Under the new arrangements (see Figure 5.2), GPs can volunteer to join Local Health Care Cooperatives (LHCCs), groups which will exist within the overarching structure of the Primary Care Trust. The objectives of the LHCCs are show in Figure 5.3. Funding of primary care within the Primary Care Trusts moves away from an individual practice model towards collective management arrangements. The LHCCs can volunteer to hold a budget for primary and community health services and there will be a management allowance to support the work of the LHCCs (Scottish Office Department of Health, 1997).

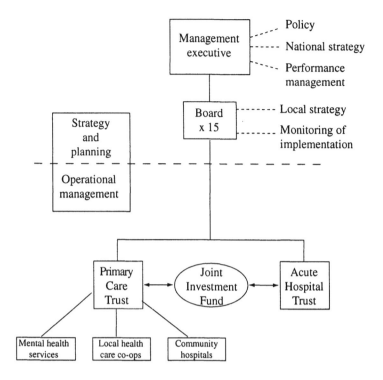

Figure 5.2   The new Scottish NHS structure

Source: The Scottish Office Department of Health, 1997, p. 14.

- provide services to their patients within an identified level of resources, including expenditure on prescribing;
- work with the support of public health medicine to develop plans which reflect the clinical priorities for the area, which take into account specific health needs of the registered patient population covered by the Cooperative;
- support the development of population-wide approaches to health improvement and disease prevention which require lifestyle and behavioural change;
- improve the quality and standards of clinical care within practices and to support clinical and professional development through education, training, research and audit; and
- support the development of extended primary care teams which are formed around the practice structure, and promote the development of clinical expertise and the emergence of specialisms within primary care.

Figure 5.3   Objectives of local health care cooperatives

Source: Scottish Office Department of Health, 1997, p. 20.

Collaborative Relationships; Evidence and Policy

GPs and NHS Trusts

It is clear from the findings that a partnership has been developing between primary and secondary care and should provide a basis for the collaborative relationship outlined in current policy. GPs and hospital clinicians recognize the value in working together to develop services and there are benefits to both parties from the joint funding that has been observed. However, there are some areas of concern. There remains a tension between some clinicians and GPs. During one meeting a senior consultant spoke of his utter distaste of the 'cherry picking' that was going on in the service because of fundholding. He believed that GPs were stealing the best and cheapest bits and leaving the hospitals with the rest. Mutual education and dialogue is essential if distrust is to be broken and true collaboration is to ensue.

Also of importance in the GP-NHS Trust relationship is the clarification of boundaries. During the meetings observed in this research, it was clear that at times, GPs were treading on the clinical territory of the secondary care clinicians. Suggestions about how services might be altered touched on the decision making domain of clinicians, threatening their professional autonomy.

The removal of much of the bureaucracy associated with contracting and invoicing ought, however, to relieve much of the friction between purchasers and providers and the antipathy of clinicians (hospital and general practice based) and business managers towards the seemingly 'endless' paper trails should be eased. Where meetings were considered to be overly concerned with money, costs to individual practices, this too may be alleviated.

GPs and Other GP Practices

Of crucial importance to the commissioning arrangement is the degree to which GPs are willing to engage in purchasing decisions and budgetary control within LHCCs and whether or not this will yield efficiencies in terms of hospital services and the organization of primary care purchasing and provision. Whilst many of the details are yet to be worked out it is in the area of potential GP collaboration where the greatest uncertainty prevails. Commenting on the White Paper, one GP welcomed the policies therein but said he just did not know how GPs would work together 'we've never had to work together before'. As noted above, professional autonomy is very important to GPs who have been independent practitioners for many years now and according to one study (Calnan and Williams, 1995) have gained increased professional autonomy since the 1990 GP contract and the introduction of fundholding.

Reaching agreement between a group of GPs was a concern to a number of those who were interviewed. One non-fundholder spoke of the difficulties in getting six GPs in the health centre to agree on building renovations never mind finding agreement in a larger group on priorities, spending and service planning. There is not a great deal of evidence upon which to draw here but some studies (D'Souza, 1995; Laing and Cotton, 1997) have reported disputes between GPs over how money should be spent and of difficulties in managing the balance of power in decision making within GP consortia.

It is important to note that in only one case (that of the total purchasers) collaboration was for the purposes of providing primary care as well as for purchasing. In all the other settings, collaboration was in purchasing only. Whilst on some purchasing issues GPs were able to speak with one voice, this was not always the case and they did not express a particular desire to collaborate in providing services. Benefits from collaboration were those of learning from one another's experience and increasing buyer power. In Area C though, increased buyer power was thought to be of limited value because provider problems were more deep-rooted than any purchasing group would be able to affect.

One underlying reason for the potential difficulties associated with locality budgets as proposed within the LHCCs is that of differing attitudes towards the effectiveness of financial incentives. Some GPs believe that fundholding has been effective, however crude the contracting mechanism may have been, because people respond to financial incentives:

> In the past you could go along to committees and complain that something was dreadful and they would try and look into it but they would but they didn't have any leverage, but economic self interest is what we respond to by and large (GP, GPFH).

There was a fear that without money and the ability to move contracts, GPs would be locked into committee discussions with no means of stimulating action whereas with practice-based budgets, if negotiations failed, practices could go elsewhere. The above quote also implies a belief that GPs respond to economic self interest or financial incentives. Another fundholder took this further pointing to a potential disincentive in a locality budget scheme:

> I think there needs to be a practice-based budget ... There has to be responsibility down to the local clinician ... if, say in Area A of Glasgow, there was a large

commissioning group ... 'where's the responsibility?'. If in my practice I reduce my dermatology referrals because I've done a bit of dermatology and I do extra work in my practice, but all the other practices decide that they want to spend the money by sending their patients off to hospital and they don't restrict their referrals then in a practice-based budget situation, if I make savings by reducing the number of referrals to put to something else, and I get ownership of putting it into something else then in that situation there's a clear win win situation for ourselves and out patients. But if other practices take that efficiency away in a locality situation then all my efforts come to naught and therefore efficient people end up paying the bill ... The easiest thing in the world for a GP would be to see the patient and send them to the hospital. You could do that with everybody and then go off for a game of golf! ... Therefore there has to be professional responsibility. I'm not saying in any way that GPs are not doing that but there needs to be incentives for that to happen ... (GP, GPFH).

There are, however, advantages to be gained from working together. In this study GPs spoke of their desire to learn from others who had more purchasing experience. Although not reported here, the role of information sharing between GP practices proved crucial to informing purchasing decisions. They shared formal and informal information which had been obtained through official channels of communication as well as through other professional networks and incidental encounters with hospital clinicians, other GPs and so on (see Fischbacher, 1997). In an environment (market or otherwise) where the level of information about services is low, the importance of this form of information sharing should not be underestimated.

Quality and Cost

Contracts were intended to be instruments to measure quality and cost, thereby improving efficiency. None of the practices studied in this research engaged in sophisticated contracts. Indeed, contracts were often written by the Trust on the basis of the previous year's figures – the GPs signed in the appropriate place. When interviewed, GPs often said that they were not concerned with the efficiency of their providers, but this was concluded to be a misunderstanding of the term because they were exercised to tackle overly-long waiting lists and actively encouraged one-stop shops and direct access services which were ultimately more efficient means of operating secondary care services.

GPs were largely concerned with functional quality or, as Llewellyn and Grant (1996) call it, care management, i.e. the patient experience or service process as opposed to the technical quality or clinical skills, expertise and outcomes. They were not disinterested in technical quality but clinical outcomes, etc. are difficult to agree and are part of a broader and ongoing debate within health boards, Royal Colleges and so forth. Functional quality, however, is immediate and more readily definable both in a discussion and in a contract.

Conclusions

Government policy has shifted its emphasis from a market approach to a collaborative, joint planning and design approach based on partnerships between PHCTs, acute trusts and health boards. The evidence presented in this paper shows that a firm basis for good working relationships between primary care and acute providers has been established within Glasgow. Communications have improved, innovations have been stimulated and partnerships have developed. Furthermore, primary and secondary care clinicians have already become involved in joint service design. Collaboration at this level therefore, looks likely to be readily achieved.

Collaboration between GPs, however, may prove problematic. Professional autonomy or the ability to 'control' their own working environment was particularly important to the practices in this study. Where they had collaborated, they had done so on the basis of their purchasing activities and not with a view to primary care provision. Practices continued, despite joint negotiations, to place individual contracts with providers thereby retaining their autonomy. They expressed grave doubts about their ability to work together across a locality.

The new LHCC arrangements place upon primary care, the need to develop new organizational forms based upon service provision. Coupled with the loss of standard fundholding budgetary control, this will prove a significant challenge to general practitioners. There are some GPs who are optimistic and willing to rise to the challenge but it is unlikely that the transition will be smooth as inter-practice relationships have not developed in the same way as primary-secondary care relationships. As policy-makers continue to develop the detailed plans for the new structure, they need to be mindful of the objectives, behaviour and philosophies of GPs if they are to create a framework which will move primary care forward and not be hampered by inter-practice conflict and continual impasses over locality-wide priorities and service plans.[1]

Note

1   The authors would like to thank the GPs and other health care professionals who participated in this study. We are especially grateful to the GPs and Trust business managers who made access to purchasing and commissioning meetings possible and who gave helpful comments on the findings.

References

Alderslade, R. and Hunter, D.J. (1994), 'Commissioning and Public Health', *Journal of Management in Medicine*, 8 (6), pp. 20–31.
Audit Commission (1996), 'What the Doctor Ordered', report on GP fundholding in England and Wales, HMSO.
Bachmann, M.O. and Bevan, G. (1996), 'Determining the Size of a Total Purchasing Site to Manage the Financial Risks of Rare Costly Referrals: Computer simulation model', *British Medical Journal*, 313, 7064, 26 October, pp. 1054–7.
Bartlett, W., Propper, C., Wilson, D. and Le Grand, J. (eds) (1994), *Quasi-Markets in the Welfare State*, SAUS Publications, Bristol.
Benton, D. (1995), '2001 Commission Impossible', *Nursing Management*, 1 (9), pp. 10–11.
Bowie, C. and Harris, T. (1994), 'The fundholding fandango', *British Journal of General Practice* 44 (January), pp. 38–40.
Calnan, M. and Williams, S. (1995), 'Challenges to Professional Autonomy in the United Kingdom? The Perceptions of General Practitioners', *International Journal of Health Services*, 25 (2), pp. 219–41.
Carruthers, I., Fillingham, D., Ham, C. and James, J. (1995), 'Purchasing in the NHS: The Story so Far', Discussion Paper 34, Health Service Management Centre, University of Birmingham.
Coulter, A. (1995), 'General Practice Fundholding: Time for a cool appraisal', *British Journal of General Practice*, March, pp. 119–20.
Coulter, A. and Bradlow, J. (1993), 'Effect of NHS Reforms on General Practitioners' Referral Patterns', *British Medical Journal*, 306, pp. 433–7.
Deakin, N. and Walsh, K. (1996), 'The Enabling State: The Role of Markets and Contracts', *Public Administration*, 74, Spring, pp. 33–48.
Department of Health (1989), *Working for Patients*, HMSO Publications.
Department of Health (1997), *The New NHS: Modern – Dependable*, Cmd 3807, December, The Stationery Office, London.
D'Souza, M.F. (1995), 'The Multifund and Outcome Research', *International Journal of Epidemiology*, 24, 3, Suppl. 1, S113–18.
Ellwood, S. (1996), 'How did Fundholding Doctors Respond to the Market?', *Management Accounting*, September, pp. 24–8.
Ellwood, S. (1998), 'GP Fundholder Admissions and the New NHS', paper presented at the Third International Conference Strategic Issues in Health Care Management, St Andrews.
Fischbacher, M. (1997), 'Relationships, Innovation and Information', working paper for British Academy of Management Conference, London.

Fischbacher, M. and Francis, A. (1998), 'Purchaser Provider Relationships and Innovation: A Case Study of GP Purchasing in Glasgow', *Financial Accountability and Management*, 14 (4), November, pp. 281–98.

Glennerster, H. (1995), 'Internal Markets: Context and Structure' in M. Jerome-Forget, J. White, and J.M. Wiener (eds), *Health Care Reform Through Internal Markets; Experience and Proposals*, Brookings Jnstitution, Washington DC.

Glennerster, H., Matsaganis, M., Owens, P. and Hancock, S. (1994), *Implementing GP Fundholding; Wild Card or Winning Hand?*, Open University Press, Buckingham.

Gosden, T. and Torgerson, D.J. (1997), 'The Effect of Fundholding on Prescribing and Feferral Costs: A review of the evidence', *Health Policy*, 40 (2), pp. 103–14.

Gosden, T., Torgerson, D.J. and Maynard, A. (1997), 'What is to be Done about Fundholding?', *British Medical Journal*, 315, 7101, 19 July, pp. 170–1.

Ham, C. (1994), 'The Future of Purchasing', *British Medical Journal*, 309, 22 October, pp. 1054–7.

Hudson, B. (1995), 'A Little Local Difficulty', *Health Service Journal*, 1 June, pp. 24–5.

Laing, A. and Cotton, S. (1997), 'Partnerships in Purchasing: Development of Consortia Based Purchasing Amongst GP Fundholders', *Health Services Management Research*, March.

Lapsley, I., Llewellyn, S. and Grant, J. (1997), *GP Fundholders: Agents of Change*, The Institute of Chartered Accountants of Scotland, Edinburgh.

Le Grand, J. and Bartlett, W. (eds) (1993), *Quasi-Markets and Social Policy*, Macmillan Press Ltd, Basingstoke and London.

Llewellyn, S. and Grant, J. (1996), 'The Impact of Fundholding on Primary Health Care: Accounts from Scottish GPs', *Financial Accountability & Management*, 12, 2, May, pp. 125–40.

Matsaganis, M.A. and Glennerster, H. (1994), 'Cream-Skimming and Fundholding' in W. Bartlett, C. Propper, D. Wilson and J. Le Grand (eds), *Quasi-Markets in the Welfare State*, SAUS Publications, Bristol.

Propper, C. (1993), 'Incentives in the New UK Health Care Market', *The Economic Review*, pp. 15–18.

Robinson, R. (1996), 'The Impact of the NHS Reforms 1991–1995: A review of research evidence', *Journal of Public Health Medicine*, 18 (3), pp. 337–42.

Scottish Office Department of Health (1997), *Designed to Care; Renewing the National Health Service in Scotland*, Cmd 3811, December, The Stationery Office, Edinburgh.

Shapiro, J., Smith, J. and Walsh, N. (1996), 'Approaches to Commissioning: The dynamics of diversity', Research Paper 22, National Association of Health Authorities and Trusts, Birmingham.

Teeling Smith, W. (1986), *The Politician's Dilemma*, Office of Health Economics, London.

Wainwright, D. (1996), 'The Best of Both Worlds', *Health Service Journal*, 25 January, pp. 30–1.

Whynes, D.K., Heron, T. and Avery, A.J. (1997), 'Prescribing Cost Savings by GP Fundholders: Long-Term or Short-Term?', *Health Economics*, 6, pp. 209–11.

6 Towards More Equitable Resource Allocation to GP Practice

XIAO-MING HUANG,[1] JACKIE GREEN,[2] DICK BEATH[2] AND
JOHN E. CLARKE[3]

1   GE Capital Global Consumer Finance Ltd, Leeds
2   Avon Health Authority, Bristol
3   Scottish Homes, Edinburgh

Introduction

The expenditure on health services has increased sharply over the last 10 years and it is now the second largest area of public spending, after social security (Appleby, 1997). How to allocate resources to reflect population health needs has always been and still is a great challenge for both health policy makers and health researchers.

The recently-published government White Paper (1997) once again stressed the importance of allocating scarce NHS resources based on needs of populations, including the impact of deprivation. A newly revamped Advisory Committee on Resource Allocation in the health service is remitted to improve the resource allocation in both primary and secondary sectors. It has called for more studies, in particular, to look at the resource allocation 'below Health Authority level'. The government's intention is to develop a national formula which will set fair shares for the primary care groups (PCGs), as the York formula (Carr-Hill et al., 1994) now does for Health Authorities (HAs). So far, in absence of an appropriate sub-HA resource allocation formula, the York formula has sometimes been chosen to provide a general guide to action despite its limitations (Sim et al., 1997).

The latest developments indicate that it is timely to revisit the York formula and to understand its implications and limitations in both national and local

Controlling Costs: Strategic Issues in Health Care Management, H.T.O. Davies, M. Tavakoli, M. Malek, A. R. Neilson (eds), Ashgate Publishing Ltd, 1999.

resource allocation. It is equally, if not more, important to explore the possibility of developing a more locally relevant formula for resource allocation below Health Authority level, particularly to GP practices. Once the fair share for each practice is known, the fair share for a primary care group could be derived because a primary care group is more likely to consist of GP practices and to serve population registered on member practices' lists rather than serving individuals living within a certain geographical boundary.

In this paper, we shall discuss the major limitations of the York formula, particularly when it is used for setting up budget targets for GP practices. We shall then describe a study in which a statistical model is developed in Avon Health Authority with enumeration district (or ED, i.e. a geographical small area consisting of about 200 households) level information and the need indicators standardized to age, sex and 'lifestyle' using geodemographical methods. Local population needs can therefore be better reflected when determining each GP practice's fair share of the Hospital and Community Health Services (HCHS) 'acute and general' budget. Finally we shall summarize the major points.

York Formula

The York formula is in fact a weighted capitation formula. As a principle, the weighted capitation formula proposed by the Resource Allocation Working Party (RAWP) has been widely accepted and has remained intact since it was first reported in 1976. However, the early RAWP formula suffered from several crucial deficiencies.

The review of the RAWP formula completed in 1988 sought to address the concern about the measurement of needs (Department of Health and Social Security, 1988). The proposed augmentation of standardized mortality ratios with an index of social deprivation was intended to capture aspects of needs not reflected in mortality measures, although the social deprivation index was later dropped from the modified formula introduced by the government in 1990. This review, however, also attracted criticism, in particular the model structure and the statistical methods used (Sheldon and Carr-Hill, 1992).

The NHS Executive commissioned a study from the University of York to address these difficulties, and the new model was based upon a better theoretical underpinning supported with more comprehensive data and used more advanced statistical methods. This study was completed in 1994 and the new formula, widely known as the 'York formula', has been used in 'general and acute' resource allocation to Health Authorities since then.

As a weighted capitation formula, the York formula derives the relative shares using weighted population (WP). The latter is calculated as:

$$WP = POP * a * n * c \qquad\qquad (1)$$

Where

POP   – the HA's crude population;
a   – the HA's age-related need factor;
n   – the HA's additional need factor;
c   – the HA's geographical cost factor.

The age-related need factor is derived from the age cost curve which measures the national average expenditure per annum per head for each age band (see Figure 6.1). The additional needs factor is derived from the statistical formula developed by York University and the geographical cost factor is derived from various market force factors (MFFs) (NHS Executive, 1997).

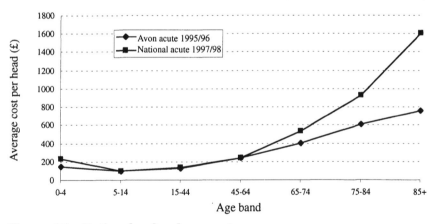

Figure 6.1   National vs local age cost curves

The York formula is undoubtedly the best model developed so far for resource allocation to HAs, as a result of a sophisticated statistical analysis. However, it is important to understand its implications and potential limitations in order to assess its impact and appropriateness, particularly when applied to sub-HA level. A more thorough discussion on this will be the subject of another paper (Huang and Prothero, 1998). We shall briefly discuss here the major aspects in the York formula which require attention.

1   Firstly, from practical experience, people know that the York formula may not work well when there is a large proportion of elderly people in a population. When applied to local level, an unusually high proportion of students in a population will also cause difficulty (Sim et al., 1997). This could be because of the underlying assumption in the York formula that there is no interaction between age-related needs and the additional needs-related to general health and socioeconomic circumstances, and therefore that a single age-cost curve is able to reflect the age-related needs. The way in which statistical formula for deriving the additional needs factor was developed implies that the York formula, when used to allocate resources, tends to underestimate population needs in more deprived areas. The effect becomes greater when there are many elderly people in a population. As a result, the needs of a population with a large proportion of deprived elderly people tend to be underestimated. Similarly, the needs of a population with large proportion of affluent elderly people tend to be over estimated. For similar reasons, one could explain the difficulty with an unusually high proportion of students.

   This problem might be alleviated when the York formula is applied locally (setting other issues aside for the time being) at sub-HA level where local age cost curve is used, provided that the age cost curves among different local populations are more similar.

2   Secondly, the York formula was developed for resource allocation to HAs and its purpose is to decide how to distribute resources to HAs so that each HA will have the fair amount of resources for the provision of services to that population based on its needs. However, the objective of resource allocation at sub-HA level is different. It is not about the distribution of resources to provide, but to purchase the services based on needs because the GP practices or primary care groups within the same Health Authority mainly use the same hospitals. Therefore, local resource allocation should take into account the different service pricing structures among different hospitals as well as the different patterns of demand for services in each local hospital by different GP practices or primary care groups.

   It is not clear how this difference will affect the validity of York formula when applied below HA level. However, it can be expected that the more the prices reflect the true costs (e.g. setting prices at HRG level), the less the impact will be.

3   Thirdly, the York formula was developed using data aggregated to electoral

ward level and a ward consists typically of 5,000 households, hence the problem of ecological fallacy (which means it is impossible to infer attributes of individuals solely from an analysis of aggregated observations). Although not all people living in any small area will have the similar health status and level of deprivation, a ward represents much too large an area to be used in deriving the health and socioeconomic characteristics of a GP practice's population. An enumeration district (ED) which consists of typically 200 households is more homogenous and hence more appropriate for health or socioeconomic studies of GP practice populations (Majeed et al., 1996).

4   As a general principle, a model developed at one level of data aggregation will not necessarily be valid when applied to another level of data aggregation. Hence, the general validity of the York formula is in doubt when it is applied directly at sub-HA level, particularly to GP practices even though ED level data are available and used.

Methodology

Level of Aggregation

Enumeration districts are more homogenous than electoral wards, and the effect of ecological fallacy is therefore less damaging. But data at ED level have their own problems, namely (Buckingham, 1996):

1   small sample problem: for small areas like an ED, many units may register no event such as death, permanent sickness or pensioner living alone while others register relatively large numbers. Any health or socioeconomic indicator for a GP practice population derived from ED level data may be thereby less robust;

2   Barnardization of census data: census data at ED level has been deliberately corrupted by randomly adding -1, 0, +1 to counts to protect confidentiality. This will result in less accuracy of any health or socioeconomic indicator derived.

It seems that we are now facing a dilemma: ward level data is too vulnerable to ecological fallacy but ED level data is not robust and reliable enough. The ideal solution is to preserve the merits of both ward and ED by grouping similar EDs into 'area types' and then derive the required indicators from such 'area types'.

Fortunately, such groupings already exist in the form of 'super profiles'. Through multivariate statistical analysis mainly based on census data, EDs are first grouped into 160 'clusters' whose members possess homogeneity in the predominant socioeconomic characteristics of their populations. These 'clusters' are further grouped into 40 'target markets' and 10 'life styles'. A computer software has been marketed by CDMS Ltd, which is part of the Liverpool-based Littlewoods organization (CDMS, 1994).

Hennell and colleagues (Hennell et al., 1994) published their pioneering work of applying 'super profile' methodology in primary care resource allocation. They first derived the long-term illness ratio for each of the 30 'Mersey area types' (similar to 'target markets') and then consolidated these ratios for the entire population of a GP practice to obtain a Synthetic Practice Illness Ratio, or SPIRO score. Such scores were then applied as needs indicator to explain the GP practices' drug prescribing expenditures.

In simple terms, a SPIRO score is the expected long-term illness ratio for a practice population standardized to age, sex and 'target market'. We have adopted a similar approach in deriving the health and socioeconomic indicators used in our modelling work.

Data Collected

The data required for statistical analysis and modelling can be categorized into: 1) hospital service utilizations and prices; 2) health and socioeconomic indicators; 3) GP practice characteristics; and 4) measure of accessibility to hospitals.

Hospital service utilizations and prices Hospital services were measured respectively by number of outpatient consultations, day cases, elective inpatient finished consultant episodes (FCEs) and emergency inpatient FCEs. Data on utilization of hospital services in four local hospitals by individual patients during 1995/96 financial year were downloaded from the computer systems. The data were analyzed to obtain the utilization of hospital services by each practice population, grouped by hospital, specialty and service types, i.e. outpatient, day case, elective inpatient and emergency inpatient. The actual prices charged by each hospital, in each specialty and for each service type were available from the Health Authority's financial system. The total hospital service expenditure for Avon was first analysed by patient age bands. Then, an Avon wide age-cost curve was derived to measure the average cost per Avon resident per annum for purchasing the hospital services required. Two variables were also derived from these data:

ACTUAL   – actual acute expenditure in 1995/96 for each GP practice;

MFF   – market force factor for a GP practice, which is defined as the ratio between the actual acute expenditure and the expected acute expenditure if the HA wide average prices were applied to the services utilized by its population.

Health and socioeconomic indicators The individual birth and death data were available from ONS annual district birth and death extract files that include postcodes. Postcodes were then mapped to an ED. Small area statistics at ED level were extracted from 1991 census, including: long-term illness, permanent sickness, social class, pensioners living alone, single carer households, unemployment status, housing tenure and ethnic groups. These items were chosen because they represent the most commonly used indicators for health and socioeconomic conditions and were found to be the most important factors in the York study. Applying a standardization process similar to SPIRO methodology, we calculated the following synthetic practice ratios:

Synthetic Practice Illness Ratio (SPIRO)

LONG_ILL   – SPIRO score for 'proportion of total population with limiting long term illness';

LOW_BWGT   – SPIRO score for 'proportion of low weight births';

PERM_SICK   – SPIRO score for 'proportion of residents of working age permanently sick';

SMR   – SPIRO score for 'all-cause mortality ratio'.

Synthetic Practice Deprivation Ratio (SPIDER)

MANU_CLASS   – SPIDER for 'proportion of persons in households with head in manual social classes';

LONE_PENS   – SPIDER for 'proportion of those pensionable age living alone';

SINGLE_CARER   – SPIDER for 'proportion of dependants living in single carer households';

UNEMPLOYED   – SPIDER for 'proportion of persons economically active unemployed';

PRIV_RENT   – SPIDER for 'proportion of persons in private rented accommodation';

NOT_BLACK   – SPIDER for 'proportion of persons from non-black ethic groups'.

All indicators except LOW_BWGT and SMR were standardized to 'target markets'. Because of the relatively small numbers of births and deaths, LOW_BWGT and SMR were standardized to 'lifestyles' instead to improve robustness of the estimates.

GP practice characteristics Data were also collected on GP practice characteristics including:

GP_NO   – number of GPs in a practice;

GP_WTE   – number of GP whole time equivalents in a practice;

GPFH_9596   – fundholding status of the practice in 1995/96;

POP   – average number of Avon residents registered on the practice list in 1995/96;

TEMP_RESID   – average number of temporary residents registered on the practice list in 1995/96.

Measure of accessibility to hospitals Supply of health care to a practice population may potentially affect its utilization of hospital services. Ideally, we would like to measure the accessibilities of four different health services, i.e. NHS hospital services, GP services, nursing and residential homes and private hospital services. Because of data availability, only the accessibility of NHS hospital services was derived. This accessibility measure (HOSP_ACC) was derived using a procedure adapted from the idea of spatial interaction modelling described by Wilson (1974) and the same idea was also applied by York team in their study. In particular, the following steps were followed:

1   calculate the attraction constrained spatial interaction measure T_{id} between an ED i and a local NHS hospital d:

$$T_{id} = g \, P_i \, B_d \, S_d \, h(c_{id}) \tag{2}$$

where

P_i –   the number of residents in EDi;

S_d –   the number of inpatient beds in local hospital d (inpatient bed number was used here as a measure of attractiveness of a hospital in the absence of any thing better);

$h(c_{id})$ –   a distance decay or deterrence function;

B_d –   the balancing factor to reflect the effect of competing populations:

$$B_d = \left[\sum_i P_i \, h(c_{id}) \right]^{-1} \tag{3}$$

g   –   a gravitational constant;

2   calculate the accessibility A_i of ED i to local hospital services:

$$A_i = \frac{(\sum_d T_{id})}{P_i} \tag{4}$$

3   consolidate these A_is for the entire population of a GP practice to obtain a synthetic practice accessibility indicator.

The most difficult aspect of modelling the spatial interactions is the choice of distance decay function. The purpose of this function is to measure the deterrence effect of distance on the utilization of service. In the lack of any relevant information, York team chose the function as $h(c_{id}) = c_{id}^{-2}$ rather arbitrarily, although it was noted that an empirical function could have been estimated had the information about hospital of treatment been available. We have derived the distance decay function from the actual hospital activity records included in which are both individual patient postcode and hospital of treatment. The best fit function was found to be:

$$h(c_{id}) = 1.0, \qquad \text{when } c_{id} \leq 0.895 \text{ km}$$
$$= 1.148 \exp(-0.154c_{id}) \quad \text{otherwise}$$

where, $R^2(\text{adj.}) = 0.988$ for the original untruncated negative exponential function.

Statistical Methods

There are three statistical issues needed to be addressed, i.e. model estimation technique, multi-level structure and multicollinearity problem. Generally speaking, the utilization of a health service at Health Authority level can be determined not only by the needs but also the available supply of the service. Supply of the service in turn could be affected by the utilization and possibly the characteristics of local community as well. Estimating the relationship between utilization and needs requires a more advanced statistical technique (i.e. two-stage least squares regression) in order to obtain unbiased results. This was in fact the major criticism of the review of RAWP formula and the important consideration in developing the York formula.

However, this 'chicken and egg' situation is not expected to be a problem when analyzing the utilization of general and acute services by GP practice populations because the utilization of service by one practice population is unlikely to affect the overall supply in the local hospitals. This is very similar to the situation where the way individual patient consults is unlikely to affect overall supply of GP services (Carr-Hill et al., 1996). Under these circumstances, ordinary least squares regression is a valid technique to use for model estimation.

Another major concern in statistical analysis of this sort is the existence of systematic effects of administrative layers, or 'levels', on utilization. A good example is that wards are clustered into districts and districts are further clustered into regions. Generally, one would expect wards in the same district or region be more similar in utilization of hospital services than wards in different districts or regions. This multilevel structure and its effect were explicitly taken into account by York team in their analysis of hospital service utilization through multilevel modelling technique (Paterson and Goldstein, 1991). This technique is only appropriate however when there is a sufficient number of groups at each level (Goldstein, 1987).

In an analysis at GP practice level, one could suggest that practices can be grouped into fundholders and non-fundholders, which in turn can be grouped into localities. Since the concept of GP locality and locality commissioning is still very much an issue under discussion, locality should not affect the actual utilization of hospital services by practice populations back in 1995/96. Fundholding status might, however, affect the way hospital services are utilized because budget savings could act as an incentive for GP fundholders to reduce hospital referrals, although a study of the first wave of fundholding practices found no such evidence (Coulter and Bradlow, 1993). We modelled this fundholding effect using a 'dummy variable' which was set to 1 for fundholding practices and 0 for non-fundholding practices.

Finally, multicollinearity often presents a great challenge to statistical analysis involving health and socioeconomic variables. The fact that many such variables rise and fall almost in tandem makes it difficult to analyse and to interpret. Sheldon and colleagues (Sheldon et al., 1994) made an attempt to use routinely collected data about hospital service utilization to identify the indicators of population needs, from a wide range of health and socioeconomic variables, in the hope of deriving a needs-based formula for setting GP fundholding budgets. Despite using sophisticated statistical techniques, the authors failed to identify any such needs indicator. The most statistically acceptable model showed that though mortality, illness and several social class variables appeared to be associated with utilization, the signs and the sizes of the coefficients were contradictory. Multicollinearity was believed to be one of the major reasons for this (Judge and Mays, 1994).

Factor analysis offers a promising technical development in tackling multicollinearity problem in regressions. Factor analysis will replace the set of intercorrelated variables with a set of uncorrelated ones (i.e. common factors) which are linear combinations of the original variables. Normally, a few such factors will be sufficient to account for most of the variability in the original data. The lack of correlation between these factors is an important feature not only because it will help eliminate the multicollinearity problem encountered when the original variables are directly used in regression, but also because the factors are measuring different 'dimensions' in the data set (Manly, 1994). Interpreted properly and sensibly, this will provide us with better insight into the underlying relationship between needs and utilization. Hence, despite some reservations (Chatfield and Collins, 1980), factor analysis and a similar approach (i.e. principal component analysis) have been applied to many areas including the analysis of air quality (Henry and Hidy, 1979), water pollution (Mullis, 1994) and more relevantly, to the measurement of patient perceptions of the quality of hospital care (Thompson, 1983).

Modelling Process and Results

The modelling process started with identifying a measure for the utilization of hospital services. The actual expenditure is not satisfactory because it is determined by not only the volume and type of services utilized by a practice population but also where such services are provided because different hospitals could charge different prices for the same type of service. A better way is to measure the utilization by the expected expenditure using Avon wide average price for each service type irrespective of which hospital actually providing the service. This measure in fact can be easily derived as the actual expenditure divided by market force factor.

The next step was to calculate the age weight factor (AGE_WT) for each practice. This factor measures the ratio of age weighted average cost for a GP practice and average cost for Avon population. The former was calculated using the Avon age-cost curve.

As with the York formula, we assumed that the actual hospital service expenditure for each practice is explained by four elements, i.e. practice population, age-related need, market force factor and additional need. Hence

$$ACTUAL = POP * AGE\_WT * MFF * f(N) \tag{5}$$

where

f( )	– a function;
N	– health and socioeconomic needs variables.

From that, we derived the measure of 'age standardized average hospital service utilization' for each practice by

$$U\_AVG = \frac{ACTUAL}{(POP*AGE\_WT*MFF)} \tag{6}$$

It was our intention to identify the significant needs factors and function f(N) through statistical modelling, which could explain the needs based variations in U_AVG among practices. The basic characteristics of the available health and socioeconomic variables are summarized in Table 6.1. The means of the variables are not exactly 100 because: 1) not all Avon practices were included in the modelling exercise (Bath and North Somerset practices had to be excluded as there was no information about their financial expenditures in 95/96) and 2) not all Avon residents registered with Avon practices.

Table 6.1   Basic characteristics of the available variables

Variable	Symbol	Minimum	Maximum	Mean	Std. deviation
LONG_ILL	X1	32.23	143.53	100.39	16.37
LOW_BWGT	X2	76.59	124.76	98.91	6.80
MANU_CLASS	X3	52.95	159.02	102.54	24.59
PERM_SICK	X4	32.34	172.80	100.62	29.39
SINGLE_CARER	X5	66.51	147.33	99.37	19.62
SPIRO_SMR	X6	28.28	109.83	96.72	7.88
PRIV_RENT	X7	31.51	415.27	109.21	86.15
LONE_PENS	X8	0.00	214.53	99.69	17.71
NOT_BLACK	X9	89.79	100.10	98.60	2.14

Not surprisingly, we, like many others, also had to face the difficulty of multicollinearity existing in these variables. Correlation analysis showed that many such variables are highly correlated (see Table 6.2), in particular single carer, unemployment and permanent sickness. Three health needs indicators (except SMR) are also highly correlated each other. Because unemployment is so highly correlated to single carer ($r = 0.973$), we excluded it from factor analysis in order to obtain results which are easier to interpret.

Applying factor analysis techniques resulted in two important common factors (with eigenvalue greater than unity) which together can 'explain' 80.2 per cent of the total variance in the whole health and socioeconomic variables. The first factor is highly correlated to long-term illness, low weight birth, permanent sickness, mortality, manual class and single carer. It is not too difficult to see that this factor represents the 'needs' dimension. The second factor is highly correlated to private renting, black ethnic minority, lone pensioner and single carer. This seems to measure the 'inner city' environment in which (particularly Bristol city) there are more privately rented households, more people from black ethnic minority, more single parent families and likely more pensioners living alone as well. These two factors are not correlated to each other. The factor loadings which are also the correlation coefficients

Table 6.2   Correlation matrix of health and socioeconomic variables

	NOT_BLACK	PRIV_RENT	SINGLE_CARER	LONE_PENS	UNEMPLOYED	MANU_CLASS	LONG_ILL	LOW_BWGT	PERM_SICK	SMR
NOT_BLACK	1	-0.433	-0.577	-0.295	-0.661	-0.009	-0.364	-0.129	-0.469	0.269
PRIV_RENT	-0.433	1	0.159	0.434	0.249	-0.560	-0.197	-0.159	0.040	-0.504
SINGLE_CARER	-0.577	0.159	1	0.511	0.973	0.612	0.875	0.838	0.973	0.285
LONE_PENS	-0.295	0.434	0.511	1	0.469	0.065	0.421	0.396	0.521	0.249
UNEMPLOYED	-0.661	0.249	0.973	0.469	1	0.525	0.787	0.760	0.918	0.132
MANU_CLASS	-0.009	-0.560	0.612	0.065	0.525	1	0.741	0.724	0.653	0.453
LONG_ILL	-0.364	-0.197	0.875	0.421	0.787	0.741	1	0.896	0.945	0.646
LOW_BWGT	-0.129	-0.159	0.838	0.396	0.760	0.724	0.896	1	0.897	0.633
PERM_SICK	-0.469	0.040	0.973	0.521	0.918	0.653	0.945	0.897	1	0.476
SMR	0.269	-0.504	0.285	0.249	0.132	0.453	0.646	0.633	0.476	1

Table 6.3   Factor loadings and factor score coefficients

Variables		Factor loadings			Factor score coefficients	
Name	Symbol	NEEDS	INNER_CITY	Communality	NEEDS	INNER_CITY
LONG_ILL	X1	0.940	0.279	0.962	0.194	0.043
LOW_BWGT	X2	0.925	0.198	0.896	0.197	0.010
MANU_CLASS	X3	0.859	-0.161	0.765	0.210	-0.134
PERM_SICK	X4	0.858	0.494	0.980	0.158	0.138
SINGLE_CARER	X5	0.761	0.610	0.951	0.127	0.194
SPIRO_SMR	X6	0.753	-0.309	0.663	0.197	-0.187
PRIV_RENT	X7	-0.432	0.815	0.851	-0.163	0.373
LONE_PENS	X8	0.308	0.637	0.500	0.021	0.241
NOT_BLACK	X9	-0.085	-0.802	0.651	0.043	-0.327

(since Principal Component Analysis method was used for factor extraction) between the original variables and the two common factors are shown in Table 6.3, where 'communality' of a variable reflects the part of its variance that is related to the two common factors. It can be seen that all communalities are reasonably high and some are very high. Kaiser-Meyer-Olkin measure of sampling adequacy (KMO = 0.674) and Bartlett test of sphericity ($p < 0.000$) both suggested that it was reasonable to conduct the factor analysis to the data set (Norusis 1994).

A common factor can be expressed as a linear combination of the standardized original variables using factor score coefficients. For instance,

$$\text{NEEDS} = \Sigma w_i \left(\frac{X_i - m_i}{SD_i} \right) \tag{7}$$

where X_i is an original variable, m_i is the mean of the variable, SD_i the standard deviation and w_i the factor score coefficient as shown in Table 6.3.

Since 'age standardized average hospital service utilization' for a practice might be affected by service accessibility (S) and GP practice characteristics (G) in addition to the general health and socioeconomic circumstances (N), we proposed a structural model that

$$\text{U\_AVG} = f(\text{S, G, N}) \tag{8}$$

where S includes HOSP_ACC, G includes all GP practice characteristics indicator except practice population and N includes the two common factors, NEEDS and INNER_CITY. For the reasons discussed in the previous section, the ordinary least squares (OLS) regression method was used in estimating the model. The best fit model is as shown in Table 6.4. It is found that hospital accessibility, temporary residents, size of practice and fundholding status are not significant in explaining the 'age standardized average hospital service utilization'. Adjusted R^2 statistic shows that common factor NEEDS alone accounts for 47.7 per cent of the variance in U_AVG. It is also found that the random error term of this model is normally distributed.

We also estimated a model which included market force factor (MFF) as one of the potential explanatory variables. The hypothesis was that utilization of hospital services might be affected not only by physical accessibility to the services but more likely also by financial accessibility. For a GP fundholding practice with given annual budget on many hospital procedures, other things being equal, the more expensive the services are the less it can afford to purchase. For a non-fundholding practice, though it does not have any fixed

Table 6.4   Age standardized average hospital service utilization model for Avon practices, 1995/96

Multiple R	0.694
R Square	0.481
Adjusted R square	0.477
Standard error	33.6

Analysis of variance

	df	Sum of squares	Mean square
Regression	1	128860	128860
Residual	123	138846	1129
F = 114.2	Signif F = 0.000		

Variables in the equation

Variable	B	Std. error	Beta	t	Sig.
(Constant)	223.572	3.005		74.397	0.000
NEEDS	32.236	3.017	0.694	10.684	0.000

Table 6.5   Age standardized average hospital service utilization model with MFF

Multiple R	0.707
R square	0.499
Adjusted R square	0.491
Standard error	33.1

Analysis of variance

	df	Sum of squares	Mean square
Regression	2	133660	66830
Residual	122	134046	1099
F = 60.8	Signif F = 0.000		

Variables in the equation

Variable	B	Std. error	Beta	t	Sig.
(Constant)	357.717	64.246		5.568	0.000
NEEDS	31.924	2.98	0.687	10.711	0.000
MFF	-134.447	64.322	-0.134	-2.09	0.039

budget, the Health Authority as a whole however does have a fixed total budget on hospital services as determined by the Department of Health each year using the York formula. This financial constraint might in one way or another affect the financial accessibility of a practice to hospital services. In the absence of any better indicator to measure this financial accessibility directly, market force factor seems to offer us a possible proxy for it. Regression analysis shows that MFF is indeed a statistically significant variable together with NEEDS factor in explaining U_AVG although NEEDS factor remains to be predominant (with much higher absolute Beta value). See Table 6.5. The negative sign of MFF in the model indicates that, other things being equal, the higher MFF (i.e. practice uses more expensive hospitals for the services) the less the utilization tends to be. The random error term of the model is again normally distributed.

Obviously, financial accessibility is not a needs factor and it should not be accounted for when resources are allocated. Hence, should it be accepted that MFF does reflect the financial accessibility well, we could assume that MFF take the district average value (i.e. 100) for all practices when it is used in estimating the fair shares. This would allow us to estimate the needs based 'age standardized average hospital service utilization' for each practice under the same 'market' condition, from which relative shares can be derived. This approach is slightly different from that adopted by York team in which, once 'needs' variables were identified, the model was refitted to the 'needs' variables only so that the final formula 'is sensitive not only to legitimate health care needs, but also to supply to the extent that it reflects those needs'. Nevertheless, since we were not completely certain about the validity of using MFF as a proxy for financial accessibility and also if we had adopted York approach to refit the model, we would have obtained the same result as in Table 6.4, we decided to take the first model as our best fit model, i.e.

$$f(N) = 223.572 + 32.236*NEEDS \qquad (9)$$

Replacing common factor NEEDS by the original variables using formula (7), we obtained the following model:

$$
\begin{aligned}
f(N) = -112.982 \;&+ 0.3824\,(LONG\_ILL) &&+ 0.9347\,(LOW\_BWGT) \\
&+ 0.2753\,(MANU\_CLASS) &&+ 0.1738\,(PERM\_SICK) \\
&+ 0.2090\,(SINGLE\_CARER) &&+ 0.8066\,(SMR) \\
&- 0.0610\,(PRIV\_RENT) &&+ 0.0381\,(LONE\_PENS) \\
&+ 0.6499\,(NOT\_BLACK) && \qquad\qquad (10)
\end{aligned}
$$

Applications

To apply this model in setting hospital service budget targets to GP practices, one can follow the steps as below:

1 estimate the needs based 'age standardized average hospital service utilization', i.e. f(N), for each practice's population;

2 calculate the 'needs based demand for cash' (NBDC) for each practice:

$$NBDC = POP * AGE\_WT * MFF * f(N)$$

3 calculate the relative proportion of the 'needs based demand for cash' for each practice;

4 and finally, multiply this relative proportion to the total hospital service budget available to all practices concerned and derive the needs based fair share for each practice.

We applied this approach to derive the 1995/96 fair share estimate for each of the practices included in the analysis. Our own fair share estimates (called 'Avon' fair share estimates for convenience) were then compared to the estimates derived from York formula. It was found that the ratio between York and Avon fair shares ranged typically from 0.82 to 1.48 except for two university student health service centres where the ratios were 2.67 and 4.10 respectively (see Figure 6.2). We also compared Avon fair share estimates to the crude capitations and this time it was found that the ratio ranged typically from 0.64 to 1.36. But the two student health service centres had a ratio of 0.20 and 0.35 respectively. Since Avon fair shares for the two practices were much closer to their actual expenditures while York estimates were three or more times higher, it is clear that York Formula had overstated the needs of these two practices. Both York and Avon fair share estimates were also compared to the actual practice expenditures in 1995/96 (see Figure 6.3).

The comparative information together with various health and socioeconomic characteristics indicators were compiled for all practices. This package of comparative information is valuable in helping people gain better insight into needs based resource allocation at practice level and also helping identify areas for further investigation to understand how resources are currently being used.

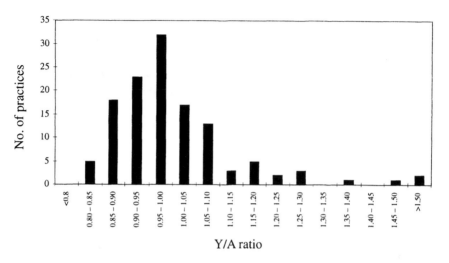

Figure 6.2 Frequency distribution of York/Avon share estimate ratio

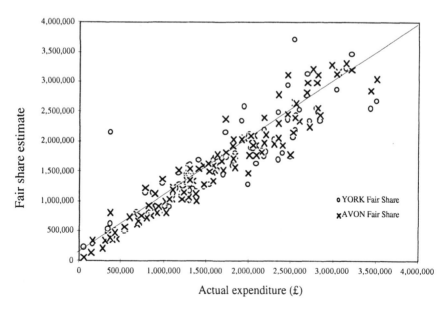

Figure 6.3 Comparison between York and Avon fair share estimates

Conclusions

Allocating resources at sub-HA level based on population needs is now one of the top priorities specified in the latest government White Paper which sets out the government vision on the 'new NHS'. Although government intends to develop a national formula to set fair shares for the primary care groups, it is almost foreseeable that this will not be an easy task. A primary care group is more likely to consist of a group of GP practices whose populations scatter across the boundaries of wards and/or EDs. Hence, any attempt to allocate resources to PCGs based on wards (as York formula does to Health Authorities) is bound to result in mismatches between needs and resources. A typical PCG will serve 100,000 population while a GP practice could serve a population ranging from a few thousands up to 15,000. It will therefore not be surprising to find from time to time that the mismatch is too significant to ignore.

Since GP practices are the basic building blocks in this structure, it is vitally important to understand the population needs at this level. The challenge is that ward is too large a geographical area to identify population needs of a practice and on the other hand, ED is too small an area which is vulnerable to the small sample and Barnardization effects. We solved this problem by grouping EDs to 'target markets' and / or 'lifestyles' using geodemographical approach so that more robust health and socioeconomic characteristics indicators can be derived for EDs, which were then used to derive the similar indicators for a practice population.

Another problem often experienced in a statistical modelling (e.g. regressions) involving health and socioeconomic variables is that such variables tend to be highly correlated. This problem of multicollinearity makes the modelling very difficult and sometimes impossible. We have applied multivariate statistical method, i.e. factor analysis, to identify the underlying not-directly-measurable 'common factors' from these variables. These common factors were not correlated and were then used in our statistical modelling. Two important common factors were identified. One appeared to reflect the health needs for both health and socioeconomic reasons. The other appeared to reflect the level of urbanization (i.e. inner city environment). Our study showed that only the first factor affected the utilization of hospital services in Avon.

An underlying assumption of the York formula is that there be no interaction between age and general health and socioeconomic circumstances as far as needs for hospital services are concerned. This assumption may not be true and hence bias could arise as a result. So far we have adopted a rather pragmatic approach in the sense that we followed the same philosophy as that of the York formula by assuming there be no such interaction effect. Since the York formula has been widely accepted and applied, we believe that a local formula developed on the same principle will have a better chance to be understood and accepted by local GP practices. However, this implies that our formula may still result in some degree of bias in the estimate of a practice's fair share. In particular, the needs of a practice serving more deprived elderly population might be underestimated and equally, the needs of a practice serving more affluent elderlies might be overestimated.

Our main focus here is to develop a needs-based resource allocation formula which is more locally relevant and responsive than the York formula, based upon information at ED level. In fact, it is possible to take into account the aforementioned interaction effect in resource allocation. To achieve this, one could first derive an age-cost curve for each 'target market' (or 'lifestyle') and the age-related needs element could be derived using such target market specific age-cost curves. Similar approach as discussed before could then be applied in developing a model for additional needs.[1]

Note

1   This paper is based on the research conducted in Avon Health Authority when Dr Xiao-Ming Huang was working as Information Development Manager and Dr John E. Clarke as GIS Development Officer. The authors would like to thank their colleagues in Avon Health Authority for their valuable comments and discussions, particularly Michael Shephard, David Prothero, Kieran Morgan, Robert Mullis and Christine Hine. We also thank the anonymous referees for their helpful suggestions.

References

Appleby, J. (1997), 'Financing the NHS', *1997/98 NHS Handbook*.

Buckingham, K. et. al. (1996), *Interim Needs Indicators for Community Health Services*, University of Kent, Canterbury.

Carr-Hill, R.A. et al. (1994), *A Formula for Distributing NHS Revenues Basedon Small Area Use of Hospital Beds*, University of York, York.

Carr-Hill, R.A., Rice, N. and Roland, M. (1996), 'Socioeconomic Determinants of Rates of Consultation in General Practice Based on Fourth National Morbidity Survey of General Practices', *British Medical Journal*, 312, pp. 1008–13.

CDMS (1994), *Super Profiles*, promotion brochure, CDMS Ltd, Liverpool.

Chatfield, C. and Collins, A.J. (1980), *Introduction to Multivariate Analysis*, Chapman & Hall, London.

Coulter, A. and Bradlow, J. (1993), 'Effect of NHS Reforms on General Practitioners' Referral Patterns', *British Medical Journal*, 306, pp. 433–7.

Department of Health (1997), *The New NHS: Modern – Dependable*, The Stationery Office, London.

Department of Health and Social Security (1988), *Review of the Resource Allocation Working Party Formula: Final Report by the NHS Management Board*, London.

Goldstein, H. (1987), *Multi-level Models in Educational and Social Research*, Griffin Publishing Co., London.

Hennell, T., Knight, D. and Rowe, P. (1994), *A Pilot Study into Budget Setting Using Synthetic Practice Illness Ratios (SPIRO Scores) Calculated from 'Super Profiles' Area Types*, Working Paper 43, The Urban Research and Policy Evaluation Regional Research Laboratory, NHS Executive – North West.

Henry, R.C. and Hidy, G.M. (1979), 'Multivariate Analysis of Particulate Sulfate and Other Air Quality Variables by Principal Components – Part I: Annual data from Los Angeles and New York', *Atmospheric Environment*, 13, pp. 1581–96.

Huang, X.M. and Prothero, D.L. (1998), *York Formula: Its implications and limitations in national and local resource allocations*, in preparation.

Judge, K. and Mays, N. (1994), 'A New Approach to Weighted Capitation', *British Medical Journal*, 309, pp. 1031–2.

Majeed, F.A., Martin, D. and Crayford, T. (1996), 'Deprivation Payments to General Practitioners: Limitations of census data', *British Medical Journal*, 313, pp. 669–70.

Manly, B.F.J. (1994), *Multivariate Statistical Methods: A Primer*, Chapman & Hall, London.

Mullis, R.M. (1994), *The Ecotoxicological Impacts of Urban Discharges*, PhD thesis, Middlesex University.

NHS Executive (1997), *HCHS Revenue Resource Allocation to Health Authorities: Weighted Capitation Formulas*, Department of Health, Leeds.

Norusis, M.J./SPSS (1994), *SPSS Professional Statistics 6.1*, SPSS Inc.

Paterson, L. and Goldstein, H. (1991), 'New Statistical Methods for Analysing Social Structures: An introduction to multilevel models', *British Educational Research Journal*, 17 (4), pp. 387–93.

Sheldon, T.A. and Carr-Hill, R. (1992), 'Resource Allocation by Regression in the National Health Service: a Critique of the Resource Allocation Working Party's Review', *Journal of Royal Statistical Society*, A, 155 (3), pp. 403–20.

Sheldon, T.A., Smith, P., Borowitz, M., Martin, S. and Carr-Hill, R. (1994), 'Attempt at Deriving a Formula for Setting General Practitioner Fundholding Budgets', *British Medical Journal*, 309, pp. 1059–64.

Sims, A. et al. (1997), 'Funding a Primary Care Led NHS: Achieving a model for more equitable allocation of healthcare resources at a sub-district level', *Journal of Public Health Medicine*, 19 (4), pp. 380–6.

Thompson, A.G.H. (1983), *The Measurement of Patient's Perceptions of the Quality of Hospital Care*, PhD thesis, University of Manchester.

Wilson, A.G. (1974), *Urban and Regional Models in Geography and Planning*, Wiley, Chichester.

7 Impact of Financial Exclusion on Health Care Utilization: Is Insurance the Answer? The Case of Kissidougou in Rural Guinea-Conakry

BART CRIEL,[1] MOUSSA SYLLA,[2] XAVIER DE BÉTHUNE,[1]
MOHAMMED LAMINE YANSANÉ,[3] YÉROBOYE CAMARA,[4]
SÉKOU CONDÉ[4] AND MICHEL GODY[4]

1   Department of Public Health, Institute of Tropical Medicine, Antwerp,
     Belgium, and Medicus Mundi Belgium consultant to the PRIMA project
2   PRIMA (Projet de recherche sur le Partage des Risques-Maladie), Medicus
     Mundi Belgium, Kissidougou, Guinea
3   PSR (Projet Santé Rurale), GTZ (Gesellschaft für Technische
     Zusammenarbeit) and Ministry of Health, Conakry, Guinea
4   Ministry of Health, Conakry, Guinea

Introduction

The Kissidougou district counts 178,382 inhabitants (1996) of whom more than two-thirds live in rural villages. The district health services system is based on two tiers: a network of decentralized health centres and a district hospital. There are few private health care providers except in the informal (often illicit) and traditional sectors. The hospital enjoys a position of virtual monopoly.

The principal source of revenue is the commercialization of agricultural crops. Rice, coffee, and cola are harvested at the end of the year; part of the harvest is sold at the beginning of the dry season in December/January. February, March and April are the months when most of the traditional feasts

Controlling Costs: Strategic Issues in Health Care Management, H.T.O. Davies, M. Tavakoli, M. Malek, A. R. Neilson (eds), Ashgate Publishing Ltd, 1999.

and ceremonies take place, consuming a considerable amount of the household resources. The bulk of the rice harvest is stored. It is used for household consumption but also constitutes a potential source of cash income that can be mobilized in case of need. For a substantial number of households in the Kissidougou area, this reserve is at its lowest during the third quarter of the year.

Hence, part of the population faces a problem of partial financial exclusion in the second half of the year (which coincides with the rainy season), more particularly during the months of July, August, and September. In 1991, the per capita income of a rural household in that part of the country was estimated at US $200 (Centre International de Développement et de Recherche, 1994). This is not evenly distributed over the year: in the second semester it is only half of what it is between January and June (Galland, 1996).

There are different types of exclusion (Centre International de Développement et de Recherche, 1994; de la Rocque, 1996; Galland, 1994; Galland et al., 1991 and 1997). A first distinction can be made in terms of the duration of the exclusion (*temporary* versus *permanent* exclusion); a second is made in terms of the importance or size of the exclusion (*partial* versus *total* exclusion). They are illustrated in Figure 7.1. Some households may be able to face all kinds of health expenditures the whole year; others may have difficulties in paying for major, or for major and minor expenditures, the whole or part of the year.

Temporary exclusion occurs when households lack money during part of the year. In the *Region Forestière* in Guinea-Conakry it was reported to arise in about 40–50 per cent of the households (Soucat et al., 1997). Temporary exclusion can either be partial or total; the former being generally more frequent. Some people can be excluded on a permanent basis, i.e. they *always* lack (partially or totally) money to purchase health care. In the *Région Forestière* of Guinea, some 5 per cent of the general population are reported to face such a situation (Galland, 1996). This type of exclusion is rarely limited to a mere phenomenon of financial or economic exclusion. Very often it is also of social nature.

What is the Impact of Exclusion on Health Care Utilization?

The Context

As elsewhere in the country, government health services in Kissidougou have

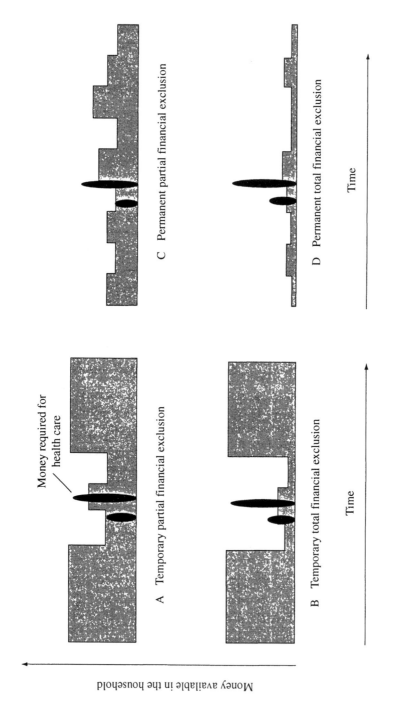

Figure 7.1   Different types of exclusion, for households confronted with a minor and a major (e.g. hospitalization, expensive treatment) health care expenditure

a user fee system that is a compromise between a flat fee and fee-for-service payments. The total (official) flat fee charged for a hospital admission varies between US $10 and US $30 depending on the patient's age and the nature of the health problem; at health centre level the fee charged for an episode of care varies between US $1 and US $5 (Ministre de l'Intérieur et de la Sécurité et al., 1993). The rates are different for adults and children, for curative and preventive care, for problems needing certain drugs or requiring laboratory investigations, etc. Hence, the magnitude of the flat rate is anything but transparent to the user.

This complex payment system is abused by a majority of health workers who charge 'under the counter' payments in addition to the official fee (Criel, 1996). These payments – which are locally called 'over-billings' – often largely exceed the official fees and constitute an important additional financial burden to patients. They create yet another source of uncertainty since they make it difficult for patients to anticipate the precise amount of money that they will need to pay in case of health service utilization. The phenomenon of over-billing, virtually generalized at health centre level, also exists at hospital level.

Senior staff of the Kissidougou District Health Team indicate that over-billing is more common in the case of patients coming from remote rural areas. These patients constitute an easier 'target': they are generally less well informed about existing official fee schedules, they often are less assertive in the negotiation process with health care providers, and they can not rely upon social networks in town. Currently, the community is not sufficiently well organized to challenge this behaviour openly and attempts to 'regulate' it have largely failed.

The PRIMA project in Kissidougou aims to investigate the possibilities of introducing insurance schemes. In the pre-operational phase the social perception and impact of exclusion were studied, as well as the effects of the reported lack of financial resources, at a specific time of the year, on utilization levels of institution-based health care.

Methods

On the one hand, the *PRIMA* research team carried out a community-based survey using a 'rapid rural appraisal' methodology (RRA) in three villages of the Yendé health centre area. RRA is an anthropological method that is being used increasingly in public health (Gueye and Schoonmaker Freudenberger, 1991; Desclaux, 1992). The RRA was carried out in May 1997 and took about four days. The purpose of this investigation was to gain more insight into the community's perception of the problem of exclusion and on existing coping mechanisms. A detailed account of the findings of the RRA is available elsewhere (Projet de Recherche sur le Partage des Risques-Maladie, 1997): here only the most important results concerning the village of Touffoudou are presented. It is a small village of 49 households (376 inhabitants), at eight km from the Yendé health centre.

On the other hand, the PRIMA team looked at seasonal patterns of health care utilization so as to check whether temporarily reduced income actually affects utilization. For that purpose the routine health information system of the government health services was analysed. Utilization data for curative services (separately for under-fives and for total new cases) at the rural Yendé health centre in the Kissidougou district were retrospectively analysed for the year 1996. As mentioned above, the crucial months in terms of financial exclusion are July, August and September. Utilization rates in the third trimester (data extrapolated to 12 months) were compared with utilization rates in the three other trimesters (also extrapolated to 12 months). No information was collected on the utilization of private first line health care providers operating in the same health centre area. Hospital inpatient utilization was analyzed for the three-year period 1994–96. The routine hospital recording system made it possible to identify the patient's residence in virtually all cases. In Kissidougou district there are three urban sub-districts which were grouped (total population of 56,628 in 1996) and 12 smaller rural sub-districts (total population of 121,754 inhabitants in 1996). Patients coming from other districts (less than 5 per cent of inpatients) were excluded from the analysis. The data for the period 1994–96 were pooled and admission rates were calculated separately for the 'exclusion' period (months of July, August and September) and the 'normal' period (i.e. the remaining months of the year). In order to cope with the different lengths of the two periods compared in the time-span 1994–96 (27 months for the normal period and nine months for the exclusion period), the average number of admissions/10,000 inhabitants/month was calculated for both periods. The calculation of hospital admission rates was carried out separately for urban and rural populations. Indeed, an important part of the urban population is less subject to the phenomenon of seasonal exclusion because its income is not dependent only on agriculture. Relative risks (RR) were calculated in order to appreciate to what extent utilization in the normal period is higher than in the exclusion period. Inpatient utilization was also assessed for each single department and separately for exclusion and normal periods. Hospital utilization was further assessed for two specific health problems for the same period 1994–96: major surgery for obstetrical problems (mainly Caesarean sections) and strangulated inguinal hernias.

Results

Exclusion in Kissidougou as assessed by the population The RRA confirmed that the exclusion period lasts from June to October, with a peak in the months of July, August and September. From October on, potential 'mobilizable' household income slowly starts to rise to reach its peak in the period March/ April. Three people of the village (two men and one woman) were asked to establish a socioeconomic classification of all the 49 households of the village according to a set of criteria identified by themselves. Every single household was 'assessed' according to the following criteria: size of land and livestock property; capacity of the household to lend money to others; capacity of the household to hire labour; perceived solvency of households when they borrow money from others. A classification in three different categories was established: the 'rich', the 'self-sufficient' and the 'poor'. In the local Kissi language, the following denominations were proposed by the three 'reviewers': the rich 'vana bolofa bendua' or 'vana bolofa pomboa'; the self-sufficient 'vana bolofa lendapila'; the poor 'vana balafondoa'.

The ranking of each household was carried out independently by the three local reviewers and was remarkably consistent in terms of results. The data are presented in Table 7.1. This classification was validated by a village assembly at the end of the survey.

Table 7.1   Socioeconomic classification of households in Touffoudou

Socioeconomic class	Number of households
Class I: the 'rich'	18 (37%)
Class II: the 'self-sufficient'	13 (27%)
Class III: the 'poor'	18 (37%)
Total	49 (100%)

The survey indicated that the rich households face no particular problems in paying for health care in the exclusion period. Moreover, they are capable in that very period to lend money to other households, or to hire labour force to work on their land. The self-sufficient sometimes face problems in the period July to September but they can easily obtain loans (generally without interest) from the rich, and reimburse these loans in the first semester of the following year. The group of poor face considerable problems during the exclusion period, not only for health care utilization but also for finding the necessary food to overcome the most difficult months. They are not always sufficiently creditworthy to obtain substantial long-term loans and are then forced to sell their labour to the rich in the village. In fact, the survey indicated that already from the end of May on, the self-sufficient and the poor start to solicit the more wealthy households for loans and for work (Figure 7.2).

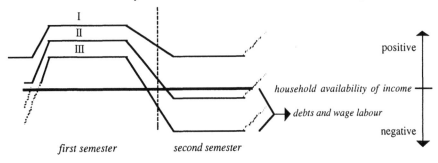

Figure 7.2 Household availability of income per socioeconomic class in the Touffoudou village

No households were identified as destitute. This suggests that the households in class II and III actually manage to return – after the exclusion period – to a threshold (close or similar to their previous level of household income availability) where they are in a position to pay back their debts and where they again are creditworthy. It is unlikely that this is always the case. It is possible indeed that poor households do *not* manage to return to the prior level of income availability. Debts are then made in a context where the borrowing household did not succeed in repaying previous debts to the lender. In such a situation the borrower gets into a vicious cycle where his debts increase every year up to a point where nobody will be willing to lend him money. Admittedly, this scenario is speculative and other scenarios are possible. For instance, households of group III might very well remain in the 'circuit' after the death of one or more children, or after the death of the mother. Other less catastrophic events, like for instance the decision not to make use of education or other services in order to save resources, may also enable households to remain solvent. At any rate, the consequences for the general well being of the household are substantial.

The Effect of Exclusion on Health Care Utilization

Health centre utilization The number of new cases (under-fives and total) per month is presented in Figure 7.3. At first glance, there is no clear pattern. Health centre utilization is somewhat lower during the second half of the year: 0.42 new cases/inhabitant in the first semester and 0.37 in the second; (RR = 1.13; CI: 1.1–1.2), but such small differences may well be explained by local seasonal epidemiological variations. The absence of clear pattern remains when one looks at the crucial period in terms of financial exclusion: the months of July, August and September.

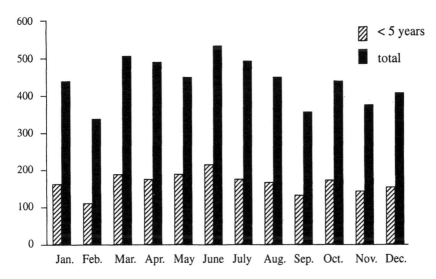

Figure 7.3 Utilization of curative services in Yendé health centre (1996)

Hospital utilization The numbers of admissions per month in the hospital for the years 1994, 1995 and 1996 show two trends (see Figure 7.4).

First, the number of admissions has increased over the years. Indeed, the yearly hospital admission rates are 17.8 per cent, 19.6 per cent and 20.7 per cent for 1994, 1995 and 1996 respectively. Second, there is a slight drop in admissions during the exclusion period (Table 7.2). This decrease is somewhat more pronounced for the rural sub-districts (Figure 7.5). This is more pronounced in the years 1995 and 1996 when overall hospital utilization was higher. The impact of exclusion on inpatient hospital utilization by the population of the entire district is relatively minor (RR of 1.07), and remains so for the rural population (RR of 1.16). Striking, but not surprising, are the high urban/rural ratios for inpatient hospital utilization in both periods (10.4 and 11.5 in normal and exclusion periods respectively). In the Kissidougou

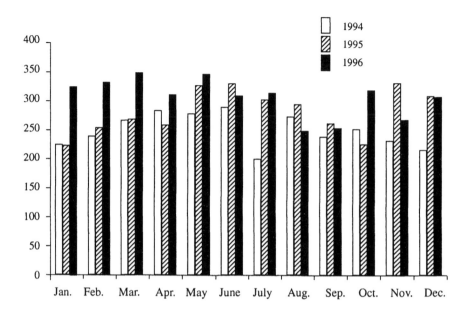

Figure 7.4   Hospital admissions per month in Kissidougou Préfecture (1994–96)

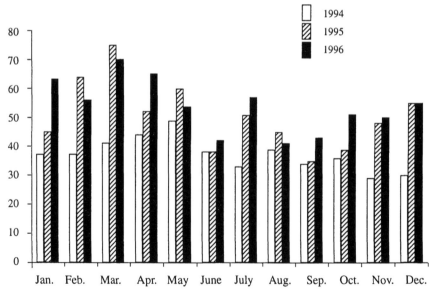

Figure 7.5   Hospital admissions per month of rural patients in Kissidougou Préfecture (1994–96)

Table 7.2   Average monthly admission rates (1994–96)

	Total préfecture	Urban sous-préfectures	Rural sous-préfectures
Average monthly admission rate (per 10,000 inhabitants) in normal period	15.91	41.5	4
Average monthly admission rate (per 10,000 inhabitants) in exclusion period	14.91	39.6	3.45
Relative risk (95%CI)	1.07 (1.02–1.12)	1.05 (1–1.1)	1.16 (1.04–1.3)

context, this urban/rural differential is not only due to the effect of distance and the costs this implies, but also to the fact that people from rural areas often have no relatives in the urban township where the majority of people belong to a different ethnic group. *We do not know anybody in town* is a complaint often voiced by the rural dwellers. Additional costs may also arise from the under the counter over-billing we mentioned earlier.

These variations are apparently not due to seasonal epidemiological variations. If they were, we would expect them to mainly affect admission rates in the paediatric and internal medicine departments (where communicable diseases are a frequent cause of admission) and less the admission rates in the maternity and the surgery departments. A separate analysis of each hospital department rules this out (Table 7.3). The rates represent the average number of admissions per month per 10,000 inhabitants. The different relative risks (RR) for the rural population – where the financial exclusion is a higher problem than in the urban area – consistently exceed the value of 1, indicating decreased hospital utilization in the exclusion period. The fact that utilization in *all* departments is affected in a similar way makes it unlikely for the lower utilization in the exclusion period to be due to seasonal epidemiological variations.

Another argument also suggests that epidemiological variations are unlikely to explain the lower utilization: there where services are free, no such seasonal pattern in hospital utilization is actually observed. The nearby N'Zérékoré *district* faces similar epidemiological disease patterns and has been hosting a high proportion of refugees from Liberia for several years. The care for the refugees was free of charge in 1995 (the costs being entirely supported by the High Commission of Refugees). Overall hospital utilization by the refugee population remained stable throughout the year, whereas for

Table 7.3   Average admission rates (*numbers*) per hospital department in the normal and in the exclusion periods (1994–96)

	Internal medicine females	Internal medicine males	Paediatrics	Maternity	Surgery females*	Surgery males*
Total:						
Normal	2.37 (*1140*)	2.56 (*1235*)	4.73 (*2277*)	3.28 (*1579*)	0.72 (*334*)	2.37 (*1097*)
Exclusion	1.93 (*310*)	2.22 (*357*)	4.82 (*774*)	3.15 (*505*)	0.64 (*103*)	2.15 (*345*)
RR	1.23	1.15	0.98	1.04	1.12	1.1
(95%CI)	(1.08–1.39)	(1.15–1.3)	(0.9–1.06)	(0.94–1.15)	(0.9–1.4)	(0.98–1.24)
Urban:						
Normal	6.02 (*921*)	6.42 (*981*)	13.39 (*2047*)	8.71 (*1332*)	1.87 (*276*)	5.35 (*788*)
Exclusion	4.96 (*253*)	5.59 (*285*)	14.07 (*717*)	8.34 (*425*)	1.67 (*85*)	4.92 (*251*)
RR	1.21	1.15	0.95	1.04	1.12	1.09
(95%CI)	(1.06–1.39)	(1.01–1.31)	(0.87–1.04)	(0.94–1.17)	(0.88–1.43)	(0.94–1.25)
Rural:						
Normal	0.67 (*219*)	0.77 (*254*)	0.7 (*230*)	0.75 (*247*)	0.18 (*58*)	0.98 (*309*)
Exclusion	0.52 (*57*)	0.66 (*72*)	0.52 (*57*)	0.73 (*80*)	0.16 (*18*)	0.86 (*94*)
RR	**1.29**	**1.17**	**1.35**	**1.03**	**1.13**	**1.14**
(95%CI)	**(0.96–1.71)**	**(0.91–1.53)**	**(1.01–1.8)**	**(0.8–1.32)**	**(0.66–1.89)**	**(0.9–1.43)**
Ratio urban/rural:						
Normal	8.9	8.3	19.1	11.6	10.4	5.5
Exclusion	9.5	8.5	27.1	11.4	10.4	5.7

In the case of surgery, the normal period covers only 26 months (the data for January 1995 were lost); in all other cases, this period covers 27 months.

the autochton population – who had to pay – it dropped significantly in the second semester of the year (Galland, 1996).

The impact of financial exclusion on the utilization of the different departments seems thus relatively homogeneous. The RR pertaining to the rural population (indicated in bold in Table 7.3) are however never significant except for the paediatric department (CI: 1.01–1.8). A level close to significance is obtained for the (female) internal medicine department (CI: 0.96–1.71). The ratios of urban/rural population admission rates remain similar in both normal and exclusion periods, except for the paediatric department where the ratio increases from about 20 in the normal period to 27 in the exclusion period. The fact that the utilization of the paediatric department is most affected by exclusion is not surprising. When resources become very scarce people obviously need to make choices and to establish priorities concerning health care and other expenditure. It is likely that more efforts will be mobilized for the health problems faced by adults. Hence, the lack of available financial resources will be overcome in some cases, in others this will not happen. Other considerations than the perception of the problem will also influence this decision-making process: for instance, the effectiveness of the technical answer the formal health services currently offer for the management of the health problem and/or the existence of technically effective solutions in the community itself. For some of the paediatric problems, reasonably effective alternatives exist to hospital-based care (for instance, self-medication and/or the utilization of local private providers).

It can be hypothesized that the relatively low admission rate in Kissidougou is an indicator of a deficit in *useful* hospital utilization – especially for the rural communities given the important urban/rural utilization differentials – and that it suggests the existence of substantial unmet need. Data from Kissidougou on admissions for strangulated inguinal hernias and for major obstetrical interventions support this hypothesis (patients from out of the district were excluded). It is unlikely that their respective incidences would be significantly different in the urban and rural population of Kissidougou. The existence of supply-induced surgery for these kind of health problems also is unlikely, certainly for strangulated hernias.

In the 36 month period 1994–96, 168 strangulated hernias were admitted: 98 patients came from the urban *sub-districts* and 70 from the rural ones. The average yearly admission rate was 31.4/100,000 for the total population; 57.7/100,000 for the urban population; and 19.2/100,000 for the rural population. The urban/rural ratio thus equals 3. In the same period, 301 pregnant women underwent surgery (mainly Caesarean sections) because of major obstetrical problems: 202 urban and 99 rural women. The average yearly admission rate (with the number of expected pregnancies as denominator) for the period 1994-96 is 1.25 per cent for the total population; 2.64 per cent for the urban population; and 0.6 per cent for the rural population. The urban/rural ratio is 4.4.

Discussion

The Effect of Exclusion on Utilization is Limited

There was virtually no impact on the utilization of curative outpatients clinics at health centre level. This does however not mean that there would be no problem at the household level, at the stages *preceding* utilization. In a survey carried out in 1994 in the Kissidougou district, patients indicated that the delay before resorting to health centre utilization was much higher in the 'exclusion' period than during the rest of the year (Centre International de Développement et de Recherche, 1994).

The impact on inpatient hospital use is more pronounced, especially at the level of the paediatric department. This last finding needs however to be placed in a context of relatively low levels of health services utilization, especially when the hospital is concerned. Yearly admission rates of about 20 per cent of the inhabitants indeed are relatively low compared to what is observed in other African district hospitals (Van Lerberghe et al., 1992; Petit and Van Ginneken, 1995).

In a context of low utilization (when life-threatening problems for which the health services can offer a technically effective solution will receive priority) it is unlikely for seasonal exclusion significantly to decrease further the level of inpatient hospital utilization. Future measurements of hospital use, in both exclusion and normal periods, would enable us to appreciate whether the impact of exclusion – which is low in a situation of low utilization – would actually increase when the Kissidougou inpatient hospital utilization grows further.

Coping with Exclusion

The Touffoudou investigation illustrates that utilization of health services in the exclusion period is often only possible because a variety of fund raising strategies are mobilized. A same level of utilization (of either health centre or hospital) at different periods of the year has different implications on the overall household economy. The most common strategies consist of borrowing from more wealthy people in the community, selling labour, and in last resort selling food stocks and/or other personal assets. The opportunity cost related to seasonal debt remains manageable as long as the poor can repay the incurred debts before the next exclusion period. The picture is different when debts cannot be refunded: in such a situation the appropriate care for the grandfather's strangulated hernia or for the mother's obstructed labour (both problems scoring high on people's priority list) may take place at the expense of the (future) well-being of the entire household.

Seasonal variation in household income is a common feature in rural communities of the developing world and may contribute to exclude people from health care in settings where they have to pay at the time of use. The Kissidougou case clearly illustrates that health care utilization is affected by a variety of factors. Financial barriers are rarely an isolated phenomenon. A variety of mechanisms are developed by the community to cope with a lack of resources at specific periods of the year. It remains to be seen whether, and to what extent, insurance-based financing has a potential to further limit the effects of exclusion.

Conclusion: Is Health Insurance an Answer to the Problem of Exclusion?

In a situation of temporary financial exclusion, as is the case in about half of the Kissidougou population, the main problem people face is uncertainty concerning the question of when to pay. An insurance mechanism may then seem an adequate answer. It carries the added advantage that the health care providers face fewer problems of 'solvency' of their clients. For instance, in the district hospital of the neighbouring Guéckédou district, up to one quarter of the hospital bills could not (or could only partially) be honoured during the second half of the year when little cash is available (Criel, 1996). This was far less a problem during the first half of the year.

The problem of people in a situation of permanent exclusion is more complex. A pure insurance mechanism may not be a feasible option in a context where people permanently lack the necessary financial resources for the payment of the subscription premiums. In these situations an element of income-solidarity needs to be introduced to reduce the uncertainty of these population subgroups. Insurance then needs to be combined with solidarity.

Solidarity with people who are not only economically but also socially marginalized is not obvious. This discussion definitely goes beyond the mere technicalities of health insurance: it raises the issue of values a society stands for and, consequently, of its choices concerning the destitute.

Kissidougou illustrates the potential, but also the limits, of financing health care through an insurance mechanism. Only some of the important constraints that transform temporary lack of cash in insurmountable barriers to hospital utilization, specifically for the rural dwellers, are vulnerable to a health care insurance scheme. The strong urban/rural differential observed in the utilization of hospital services throughout the year (indicative of a deficit in hospital utilization by the rural dwellers) is only to some extent due to a lack of financial resources to pay the fee(s) charged. Several other elements influence utilization of the hospital. What are the most relevant ones? Are they vulnerable through an insurance mechanism? If not, what other mechanisms could be considered?

Physical Accessibility

The issue of transport costs – often a bigger barrier than the fees – to the hospital is important. These costs could theoretically be tackled in the frame of a local insurance scheme. For instance, one could consider a design where the package of benefits includes (or is even restricted to) the payment of a lump sum of money to insured patients as (partial or total) compensation for the indirect costs incurred by a hospital admission. Such a design, however, would not address the scarcity of means of transport in remote areas, certainly in case of an emergency situation during the night.

The general condition of the local road network is more problematic in the second semester, with the start of the rainy season. This is obviously not vulnerable to an insurance system. One may argue that investing more local resources in the development of communication and transport infrastructure – rather than in an insurance plan – would have a greater impact on the accessibility of hospital based health care. In theory this is correct, but in practice the levels of investment that are needed would be of a different order of magnitude.

The opportunity cost of an admission is higher in the second half of the year because it is a period of intense land labour activity, at least for these (rural) households living from agriculture. It is then more difficult to find relatives who can accompany the patient. Again, this is a constraint that is not vulnerable through an insurance mechanism.

People from rural areas with no relatives in town seem reluctant to undertake a trip to the hospital. This barrier to hospital utilization – which does not exist for health centre utilization – again does not seem vulnerable through an insurance scheme. Other strategies would need to be designed for that purpose. One of them could be to provide a place to stay next to the hospital for patients and their companions. Such a 'hostel' could double as a 'self-care' unit. Such solutions were already being advocated by Maurice King in the 1960s (King, 1966).

Financial Access and Social Conflicts

There is the generalized behaviour of over-billing leading to uncertainty for patients concerning the amount of the fee(s) to be paid. To some extent, this issue could be tackled by an insurance system. An insurance system would clarify to patients and health care providers that no fee – except perhaps for the co-payment – is to be paid by the insured patients. The fact that such an arrangement potentially leads to conflict – health care providers would lose part of their revenue – definitely merits close consideration in the preparation, design, and organization of the insurance scheme.

A locally managed insurance scheme, however, possibly with a split between provider and purchaser functions, may boost local social organization and eventually constitute a stronger leverage in the quest for more accountability of the health service. An insurance-based mechanism has, in that respect, a higher potential than a simplification of the current flat rate where only the sick pay. This precisely is one of the hypotheses the PRIMA project intends to test in the future.

The introduction of an insurance mechanism for health care may affect, possibly even disturb, local social organization patterns. The prevailing interactions between different social categories – in terms of money raising strategies – were illustrated by the Touffoudou investigation. Genuine solidarity may be at the basis of the existing mutual aid mechanism mobilized in case of exclusion. But another logic, perhaps a less generous one, may also underlie this aid mechanism: for instance, the creation of sustained allegiance from the poor to the rich, or the desire for profit. It seems reasonable to anticipate that health insurance would interfere with this 'community-help' dynamic – for the worse or for the better.

Ability to Pay

Insurance may constitute a partial answer to people's problems in the exclusion period, certainly when the households' capacity to mobilize resources is limited or when they cannot (or insufficiently) rely on existing social mutual aid mechanisms. However, a major issue in the design of such a scheme would be to set affordable premiums for the ones who would most benefit from joining it. Hence, the effectiveness of insurance in reducing genuine exclusion, returns to the question of effectiveness of exemption mechanisms.

A crucial issue is the question whether a health insurance scheme would be more effective than what is already there. There would be no point indeed in replacing reasonably effective existing mutual aid mechanisms by a technical fix. The PRIMA research so far succeeded in developing awareness that health insurance is not a socially neutral phenomenon. It did this among health planners at district, but also at national level. Health insurance is much more than merely a matter of administrative technique where financial transfers are organized between individual households or between different population groups.[1]

Note

1   The authors wish to thank Mrs A. Barry and Ms P. Scheuerman of the PRIMA team in Kissidougou for their help in the data collection. Thanks also to Professor W. Van Lerberghe of the Public Health Department of the Institute of Tropical Medicine, Antwerp, for his suggestions and comments on an earlier draft of this paper.

References

Centre International de Développement et de Recherche (1994), *Etude de Prefaisabilité Mutuelle De Santé. Projet Santé Rurale Kissidougou et Gueckedou*, CIDR/GUINEE/BG/CJ/N°49bis, 1-83, CIDR.

Criel, B. (1996), 'Projet de Recherche-action Portant sur le Développement de Systèmes de Partage de Risque en Matière de Financement Communautaire des Soins de Santé', *Consult.Medicus Mundi Belgique*, document de travail, pp. 1–19.

de la Rocque, M. (1996), 'Equité et Exclusions des Services de Santé. De la Recherche à l'Action, l'Expérience d'une ONG', *Cahiers Santé*, 6, pp. 341–4.

Desclaux, A. (1992), 'Le 'RAP' et les Méthodes Anthropologiques Rapides en Santé Publique', *Cahiers Santé*, 2, pp. 300–6.

Galland, B. (1994), 'Les Services de Santé et la Population: Relations économiques, financières et institutionelles', Manuel de réflexion, 1–160, CIDR–GTZ, Eschborn, Autrèches.

Galland, B. (1996), 'Création de Mutuelles de Santé en Guinée Forestière Etude d'Opportunité', rapport préliminaire, CIDR.

Galland, B., Kaddar, M. and Debaig, G. (1997), 'Mutualité et Systèmes de Prépaiement des Soins de Santé en Afrique sub-Saharienne', *L'Enfant en Milieu Tropical*, 228, pp. 9–22.

Galland, B., Werner, H. and Camara, M. (1991), 'Etude Socio-économique et Budgetaire dans le Cadre du Projet Santé Rurale Kissidougou/Gueckedou, Guinée', GTZ, Eschborn.

Gueye, B. and Schoonmaker Freudenberger, K. (1991), *Introduction à la Méthode Accelerée de Recherche Participative (MARP), Rapid Rural Appraisal. Quelques Notes Pour Appuyer Une Formation Pratique*, 2nd edn, International Institute for Environment and Development.

King, M. (1966), *Medical Care in Developing Countries*, Oxford University Press, Oxford.

Ministre de l'Intérieur et de la Sécurité, Le Ministre de la Santé Publique et Affaires Sociales and Le Ministre du Plan et des Finances (1993), *Arreté Interministériel Fixant les Tarifs-Plafonds des Formations Hospitalières Publiques en République de Guinée*, Ministère de la Santé Publique et des Affaires Sociales, Conakry.

Petit, P.L.C. and Van Ginneken, J.K. (1995), 'Analysis of Hospital Records in Four African Countries, 1975–1990, with emphasis on infectious diseases', *Journal of Tropical Medicine and Hygiene*, 98, pp. 217–27.

Projet de Recherche sur le Partage des Risques-Maladie (PRIMA) (1997), *Points sur les Activités de PRIMA. Période Janvier – Mai*, PRIMA.

Soucat, A., Gandaho, T., Levy-Bruhl, D., de Béthune, X., Alihonou, E., Ortiz, C., Gbedonou, P., Adovohekpe, P., Camara, O., Ndiaye, J.M., Dieng, B. and Knippenberg, R. (1997), 'Health Seeking Behaviour and Household Health Expenditures in Benin and Guinea: The equity implications of the Bamako Initiative', *International Journal of Health Planning and Management*, 12, S137–63.

Van Lerberghe, W., Van Balen, H. and Kegels, G. (1992), 'Typologie et Performances des Hôpitaux de Premier Recours en Afrique Sub-Saharienne', *Annales de la Société Belge de Médecine Tropicale*, 72, pp. 1–51.

8 Supporting Purchasing in Acute Specialties in the Trent Region

NICK PAYNE, RON AKEHURST, STEVE BEARD, ALAN
BRENNAN, NEILL CALVERT, JIM CHILCOTT, CHRIS McCABE,
SUZY PAISLEY AND SUE WARD
*Trent Institute for Health Services Research – Sheffield Unit, School of Health and
Related Research, Sheffield University*

Introduction

Those responsible for purchasing or commissioning health services are faced with some important but difficult decisions about new interventions. Currently, the development of new pharmaceutical products, new surgical techniques and new diagnostic and imaging technology is proceeding at a very fast rate (Jennet, 1992; Hoare, 1992). The last few years have seen a rate of emergence of such interventions, even those of well substantiated clinical effectiveness, such that the combined costs of their purchase by the health service would exceed by several times any increase in funding available (Snell, 1997). Note that throughout this chapter the term purchasing is used for the process by which Health Authorities determine the services to be provided for their populations. In this context it is synonymous with the term commissioning, which is now becoming more widely used (Department of Health, 1997).

Purchasers have not only to make judgments about the effectiveness of new interventions, they also need to make assessments about their cost-effectiveness as an important part of the decision about how high a priority each should be given in the competition for limited new funds. In most Health Authorities, however, there is a limited number of staff of sufficient training and experience to advise on these decisions. Often one public health physician will be relied on to give advice in respect of all the acute specialties. While

Controlling Costs: Strategic Issues in Health Care Management, H.T.O. Davies, M. Tavakoli, M. Malek, A. R. Neilson (eds), Ashgate Publishing Ltd, 1999.

advice can, of course, be sought from specialist clinicians working in the provider units, all too often (although perhaps understandably) such advice is biased in favour of their particular patient group.

It is quite proper that each Health Authority should consider the needs, and therefore the priorities, for treatment and care of the particular population for which it is responsible. That is, the assessment of the importance of a particular intervention is a local decision influenced by local circumstances. By contrast, assessment of the scientific evidence for the effectiveness of an intervention and of its costs is a task which, done properly once, could inform all Health Authorities. Repetition of these assessments by all Health Authorities (or primary care groups) leads to wasteful duplication of effort, poor quality of work, and large numbers of interventions unevaluated in any systematic way.

For these reasons, a network was set up in the Trent region to allow purchasers to share research knowledge about the effectiveness and cost-effectiveness of acute service interventions and to inform collectively their purchasing policy. This network, the 'Working Group on Acute Purchasing' is facilitated by the Sheffield Unit of the Trent Institute for Health Services Research (which is based in Sheffield University's School of Health and Related Research – ScHARR). Its activities are partly supported by Health Authority staff and partly by funds provided by the Trent Regional Office of the National Health Service Executive.

This chapter describes the structure, process and outcomes of this network, and reviews how it might develop in the future.

Methods

The main steps in the process are summarized in Figure 8.1 and set out in more detail below. In principle the process is in two parts:

a) production of a draft report 'Guidance Notes for Purchasers'; and

b) peer review, discussion of these drafts and consideration by the Trent Development and Evaluation Committee (DEC).

Choice of Topics

At the beginning of each year each Health Authority in the Trent region is

Choice of topics based on purchasers' priorities

↓

Preliminary literature search to help define precise question

↓

Formation of team to produce Guidance Notes

↓

Definitive literature search

↓

Analytical work and writing of draft Guidance Notes

↓

Peer-review of draft Guidance Notes

↓

Working group on Acute Purchasing presentation and discussion

↓

Revision of draft report consequent on WGAP discussion

↓

Presentation and discussion at Trent Development and Evaluation Committee

↓

Incorporation of DEC decision and publication of Guidance Notes

Figure 8.1   The main steps in the process of choosing topics, production of Guidance Notes for Purchasers, and their options and recommendations being considered by the Trent Development and Evaluation Committee (DEC)

asked to nominate topics it would like to have examined by the Working Group on Acute Purchasing. Input is also sought from the Regional Pharmaceutical Adviser in respect of new pharmaceutical products which have not yet come to the attention of purchasers because they are still finishing their route through the licensing process. A preliminary literature search is carried out to give an indication of the quantity and quality of information available on each topic.

When all the possible topics have been collated, each Health Authority is asked to apportion a total of 100 points to those on the possible list in order that those of greatest relevance and importance can be selected. Information is sought on work already carried out or in progress elsewhere and fed back to purchasers.

Once a selection of topics has been made, a small topic-specific team is set up to work on each of those selected. This team usually consists of at least one of:

- a public health consultant from a purchasing authority;
- an analyst with health economics and/or operational research expertise;
- a specialist clinician from the relevant discipline.

This group initially defines the question in more detail and decides what work is required by whom.

A team from ScHARR consisting of a Senior Lecturer in public health medicine, an information specialist and a publications officer provide support for the whole process.

Literature Search

Information is sought from the published and 'grey' literature on three main aspects of each topic.

- Incidence/prevalence of the disease process for which the new intervention is intended.
- Evidence for effectiveness of the new intervention compared with existing treatment.
- Assessments of cost-effectiveness – particularly comparing the costs to the health service of the new intervention with existing treatment and in relation to any additional clinical benefits to patients.

Assessing Effectiveness

The approach has been to endeavour to categorize evidence in a hierarchy (Deeks et al., 1996), using that from randomized controlled trials (RCT) wherever possible, but in several instances, observational studies have had to be relied on because of the absence of RCT evidence. We consider in this article problems still encountered even if RCT evidence in its usual format is available.

Health Economic Modelling Methods Used

Having made an assessment of the effectiveness of the new intervention, an attempt is made to assess the relationship between its cost and its associated health benefits. This work is divided into the following components:

- costing the intervention, both at an individual level and at a Health Authority level, taking into account the size of the population that might be suitable for and be offered the intervention;
- turning estimates from clinical trial data on benefits – for example, survival, such as the relative risk or odds ratio of this benefit at the end of the trial – into an assessment that can be used ideally to determine life years or, where relevant, quality adjusted life years (QALYs) gained. Such assessments are essential to determine cost-utility ratios but are often lacking from the data available in clinical trials.

The economic analysis is undertaken with a health service perspective and usually aims to determine the entire cost to the health service, for example, the costs of a new and expensive drug netted against any potential reductions in costs associated with it as a result of fewer hospital admissions. Financial costs and benefits to patients or their carers or society in general are not included in these calculations, but are rather regarded as benefits in the same way as, for example, gains in life-years in the treated group. Where appropriate the economic analyses are carried out both with and without discounting of costs and benefits and, whenever possible, a sensitivity analysis in respect of all key assumptions is carried out. Where significant changes in costs and savings are expected, attempts are made to show how these vary over time. Attention is also drawn to circumstances where the introduction of a new intervention will result in changes in the balance of resources required in the NHS, for example between hospital and primary care budgets.

Peer Review and Assessments of the Recommendations from the Guidance Notes for Purchasers

A draft Guidance Note for Purchasers on the new intervention in question is prepared and circulated to representatives (usually public health physicians) from each Health Authority in Trent and to clinical specialists in the relevant discipline. A seminar is held at which these reports are presented and discussed. Usually both a 'protagonist' and 'sceptic' clinician in respect of the new intervention is invited to try to balance the debate, and often up to eight clinicians involved with the service in question will attend.

Following amendments to the draft report, and further analysis where necessary, the Guidance Notes are considered by the Trent Development and Evaluation Committee. This is comprised of members appointed on the basis of their individual knowledge and expertise, and includes non-clinically qualified scientists and lay members. The committee recommends, on the basis of the appropriate evidence and analyses from the draft Guidance Notes, priorities for: direct development of new services on a pilot basis; or service developments to be secured by Health Authorities. Finally, with the Trent DEC's summary and decision added, the Guidance Notes are published by the Trent Institute for Health Services Research.

Results

Topics Analysed

The topics that have been considered and for which Guidance Notes are published so far are listed in Table 8.1. Eight of these deal with pharmaceutical products, three with surgical techniques, one with a diagnostic imaging intervention, and one with a blood product and its replacement.

Literature Searching

The results and lessons learned from the literature searching process are dividable into 'successes' and 'problems'.

Successes

• Searching is approached from more than one angle in an attempt to inform

Table 8.1   Topics considered to date, with summary of DEC recommendation (when made), approximate annual costs of following this recommendation and approximate possible costs if no prioritization process had been carried out. An average Health Authority (HA) is taken as having a population of 500,000

Topic	Recommendation of the Trent Development and Evaluation Committee (DEC)	Annual extra cost to an average HA of following DEC's recommendation	Annual extra cost to an average HA without this prioritization process
The use of DNase in cystic fibrosis	Not considered	~£90,000	~£90,000
The use of cochlear implantation	Not considered	~£138,000	~£138,000
The use of HMG Co-A reductase inhibitor (statin) treatment in the prevention of coronary heart disease	Purchase for secondary prevention and high risk primary prevention	~£5,490,000	~£34,000,000
The use of computed tomography in the management of transient ischaemic attack	Supported use of CT scanning	~£130,000	~£130,000
The use of prostacyclin and iloprost in the treatment of primary pulmonary hypertension	Recommended should be purchased only as part of a national programme	—	~£45,000
The use of riluzole in the treatment of amyotrophic lateral sclerosis (motor neurone disease)	Not supported as evidence of effectiveness was insufficient	—	~£100,000
The use of recombinant factor VIII versus plasma derived factor VIII in Haemophilia A	Supported only for newly-diagnosed patients	~£65,000 in five years	~£255,000
The use of cisplatin and paclitaxel as first line treatment in ovarian cancer	Supported mainly for use within clinical trials	Up to ~£260,000 if treated all suitable patients	~£260,000
The use of bone-anchored hearing aids	Supported limited use	~£20,000	~£20,000
The use of alpha interferon in chronic myeloid leukaemia	Not recommended as not a cost-effective treatment	—	~£160,000
The use of donepezil in Alzheimer's disease	Supported for use in trials only	~£240,000	~£2,400,000
The use of growth hormone in hormone deficient adults	Supported in severely affected individuals	~£65,000	~£130,000
The use of spinal cord stimulation in chronic pain	Not recommended outside trials	—	~£40,000
Total costs		~£6,498,000	~£37,768,000
Total costs less statins		~£1,008,000	~£3,768,000

not just the clinical effectiveness aspect but all aspects of the topic.

- Access to the Internet and to electronic databases, which include health sources, 'non-health' sources and grey literature, allows very wide ranging searches to be carried out. This is particularly important considering the scattered nature of evidence on new technologies.
- Knowledge of current research programmes, guidelines and health technology assessment organizations reduces duplication of work and informs project teams of major current research relevant to priority topics.
- Search methodologies to identify systematic reviews and RCTs facilitates the identification of good quality evidence to inform the summary of evidence of effectiveness (Dickersin, 1994; NHS Centre for Reviews and Dissemination, 1996).

Problems

- There is a lack of established methodologies for identifying evidence or information on other aspects of topics, especially incidence/prevalence and cost-effectiveness.
- Due to the above, and to the varying nature and amount of information relevant to the disease process and the intervention, is it difficult to establish a standardized system or method of searching and data collection which would inform all aspects of each topic.
- The identification of current research and guidelines is a time-consuming process. Further development of collaborative initiatives in this area would improve the quality of this type of information, as well as the coordination and communication of its retrieval.

Format of Guidance Notes

We have found that the following format is useful for communicating the results of the analysis and setting out the Guidance Notes for Purchasers.

- *Introduction*: this considers: incidence and pathology; prognosis and mortality; current standard treatment options; scale of the problem in a typical health district.
- *Summary of evidence of effectiveness*: this summarizes the current research evidence of the effectiveness of the new intervention compared with existing treatment drawing on controlled trials and observational studies.
- *Cost and benefit implications of adopting the intervention*: this interprets

the evidence for effectiveness and on marginal costs (both total and net) of treatment in terms relevant for informing purchasing decisions. Modelling techniques are used where necessary to draw together the available evidence, highlighting gaps in knowledge or information, and facilitating the incorporation of expert judgment from relevant clinicians. These techniques allow an estimation of the cost-effectiveness or cost-utility of the new intervention compared with standard treatment.

- *Options for purchasers and providers*: a set of options is generated, usually ranging from do not purchase at all, purchase only within further trials, to purchase to permit widespread use.
- *Discussion and conclusion.*
- *Summary matrix*: including, where appropriate, criteria for adopting, continuing and discontinuing treatment.
- *References.*

Analytical Problems

The main problems that are encountered with the evidence are listed, with examples of their occurrence from topics examined so far.

- Insufficient information is available of the incidence or prevalence of the relevant condition to be able to give an indication of the size of the problem in an average Health Authority (e.g. numbers suitable for spinal cord stimulation for treatment of chronic pain; numbers suitable for statin cholesterol-lowering treatment).
- No randomized clinical trial data are available (e.g. use of bone-anchored hearing aids).
- Trials have been carried out but either are unpublished (and the data are 'held on file' by pharmaceutical companies) or available only in abstract form (e.g. use of riluzole in motor neurone disease).
- Clinical trials are of insufficient duration to assess adequately whether a worthwhile effect is likely to be obtained, or do not provide evidence on the most appropriate or significant end points such as mortality (e.g. use of DNase in cystic fibrosis), or quality of life for patients and carers (e.g. anti-dementia drugs). Thus, the clinical end-points in trials often do not relate to the functional end-points necessary for purchasing decisions.
- Trial data are presented such that an effect of treatment (usually a favourable relative risk or odds ratio) is given after a period of time. This, however, does not allow an assessment of the difference in the areas under the survival

curves of intervention and control groups which is necessary to determine cost-effectiveness in terms of a ratio such as cost per life years gained (use of cisplatin and paclitaxel in ovarian cancer; use of alpha-interferon in leukaemia; riluzole in motor neurone disease; use of statins).
- Information from trials on quality of life is insufficient to assess or calculate the cost utility of treatment, for example as cost per quality adjusted life year (e.g. use of growth hormone replacement therapy in adults).

Survival Analysis and Its Modelling

In order to make an estimate of life-years gained in situations where the new intervention reduces mortality, several analytical approaches have been taken, including.

- Applying intervention and placebo relative risk to all-cause mortality life-tables.
- Mathematical modelling of the published survival curve data.
- Applying trial data on changes in physiological variables to observational data on how these variables affect survival.

Clearly, none of these methods is a substitute for the appropriate data from experimental studies. However, if, as is common, these data are not available, then these approximations provide the only method of making an estimate of survival difference in terms of life-years gained such that an estimate of cost-effectiveness ratios may be produced. Sensitivity analyses, however, often reveal considerable uncertainty about our central estimates of both costs and benefits.

Cost and Saving Implications of Interventions

The total cost implications of interventions considered so far are substantial as Table 8.1 also shows. In addition, the numbers of potential patients that might be treated range from only a handful for a Health Authority to many thousands. What is also clear from Table 8.1 is how substantial the cost implications for Health Authorities would be if no prioritization process were attempted.

We have concentrated particularly on costs to the health service rather than total costs. Purchasers have felt that wider costs and savings associated with new interventions (such as those to patients and carers and society generally) should be taken account of as loss or gains of benefit rather than added to or subtracted from health service costs. Thus, any implications for changes in the purchasing power of patients, carers, etc. are taken account of qualitatively.

Working Group on Acute Purchasing Meetings

The Working Group on Acute Purchasing is relatively well attended by purchaser representatives and by clinicians from the relevant clinical disciplines. Purchasers are almost exclusively represented only by public health physicians rather than others in the Health Authority such as managers involved in contracting or from finance departments.

There is usually a high quality of debate about the technical accuracy of the draft Guidance Notes and many suggestions are made about further analysis and refinement of the draft before it is presented to DEC. One consequence of the discussion is that clinicians are often made sharply aware of the difficult prioritization questions that Health Authorities have to make and of the process by which these decisions are made.

Discussion

The approach described in this chapter follows on from a similar initiative in the Wessex (latterly South and West) Region (Stevens et al., 1995). Since then, other parts of the country have followed our lead and set up similar assessment mechanisms for new health technologies (SHPIC, 1996). At the national level, the Health Technology Assessment Programme (Advisory Group on Health Technology Assessment, 1993) has commissioned a large number of individual studies which should help to ensure that appropriate evaluations are undertaken. This programme is supplemented by the Cochrane Centre (Chalmers et al., 1992), and by other National Health Service initiatives (NHS Centre for Reviews and Dissemination, 1998). These usually undertake, however, long term work and the results are currently still limited to relatively few topics. Purchasers, however, need assessments of many more interventions, and the time scale for purchaser decision making is usually more urgent than the output of this national work. In addition, they need a cost-effectiveness appraisal, as well as simply an assessment of effectiveness, in order for essential prioritization decisions to be made (Goldberg-Wood, 1997).

Purchasers have found already that their resources in terms of expertise are inadequate to cope with individual assessments of new interventions. Already quite small organizations, they have been stretched still further by pressures on management costs so there is clearly a need for them to collaborate and share this assessment work. Moreover, purchasers also need to try to provide some uniformity in their decision-making processes to avoid 'rationing by postcode' and to ensure that these decisions are subject to adequate, unbiased, peer review.

We have found that the information required for adequate assessment can be difficult to retrieve, and is often deficient because of lack of information on disease incidence or prevalence, lack of controlled trials and lack of cost-effectiveness information to allow fair comparisons. Moreover, what evidence is available may be published too late. There is a need to develop further the process of providing analysis and advice for purchasers in the format they require. There is often a gap between the published evidence and the information needed for prioritization of scarce resources. The information required for the licensing of new drugs, for example, is not sufficient to meet these needs. We have attempted, for example with modelling techniques, to bridge this gap, but we need both improved review methodologies, and clinical trials that address questions that purchasers as well as providers need answering. There is currently a debate about the advantages and disadvantages of the modelling approach to health economic analysis. We believe modelling works on two levels: it provides a better understanding of costs and benefits than would otherwise be available to purchasers; and it identifies gaps and uncertainties in the research evidence.

Finally, although we have helped avoid duplication of assessment effort in one health region, there is a need to make this a nationwide initiative as has been recently recommended (Audit Commission, 1997). To this end, we have set up a collaboration – 'InterDEC' – with other regional initiatives such as ours to avoid still further duplication and to provide improved quality and peer-review of our reports.

A challenge for InterDEC, or whatever national initiative such as the National Institute for Clinical Excellence (NICE) is introduced, is how to develop an assessment framework for new and existing health technologies which allows improved comparison between them. We attempt to compare interventions by standard cost-effectiveness and cost-utility assessments, but Health Authorities and other purchasers need still further refinement of this approach in order for their prioritization or 'rationing' decisions to both be, and be seen to be, equitable.[1]

Note

1   Financial support for the Working Group on Acute Purchasing and the Development and Evaluation Committee is partly provided by NHS Executive Trent. The expert advice and support from Professor Sir David Hull and members of the Trent DEC is gratefully acknowledged; as is the administrative work of Pat Holmes, Mike Jacobs and Gill Rooney from the Trent Institute for Health Services Research.

References

Advisory Group on Health Technology Assessment (1993), *Assessing the Effects of Health Technologies, Principles, Practice, Proposals*, Department of Health, London.

Audit Commission (1997), *Higher Purchase: Commissioning specialized services in the NHS*, Audit Commission, London.

Chalmers, I., Dickersin, K. and Chalmers, T.C. (1992), 'Getting to Grips with Archie Cochrane's Agenda', *British Medical Journal*, 305, pp. 786–8.

Deeks, J., Glanville, J. and Sheldon, T. (1996), *Undertaking Systematic Reviews of Effectiveness: CRD guidelines for those carrying out or commissioning reviews*, CRD Report 4, NHS Centre for Reviews and Dissemination, York.

Department of Health (1997), *The New NHS*, Department of Health, London.

Dickersin, K., Scherer, R. and Lefebvre, C. (1994), 'Identifying Relevant Studies for Systematic Reviews', *British Medical Journal*, 309, pp. 1286–91.

Goldberg-Wood, S. (1997), '"Smart" rationing is possible', *British Medical Journal*, 315, p. 146.

Hoare, J. (1992), *Tidal Wave. New Technology, Medicine and the NHS*, King's Fund Centre, London.

Jennet, B. (1992), 'Health Technology Assessment', *British Medical Journal*, 305, pp. 67–8.

NHS Centre for Reviews and Dissemination (1996), *Undertaking Systematic Reviews of Research of Effectiveness: CRD guidelines for those carrying out or commissioning reviews*, University of York, York.

NHS Centre for Reviews and Dissemination: University of York, Internet WWW page at URL:http://www.york.ac.uk/inst/crd/welcome.htm (cited 28 January 1998).

SHPIC (1996), *Preventing Blindness in Diabetes*, Scottish Health Purchasing Information Centre, Aberdeen.

Snell, P.H. (1997), *Sheffield's Health into 1997. Director of Public Health's Annual Report*, Sheffield Health Authority, Sheffield.

Stevens, A., Colin-Jones, D. and Gabbay, J. (1995), '"Quick and Clean": Authoritative health technology assessment for local health care contracting', *Health Trends*, 27, pp. 37–42.

SECTION 2
ECONOMIC EVALUATION
AND ITS CONTRIBUTION TO
CONTROLLING COSTS

9 Prevention Better Than Treatment? Implementing Evidence-based Strategies

CERI J. PHILLIPS
School of Health Science, University of Wales Swansea

Introduction

One of the proposals of the government's White Papers (Secretary of State for Health, 1997; Secretary of State for Scotland, 1997; Secretary of State for Wales, 1998) is the establishment of a National Institute for Clinical Excellence, which will seek to promote high quality national guidelines for treatment, based on the most up-to-date scientific evidence. The proposal to establish such a body is part of the government's commitment to improve quality in all aspects of health care. However, while such intentions are warmly welcomed, the issue of funding health care services remains a contentious issue.

> It would be a tragedy if implementation of a vision for the organisation and provision of care that has received widespread support were to be frustrated by an approach to NHS spending that owes more to electoral expediency than the current state of the public finances (Ham, 1998).

Differentials between the resources available for the health services and demands placed on them continue to be major headaches for those at all levels of policy making, decision-making, commissioning services and the provision and delivery of health care services. The proposals contained in the White Papers are yet another attempt to address the issue of the health care dilemma (Phillips and Prowle, 1993) of ever-increasing demand against a background of constraints in supply. The development of policies and strategies based on what has been shown to be clinically effective have been advocated for some

Controlling Costs: Strategic Issues in Health Care Management, H.T.O. Davies, M. Tavakoli, M. Malek, A. R. Neilson (eds), Ashgate Publishing Ltd, 1999.

time, while terms such as evidence-based health care and clinical effectiveness are now common usage in health care circles. The extent to which they have been implemented is dubious (Walshe and Ham, 1997), but the recognition of their importance by the government should result in additional impetus, coupled by claims which argue that the way to reduce cost pressures in health care is to focus on proven quality (Marwick, 1997).

Clinicians are also increasingly being urged to practise and prescribe in a cost-effective manner. In other words they are being urged to provide interventions which will maximize the level of benefits to patients – health effects – relative to the resources available. In other countries, Australia and Canada for example, new drugs are only introduced after it has been shown that they are cost-effective, while research investigations, funded by the NHS (and other bodies), usually have to contain an economic evaluation to ascertain the resource implications if they were to be implemented.

There is an obvious relationship between clinical effectiveness and cost-effectiveness witnessed many years ago by Professor Archie Cochrane.

> The development of cost-effective health care needs hard evidence, preferably from randomised trials, that the use of each clinical procedure or drug either alters the natural history of the disease or otherwise benefits many patients at a reasonable cost (Cochrane, 1972).

However, there are a number of tensions between those who advocate the evidence-based and cost-effective approaches. Notwithstanding, the issue of whether results from clinical trials demonstrate the effectiveness of an intervention or should merely be regarded as efficacious (the increasing use of systematic reviews and meta-analyses has alleviated the issue to some extent and has provided a useful synthesis of knowledge as to what constitutes effectiveness and a good basis for economic modelling), concern has been voiced as to whether evidence-based medicine, with its emphasis on individual patients, will result in an inefficient and unethical allocation of resources (Maynard, 1997). Furthermore, it has also been argued that these 'policy drivers', evidence-based medicine and cost-effective practice together with 'preference-driven' medicine, have major limitations in seeking to provide an adequate framework for decision-making in health care (Dowie, 1996). Dowie argues for a decision-analysis based medical decision-making model, which advocates ensuring that inferences from randomized controlled trials and meta-analyses to individual patients (or patient groups) are made explicitly; paying equally serious attention to evidence on values and costs as to clinical evidence; and accepting the inadequacy of 'taking into account and bearing in mind' as a way of integrating the multiple and distinct elements of a decision. What is advocated in this chapter is that a framework be established whereby commissioners can assess the evidence for the clinical and economic impact of new technologies. The decision as to whether to commit resources to new developments obviously involves a number of factors, but information relating to the effectiveness and efficiency of an intervention can provide an extremely important contribution to the decision making process.

This chapter attempts to move towards such a framework by integrating the evidence on effectiveness with the costs likely to be incurred in providing interventions and the probable benefits generated. The explicit aim is to demonstrate how the effectiveness of an intervention, expressed in terms of numbers-needed-to-treat (NNT), combined with an analysis of its economic impact can provide commissioners with an indication of how quality improvements in health care provision and cost savings can be generated. The chapter focuses on the extent to which preventive strategies, using pharmacological interventions, for groups of high-risk patients are both effective and likely to result in budgetary savings for commissioners of health care.

Description of Strategies

One of the major factors driving up demand for health care resources is the demographic shift towards a higher percentage of elderly people. Thus strategies relating to two areas of relevance for the provision of elderly care have been selected, namely the prevention of hip fractures and recurrent strokes. Both of these areas have far reaching implications for the patient, their family and health and social services who have to provide treatment, recovery and rehabilitation services. Given the high cost of providing treatment and care for people who suffer hip fractures and strokes, it is essential that commissioners assess whether it is better to allocate resources from limited resources to new technologies, which prevent the occurrence of such events, or to adopt wait and see strategies, maintaining the status quo and incur the necessary costs as and when they arise. The increasing 'demographic shift' is likely to mean however that the 'status quo' stance brings with it additional dilemmas, which tend to reinforce the argument for considering the impact of new technologies as they arise.

The chapter will utilize studies which have demonstrated the effectiveness of new pharmacological interventions in preventing hip fractures and recurrent strokes and assess the economic impact of their adoption.

Methods

The measure used for the effectiveness of an intervention is the number needed to treat (NNT) (Laupacis, Sackett and Roberts, 1988; Cook and Sackett, 1995; McQuay and Moore, 1997). This measure provides an indication of the number of patients who need to receive the intervention in order to avoid one of them having a stroke or a hip fracture, who would have had such an event if they had not been given the intervention. It is thus possible to estimate the cost of achieving the prevented event and compare it with the cost of the alternative, that is the total costs of treating and caring for a patient with a stroke or a hip fracture.

Unfortunately, there are a number of uncertainties in the process outlined above. Firstly, NNTs are point estimates and thus attention also needs to be focused on their confidence intervals. Secondly, prices of drugs fluctuate, with new drugs including high premiums over and above out-of-patent products, while the extent of adverse effects and their associated costs which may accompany the preventive intervention need to be incorporated within the model. Thirdly, the actual cost of providing treatment and care for patients with recurrent strokes and hip fractures is subject to the limitations of the methodologies used to estimate such values. Fourthly, resource allocation decisions are bound by precedent and competing demands on limited resources which entail negotiation, accommodating a variety of perspectives and other factors in arriving at an agreed view as to how the available budgets are allocated.

Thus, the model offered in this chapter does not provide a clear-cut solution to the problems facing commissioners but rather a framework for their use in considering the validity of implementing new technologies.

The cost of prevention will be computed as:

Cost of prevention = NNT * Time period * Cost of intervention

with the costs of intervention based on the drug costs, professionals' time and costs of adverse effects, while the costs of treating and caring for patients who suffer from a hip fracture and recurrent stroke will be based on estimates from the literature.

Findings

Hip Fractures

The trial which provided evidence of a strategy to prevent the number of hip fractures was carried out in France. Over 3,000 ambulatory women aged 69 and over, with no serious medical conditions and life expectancy of at least 18 months, living in nursing homes or apartment houses for elderly people were randomized to receive 1.2g of elemental calcium plus 20μg of vitamin D_3 or placebos (Chapuy et al., 1992 and 1994). The results of the French study have been translated into numbers-needed-to-treat (NNT) (Bandolier, 1997). For example, to prevent one hip fracture 20 would need to be treated with 1.2g of elemental calcium plus 20μg of vitamin D_3. However, if the patients who died during the course of the study period were included, the NNT would be 40.

The annual cost involved in providing a daily calcium supplement and an injection of vitamin D probably costs between £75 and £250 per person. This is made up of pharmaceutical costs (Ostram 1.2g Merck – one tablet per day at 20p per tablet plus £3 for an annual injection of vitamin D (Torgerson et al., 1996)) and patient visits to the GP (using unit costs of £16 per surgery visit and £47 per domiciliary visit (Netten and Dennett, 1996)). Thus if the strategy formed part of other visits to the GP the annual cost per patient would constitute only the pharmaceutical costs, that is £75, while if four domiciliary visits by the GP were included the cost would rise to over £250.

Thus, with an NNT of 20, the cost of preventing a hip fracture over a three year period ranges from £4,500, when the cost of intervention is £75, to £15,000, when the cost of the intervention is £250.

In Table 9.1 a range of NNTs has been used against which to assess the cost of preventing hip fractures over a three year period. On the basis of Table 9.1 it is possible to predict the most optimistic scenario for preventing a hip fracture. Using the confidence intervals surrounding the NNT as best and worst case scenarios, the cost of preventing a hip fracture with an NNT of 13 ranges between £2,925 and £9,750 depending on which cost of intervention is taken. The worst case scenario for hip fractures yields an NNT of 60, which in turn yields a cost per prevented hip fracture of between £13,500 and £45,000.

These can be used with the costs associated with hip fractures to assess the potential for generating resource savings if the strategy was utilized as a preventive measure in women aged 65 and over. Given that the weekly rate for a nursing home is around £350 per week and the cost for an elderly person

Table 9.1   Cost of preventing one hip fracture over three years

	Intervention costs (£)			
	75	*100*	*125*	*250*
NNTs				
10	2,250	3,000	3,750	7,500
20	4,500	6,000	7,500	15,000
30	6,750	9,000	11,250	22,500
40	9,000	12,000	15,000	30,000
50	11,250	15,000	18,750	37,500
60	13,500	18,000	22,500	45,000
70	15,750	21,000	26,250	52,500
80	18,000	24,000	30,000	60,000

in hospital is nearly £800 per inpatient week (Netten and Dennett, 1996), it does not require extremely long periods of stay in such accommodation before a commissioner moves into a 'loss making' situation. Estimates of the costs associated with hip fractures have varied (Lane, 1996; Randell et al., 1995) but it would appear reasonable to assume that it would cost £10,000 to treat a patient with a fractured hip in the first year. This would include hospital costs, recovery and rehabilitation costs in the community but not other costs to patients and their families. The impact on quality of life has not formed any part of the 'cost of illness' approach adopted but it is clear that the elderly person with a broken hip has a much reduced quality of life over and above the trauma and hurt. In addition, it is highly probable that the growth in the elderly population will exacerbate the social and economic costs associated with osteoporosis and its manifestation in fractures of the vertebrae, wrist or hip. For example, it has been estimated that the increase in the number of hip fractures occurring over the next 30 years or so will be at least 17 per cent (Griffin, 1990) and without therapeutic and prophylactic intervention, the costs of osteoporosis will continue to rise above recent estimates.

The magnitude of any potential resources released from preventing hip fractures obviously depend on the extent of the problem among the elderly population, the cost of the prevention strategy and the costs of treatment, recovery and rehabilitation avoided.

Table 9.2 presents a series of possible scenarios based on a range of NNTs and prevention costs, and assuming that the cost of treating a hip fracture is £10,000, which represents the hospital costs, recovery costs in various settings and the on-going rehabilitation costs for one year.

Table 9.2   Potential resources released from preventing one hip fracture

	Intervention costs (£)			
NNT = 20	*75*	*100*	*125*	*250*
Cost per averted fracture	4,500	6,000	7,500	15,000
Cost of one hip fracture	10,000	10,000	10,000	10,000
Resources released	5,500	4,000	2,500	-5,000
NNT = 30				
Cost per averted fracture	6,750	9,000	11,250	22,500
Cost of one hip fracture	10,000	10,000	10,000	10,000
Resources released	3,250	1,000	-1,250	-1,2500
NNT = 40				
Cost per averted fracture	9,000	12,000	15,000	30,000
Cost of one hip fracture	10,000	10,000	10,000	10,000
Resources released	1,000	-2,000	-5,000	-2,0000

If the NNT is 20 there are potential resources released in three of the intervention cost scenarios. The 'break-even' point amounts to £167 per patient per year, that is, when the costs of the intervention are less than £167, there will be resources released as a result of implementing the strategy. With an NNT of 30 the 'break-even point' is £111 and with an NNT of 40 the 'break-even point' is £83 per patient per year.

Table 9.3 presents the 'break-even points' for the costs of the intervention with a range of treatment and other costs for hip fractures and NNT. An optimistic view of the effectiveness (reflected in low NNT) results in a break-even cost of intervention of £83, when the cost of treatment is £5,000. If the cost of treatment increases towards £15,000 the break-even cost of intervention is £250. If less optimistic views of the effectiveness are taken (higher NNT) the break-even costs of intervention are reduced.

Recurrent Strokes

The hip fracture example above demonstrates that the impact on budgets

Table 9.3   Break-even point for costs of intervention

	NNTs		
Cost of treatment	*20*	*30*	*40*
5,000	83	56	42
7,500	125	83	63
10,000	167	111	83
12,500	208	139	104
15,000	250	167	125

depends on the relative effectiveness and the relative costs of the alternative. In many situations such choices are compounded by the existence of a number of potential alternatives, each with different effectiveness and cost profiles. Such an example can be illustrated in the case of recurrent stroke prevention. In this example, comparison is made between two possible interventions and their respective impact on the budgets of commissioners.

Two large scale randomized trials (SALT Collaborative Group, 1991; Diener et al., 1996) have shown that both aspirin on its own and a combination of aspirin and modified-release dipyridamole are effective interventions in preventing recurrent strokes. The findings from these studies have been converted into NNTs (Bandolier, 1997) and these have been combined with the costs of the intervention to produce estimates of the cost of preventing a recurrent stroke, shown in Table 9.4.

Table 9.4   Cost of preventing one recurrent stroke

Treatment strategy	NNT	Duration	Cost (£)	Cost of prevention (£)
Aspirin	38 (20–319)	2 years	20.14	1,531 (806–12,849)
Dipyridamole plus aspirin	18 (13–29)	2 years	117.00	4,212 (3,042–6,786)

The issues for commissioners is thus not only one of contemplating whether prevention is better than treatment but whether it is worth incurring additional costs in order to prevent more recurrent strokes. From the budgetary perspective commissioners have to determine the point at which the cost of preventing an additional stroke is equivalent to the costs incurred in treating the event. Obviously, this does not take into account other factors which would impinge on the decision-making process.

Consider the situation if 100 stroke patients were given dipyridamole plus aspirin for a two year period, between five and six patients (NNT = 18) would not have a recurrent stroke who would have had one without the intervention. On the other hand, if 100 stroke patients were given aspirin over a two year period, between two and three (NNT = 38) would not have a recurrent stroke who would otherwise have had one. Thus, approximately three more patients will not have a recurrent stroke if dipyridamole plus aspirin is used as the intervention rather than aspirin. The cost of treating 100 stroke patients with dipyridamole plus aspirin for two years amounts to £23,400 compared to £4,028 for aspirin – a difference of £19,372. However, three additional patients would have had a recurrent stroke if they had been treated with aspirin. These patients have to be treated and therefore the question is whether it is more cost-effective to try and prevent them from having the recurrent stroke compared to the costs of providing treatment.

The costs associated with stroke have been estimated for a number of different regions and countries (Terént et al., 1994; Bergman et al., 1995; Smurawska et al., 1994; Gorelick, 1994; Dale, 1988) with a range of values presented. For example, the average lifetime costs for treating a stroke patient have been estimated at over $73,000 (1991 prices) (van Bortel and Ament, 1995) which would equate to nearly £46,000. More recent estimates have placed the value of treating a stroke patient at £6,600 for the first two years after stroke (Phillips, 1997) and £13,000 per annum (Chambers et al., undated). It is highly probable that there is a positive correlation between severity of stroke and the cost of treatment and, as recurrent strokes may be more severe, there are likely to be differences in the cost of treating initial and recurrent strokes. It would thus appear that the costs incurred to prevent the additional strokes represent a sound investment from the perspective of the commissioning authority. The analysis has been repeated using different NNTs and the results are shown in Table 9.5.

If the NNT for aspirin on its own was 22 (at the lower end of the 95 per cent confidence range) then cost savings from the implementation of a strategy of dipyridamole plus aspirin (with a NNT of 18) would result if the cost of treating a stroke was greater than £19,372. On the other hand if the NNT for aspirin on its own was 62, cost savings would be generated if the cost of treating a stroke was greater than £4,800.

Table 9.5 **Impact of changes in NNTs and costs of treating stroke on budgets**

	NNTs		
Cost of treatment	*13*	*18*	*25*
3,500	-374	-2,957	-15,872
7,000	3,126	543	-12,372
10,000	6,126	3,543	-9,372
15,000	11,126	8,543	-4,372
25,000	21,126	18,543	5,628

Discussion

The aim of the chapter has been to demonstrate how summary measures of clinical effectiveness can be linked with economic techniques for the purpose of assessing the relative worth of investing in new technologies. The adoption of relatively expensive new drugs has been dealt with in different ways by different authorities. This has resulted in patients with similar conditions being treated in different ways in different areas of the country. The introduction of a framework as advocated in this chapter can enable new technologies to be evaluated for their clinical and cost-effectiveness and placed in one of the quadrants in Figure 9.1.

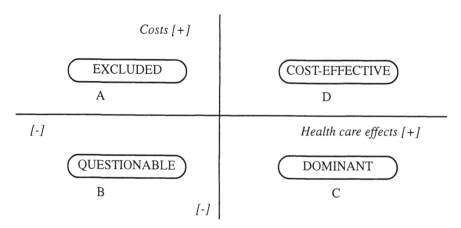

Figure 9.1   Using effectiveness and cost-effectiveness information

Basically, it can be assumed that interventions which find themselves in quadrants A and B would not be implemented, while interventions in quadrant C represent an improvement in health effects and at the same time provide additional financial resources for the authority to spend elsewhere in order to improve the health of their community. This has been shown to be the case in the areas of preventing hip fractures and recurrent strokes. But what about new interventions which are placed in quadrant D, that is interventions which improve health but at a cost?

These interventions have to be evaluated in terms of their clinical and cost-effectiveness and their cost-effectiveness ratios (CER) computed. These are compared with existing interventions and if they have a lower CER (that is cost per unit of effect) it would make economic sense if they are implemented instead of an existing programme. On the other hand if they have a higher CER they should only be implemented if additional resources are available.

Consider the situation confronting a commissioning authority who have to decide how to prioritize its expenditure to fit in with its budget. There are three possible independent programmes which it is contemplating funding. The costs and health effects of each of these is shown in Table 9.6.

Table 9.6   Cost-effectiveness of three independent programmes

Programme	Costs (£) [C]	Health effects [E]	Cost-effectiveness ratio [C/E]
C	150,000	1,850	81.08
A	100,000	1,200	83.33
B	120,000	1,350	88.89

For example, if the available budget is £150,000 then only programme C should be implemented; if the budget increases to £250,000 then programmes C and A should be implemented; if the budget is £370,000 then all three programmes should be implemented. If another intervention (programme D) becomes available for implementation, it should only be implemented if its cost-effectiveness ratio (CER) is less than 88.89 within a budget constraint of £370,000; if the budget is £250,000 it should only be implemented if its CER is less than 83.33.

In summing up, programmes in quadrants A and B should not be funded; programmes in quadrant C should be funded (as they generate both health and financial returns on the investment); while those in quadrant D should be funded in priority of their respective cost-effectiveness ratio up to the budget limit available.

Such a framework does offer commissioners an insight into the extent to which new interventions will improve the quality of care provided for patients and at the same time provide an indication of the budgetary consequences of investing in such new technologies.

Conclusion

The explicit aim of the chapter has been to demonstrate how the effectiveness of an intervention, expressed in terms of numbers-needed-to-treat (NNT), combined with an analysis of its economic impact can provide commissioners with an indication of how quality improvements in health care provision and cost savings can be generated. It has been shown that strategies designed to prevent hip fractures and recurrent strokes are both effective and result in budgetary savings for commissioners of health care. Other potential interventions, which are shown to be effective but require additional funding, need to be further assessed and compared with existing interventions to determine whether they provide additional health effects at a lower cost, that is if their CERs are lower.

The decision-making process is highly complex and involves a number of different, often conflicting, factors. The adoption of such a framework should enable decision makers to utilize the information relating to the effectiveness and efficiency of an intervention in their deliberations and enhance the quality of the commissioning making process in determining health care priorities and in ensuring that maximum quality health care is available and delivered to communities and that the most efficient use is made of resources available within health care budgets.

References

Bandolier (1997), 'NNTs for Stroke Prevention', 4 (4), No. 38, April, pp. 2–3.
Bandolier (1997), 'Calcium and Vitamin D for Preventing Hip Fractures', 4 (3), No. 37, March, pp. 5–6.
Chambers, M., Noble, I., Hutton, J. et al. (undated), *Stroke Outcome Model: Development of a decision-analytic model for economic analysis of stroke care*, MEDTAP International and Boehringer, London.

Chapuy, M.C. et al. (1992), 'Vitamin D3 and Calcium to Prevent Hip Fractures in Elderly Women', *New England Journal of Medicine*, 327, pp. 1637–42.

Chapuy, M.C. et al. (1994), 'Effect of Calcium and Cholecalciferol Treatment from Three Years on Hip Fractures in Elderly Women', *British Medical Journal*, 308, pp. 1081–2.

Cochrane, A.L. (1992), *Effectiveness and Efficiency: Random reflections on health services*, Nuffield Provincial Hospitals Trust, London.

Cook, R.J. and Sackett, D.L. (1995), 'The Number Needed to Treat: A clinically useful measure of treatment effect', *British Medical Journal*, 310, pp. 452–4.

Diener, H.C., Cunha, L., Forber, C. et al. (1996), 'European Stroke Prevention Study 2: Dipyridamole and acetylsalicylic acid in the secondary prevention of stroke', *Journal of the Neurological Sciences*, 143, pp. 1–13.

Dowie, J. (1996), '"Evidence-based", "Cost-effective" and "Preference-driven" Medicine: Decision analysis based medical decision making is the pre-requisite', *Journal of Health Services Research and Policy*, 1, pp. 104–13.

Griffin, J. (1990), *Osteoporosis and the Risk of Fracture*, Office of Health Economics, London.

Ham, C. (1998), 'Financing the NHS', *British Medical Journal*, 316, pp. 212–13.

Lane, A. (1996), 'Direct Costs of Osteoporosis for New Zealand Women', *PharmacoEconomics*, 9, pp. 231–45.

Laupacis, A., Sackett, D.L. and Roberts, R.S. (1988), 'An Assessment of Clinically Useful Measures of the Consequences of Treatment', *New England Journal of Medicine*, 318, pp. 1728–33.

Marwick, C. (1997), 'Proponents Gather Together to Discuss Practicing Evidence-based Medicine', *Journal of the American Medical Association*, 278, pp. 531–2.

Maynard, A.K. (1997), 'Evidence-based Medicine: An incomplete method for informing treatment choices', *Lancet*, 349, pp. 126–8.

McQuay, H.J. and Moore, R.A. (1997), 'Using Numerical Results from Systematic Reviews in Clinical Practice', *Annals of Internal Medicine*, 126, pp. 712–20.

Netten, A. and Dennett, J. (eds) (1996), *Unit Costs of Health and Social Care 1996*, PSSRU, University of Kent at Canterbury.

Phillips, C.J. (1997), 'The Evidence for Stroke Prevention', *Evidence Based Medicine in Practice*, December, Hayward Medical Communications, London.

Phillips, C.J. and Prowle, M.J. (1993), 'Economics of a Reduction in Smoking: A case study from Heartbeat Wales', *Journal of Epidemiology and Community Health*, 47, pp. 215–23.

Randell, A., Sambrook, P.N., Nguyen, T.V. et al. (1995), 'Direct Clinical and Welfare Costs of Osteoporotic Fractures in Elderly Men and Women', *Osteoporosis International*, 5, pp. 427–37.

SALT Collaborative Group (1994), 'Swedish Aspirin Low-dose Trial (SALT) of 75mg aspirin as secondary prophylaxis after cerebrovascular ischaemic events', *Lancet*, 344, pp. 1345–9.

Secretary of State for Health (1997), *The New NHS: Modern, Dependable*, Cm 3807, The Stationery Office, London.

Secretary of State for Scotland (1997), *Designed to Care: Renewing the NHS in Scotland*, Cm 3811, The Stationery Office, Edinburgh.

Secretary of State for Wales (1998), *NHS Wales – Putting Patients First: The future of the NHS in Wales*, Cm 3841, NHS Cymru, Cardiff.

Torgerson, D., Donaldson, C. and Reid, D. (1996), 'Using Economics to Prioritize Research: A case study of randomized trials for the prevention of hip fractures due to osteoporosis', *Journal of Health Services Research and Policy*, 1, pp. 141–6.

Van Bortel, L.M.A.B. and Ament, A.J.H.A. (1995), 'Selective Versus Nonselective b Adrenoceptor Antagonists in Hypertension', *PharmacoEconomics*, 8, pp. 513–23.

Walshe, K. and Ham, C. (1997), 'Who's Acting on the Evidence?', *Health Service Journal*, 107, No. 5547, 3 April, pp. 22–5.

10 Cost-effectiveness of Alendronate for Fracture Prevention in Postmenopausal Women

JAN JONES AND DAVID A. SCOTT
Scottish Health Purchasing Information Centre

Introduction

Osteoporosis is a common disease in which bones become brittle due to reduced bone mass density (BMD) and there is an increased risk of bone fracture. Postmenopausal women are at high risk of osteoporosis due to a deficiency of oestrogen causing reduced BMD. Fractures occur most commonly at the spine, hip, and wrist. They cause pain, loss of mobility and a reduction in the quality of life.

The risk of fractures doubles every 10 years after the menopause, and almost half of all women suffer at least one fracture by the age of 70 years (Department of Health, 1994). With an increasing elderly population the numbers suffering osteoporosis and therefore fractures will increase in future years. Fracture risk is further increased if a previous fracture has already been sustained. Fractures of the hip are associated with the greatest pain and financial cost, in addition to increased mortality (12–20 per cent of women with hip fractures die (Cummings et al., 1985)), lengthy disability (only one-third of survivors are fully mobile after six months) (Effective Health Care Bulletin, 1992), and a need for long term community or hospital care.

Options exist in both primary and secondary prevention of osteoporosis (primary prevention being the prevention of the first fracture and secondary prevention the prevention of the second or subsequent fractures). Prevention

Controlling Costs: Strategic Issues in Health Care Management, H.T.O. Davies, M. Tavakoli, M. Malek, A. R. Neilson (eds), Ashgate Publishing Ltd, 1999.

of osteoporosis aims to maintain or increase BMD. Pharmacological measures include hormone replacement therapy (HRT), the bisphosphonates (cyclical etidronate and alendronate), calcitonin, vitamin D analogues and calcium supplements. Non-pharmacological measures include exercise and diet.

Of the pharmacological measures in secondary prevention of osteoporosis, alendronate is the only drug to have proven benefit in the reduction of vertebral and non-vertebral fractures. This evidence has been obtained from a recent well-designed randomized controlled trial providing high quality evidence that alendronate provides a relative hip fracture reduction of 51 per cent and an absolute reduction of 1.1 per cent in postmenopausal women with established osteoporosis and existing vertebral fractures (Black et al., 1996).

Trials of cyclical etidronate have failed to show equivalent fracture reductions (Watts et al., 1990; Harris et al., 1993). Trials of HRT have not been conducted in established osteoporosis, or with fracture outcomes (with one exception (Lufkin et al., 1992)). Trials of vitamin D and calcium have produced conflicting results (Gillespie et al., 1997).

A number of economic evaluations of HRT have been conducted and have been recently reviewed by Torgerson and Reid (Torgerson and Reid, 1997). All are complicated by benefits of HRT additional to fracture prevention. Two estimates of the cost-effectiveness of fracture prevention using modelling techniques have found cost-effectiveness dependent on the extent and duration of fracture protection, base risk of fracture and quality of life following hip fracture (Jönsson et al., 1995; Harris and Scully, 1997).

The purpose of this paper is to present the results of a similar economic model developed to calculate the cost-effectiveness and cost-utility of alendronate in hip fracture prevention in postmenopausal women with established osteoporosis, using Scottish costs and UK prevalence data. We present the results as cost per hip fracture prevented, cost per life year gained, cost per quality adjusted life year gained.

Method

The model developed is based on a hypothetical cohort of 1,000 postmenopausal women, who have a history of fracture and allows comparison of no intervention with alendronate treatment. We include benefits associated with reduced hip fracture, i.e. life years gained, quality adjusted life years gained, 'savings' from hip fracture operations avoided and costs associated with the treatment intervention, i.e. drug costs, BMD measurements, GP visits.

All costs and benefits are discounted at a level of 6 per cent per year. We use sensitivity analysis to examine the affect of variations in: age, fracture risk, hip fracture operation cost, treatment duration, fracture protection duration, treatment efficacy, quality of life, drug cost and discount rate on the cost-effectiveness and cost-utility ratios generated.

Hip Fracture Incidence

Hip fracture incidence for women between the ages of 70 and 84 years is shown in Table 10.1. Values were derived by Torgerson (1996) from an epidemiological study of hip fractures in the female general population recently conducted in the UK (Donaldson et al., 1990). We assume that the increased risk of further fracture in women with a history of fracture is 50–100 per cent higher than the general population (Kotowicz et al., 1994; Lauritzen et al., 1993; Mallmin et al., 1993). We further assume that all fractures reported occur in osteoporotic women. A small proportion of women, aged 70–84 years, who sustain a fracture may not have osteoporosis, we have allowed for 15 per cent in the sensitivity analysis (Aitken et al., 1984). A higher fracture rate was observed in the placebo arm of the FIT trial (0.73 per cent per year) which enrolled women with low BMD and existing vertebral fractures (Black et al., 1996), this value is included in the sensitivity analysis.

Table 10.1 Fracture incidence in general population (women) derived by Torgerson

Age	Fracture incidence
70–74	0.25
75–79	0.74
80–84	1.42

Sources: Torgerson, 1996; Donaldson et al., 1990.

Outcome Following Hip Fracture

The probability of outcome after hip fracture is shown in Table 10.2. Values used were calculated by Hillner et al. (1986) and are based on published results. We assume that the frequency of each outcome is similar in the UK and have included a reduced probability of mortality of 0.1 in the sensitivity analysis.

Table 10.2 Probability of outcomes after hip fracture

Outcome	Probability
Death	0.20
No complications	0.20
Disabled	0.30
Nursing home	0.30

Source: Hillner et al., 1986.

Quality of Life

The occurrence of fractures reduces the quality of life short and long-term. The literature contains no empirical estimates of the quality of life lost due to hip fracture. We have used quality weights proposed by Hillner et al. (ibid.) shown in Table 10.3. These values were validated by a panel of experts. Again, we have assumed that equivalent utility estimates apply in the UK and have varied them in the sensitivity analysis. We have also assumed that treatment with alendronate does not adversely affect the quality of life. We have used an average life expectancy of 82 years (Information & Statistics Division, 1996b).

Table 10.3 Utility estimates

State	Utility value	Duration
Uncomplicated fracture*	0.95	1 year
Disabled	0.80	Rest of life
Nursing home	0.40	Rest of life
Dead	0.00	Rest of life

* Reduced health state for one year, then return to complete health.

Source: Hillner et al., 1986.

Cost of Fractures

The health service cost of hip fracture treatment includes operation cost, acute and rehabilitation ward costs and district nurse and physiotherapy after care. We obtained operation type and length of stay data from the Scottish Hip

Fracture Audit (Mountain and Curry, 1997). Operation and ward costs were obtained by the SHPIC costing unit from Dundee Teaching Hospitals finance department costing spreadsheet. District nurse and physiotherapy costs were estimated (Netten and Dennett, 1997; personal communication, E. Dinnes). The average costs used are shown in Table 10.4. The baseline cost is £4,757 incorporating the average cost estimates of district nurse and physiotherapy visits.

Table 10.4 Average costs included in hip fracture treatment

Item	Median duration	Average cost	Total average cost
Operation			£ 699.00
Acute stay	10.35 days	£216 per day	£2235.60
Rehabilitation stay	8.99 days	£112 per day	£1006.88
District nurse visits	24 visits	£22.58 per visit	£ 542.00
Physiotherapy	24 visits	£11.40	£ 274.00
Total			£4757.48

Little variation in the cost of different types of operation was found. The average hip fracture cost was sensitive to the length of acute and rehabilitation hospital stay as shown in Figure 10.1.

Our cost of acute and rehabilitation stay equates with other studies (French et al., 1995). Our estimation of duration of hospital stay is less than other reports in the literature. Hollingworth et al. (1995) estimated a mean of 14.58 days in an orthopaedic ward and 19.81 days in rehabilitation ward. It is possible that very frail elderly patients may have extended rehabilitation hospital stay for reasons other than hip fracture.

Therefore, taking the above into account, we estimate that the NHS costs per hip fracture range from £3,975 to £6,313. This is in agreement with other studies (French et al., 1993; Hollingworth et al., 1995).

Efficacy of Alendronate

Alendronate provides a 51 per cent reduction in the risk of hip fracture over a treatment period of three years in women with a 0.73 per cent risk of hip fracture per year (Black et al., 1996). We assume that the relative benefit is maintained across a range of hip fracture risks and that fractures are prevented and not delayed. The intervention group in the FIT trial received 5mg alendronate daily for two years followed by 10mg daily for one year (ibid.).

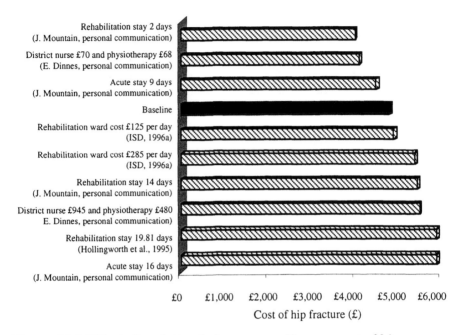

Figure 10.1 Effect of variation in key assumptions on cost of hip fracture

In our baseline model we have assumed that fracture prevention obtained following this regimen is equivalent to that obtained with 10mg alendronate daily for three years. It is logical to assume that the efficacy of alendronate is dose dependent and therefore the higher dose (10mg daily for three years) may increase efficacy. We have allowed for fracture reductions of 30 per cent and 60 per cent in the sensitivity analysis.

Duration of Treatment

There is no evidence concerning the long-term efficacy of alendronate. We conducted sensitivity analysis to determine the effect of a ten year treatment and ten year fracture protection scenario. It is likely that a waning effect will exist on the withdrawal of alendronate with further fractures prevented. We have therefore also included a three year treatment and five year fracture protection scenario. We have assumed that the extent of fracture protection remains constant over a period of 10 years.

Drug and Drug Associated Costs

Drug and drug associated costs are shown in Table 10.5. The latter include BMD measurements performed annually to monitor treatment. We have also included the cost of one visit per year to the general practitioner to review alendronate treatment.

Table 10.5   Drug and drug associated costs

Item	Cost per year
Alendronate 10mg od	£333.00*
BMD	£24.00[i]
GP visit	£10.00[ii]

*   British National Formulary.

Sources: i) Torgerson, 1996; ii) Netten and Dennett, 1997.

The lower cost of the FIT regimen (5mg daily for two years, 10mg daily for one year) is also included in the sensitivity analysis.

Results

The results for the baseline scenario describe a cohort of 1,000 women aged 70 years, with a previous history of fracture and hip fracture incidence of 0.44 per cent. Treatment with alendronate for three years (discounting at 6 per cent) with three years fracture protection results in 6.32 hip fractures avoided compared to no treatment. The cost of avoiding one hip fracture is £159,725. There are 10.41 life years saved at a cost of £97,000 per life year. When quality weights are introduced, 21.59 QALYs are saved at a cost per QALY of £46,762.

Sensitivity Analysis

We have examined the sensitivity of the results to variation in some of the key assumptions as shown in Table 10.6 and Figure 10.2.

Table 10.6   Effect of variation in key assumptions on cost per life year saved, cost per quality adjusted life year saved and cost per hip fracture avoided

Scenario	Cost/LYS	Cost/QALYs	Cost/hip Fx avoid.
3 yrs treat & 3 yrs protect	£21,726	£10,462	£28,872
75 yrs at treatment	£34,364	£16,534	£50,811
Fracture incidence 0.73% (Black et al, 1996)	£57,389	£27,666	£94,499
10 yrs treat & 10 years protect	£58,930	£28,379	£78,315
3 yrs treat & 5 yrs protect	£65,718	£31,674	£103,548
Cost of FIT (Black et al., 1996)	£65,917	£31,778	£108,542
Efficacy alendronate 60%	£82,016	£39,539	£135,053
Utility after hip Fx dec	£97,000	£41,083	£159,725
Discount rate 3%	£86,455	£42,050	£159,725
Hip Fx cost £6313 (calculated)	£96,055	£46,307	£158,169
Baseline	£97,000	£46,762	£159,725
Hip Fx cost £3975 (calculated)	£97,475	£46,991	£160,507
Utility after hip Fx inc	£97,000	£54,127	£159,725
15% Fx in non-osteoporotic women (Aitken, 1984)	£114,627	£55,260	£188,751
Mortality of 10% after hip Fx	£194,000	£56,107	£159,725
Efficacy alendronate 40%	£124,469	£60,005	£204,957
No nursing home care reqd	£97,000	£64,246	£159,725

Cost/QALY is sensitive to the absolute risk of hip fracture in women who have a history of fracture. Due to the increased risk of hip fracture in the older population, the cost/QALY of starting therapy at 75 years is significantly reduced to £16,500.

Sensitivity analysis shows that the results are marginally influenced by five years duration of fracture protection, variation of +/- 20 per cent in alendronate efficacy, adjusting the drug cost of alendronate to reflect 5mg daily doses in the first two years followed by 10mg daily in the third (Black et al., 1996), changes of +/- 0.1 in utility estimates for disability and nursing home, reduction to 10 per cent mortality following hip fracture, 15 per cent of fractures occurring in non-osteoporotic women, upper and lower estimates for the health service cost of a hip fracture, and 3 per cent discount rate.

The uncertainty of patient condition in a US nursing home (on which the outcome data are based) proffered a reallocation of these patients to the disability category which increased the cost/QALY to £64,000.

Conclusion and Discussion

It should be remembered when interpreting the above cost-effectiveness and

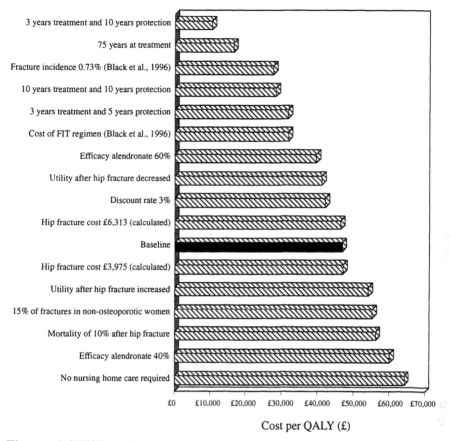

Figure 10.2 Effect of variation in key assumptions on cost per QALY saved

cost-utility figures that they do not reflect the total cost of implementation of a country-wide programme in Scotland. The total discounted cost of a programme to treat 1,000 patients amounted to £1,009,781. In the absence of additional funding, other health service programmes with a higher cost per QALY and higher total cost need to be identified and transposed to allow the new programme to be implemented.

The cost-effectiveness of alendronate in hip fracture prevention is affected principally by the absolute risk of fracture. This is in accordance with conclusions from other cost-effectiveness analysis of alendronate (Jönsson et al., 1995; Harris and Scully, 1997).

If hip fracture risk is around 1.30 per cent per year, as seen in older women (75–79 yrs) with a history of fracture, the intervention becomes borderline cost-effective (£16,500 per QALY saved) and may be considered affordable. At this age, however, there are relatively few remaining years of life and these may be affected by co-morbidities. The decision to intervene with alendronate therefore depends on the health state of the individual patient.

BMD measurements have been suggested as a tool for identifying women at increased risk of fracture. The increased risk with a 1 SD decrease in BMD is 160 per cent (Cummings et al., 1993). In such women of 70 years with a hip fracture incidence of 0.65 per cent, the cost-effectiveness of alendronate would be less favourable than in women with incidence of 0.73 per cent (Table 10.6), and would be further worsened by the additional cost of BMD screening.

Our results are based on women with a history of fracture, if a subset of women of 70 years with the highest risk of hip fracture could be identified (for example women with a number of osteoporosis risk factors including fracture history and low BMD), cost-effectiveness of alendronate treatment will increase. If hip fracture protection is maintained for a number of years after treatment is discontinued, our model suggests that cost-effectiveness increases. Currently we have no evidence to determine fracture protection duration, a scenario of five years protection provides a slight increase, whereas ten years protection although cost-effective is probably unrealistic. Likewise, the assumption that fractures are prevented and not delayed requires confirmation with trial evidence.

Our model assumes that US outcomes and utility values (Hillner et al., 1986) following hip fracture also apply to the UK. Cost-effectiveness of alendronate does not appear to be influenced by small variation in utility values, although the probability of entering a nursing home does influence our cost-effectiveness ratio.

We exclude fractures of the wrist or spine in our model because we could find no associated utility values reported in the literature. These other types of fractures, although of less financial implication, do reduce quality of life and occur more frequently than hip fractures, and if included in the model could be expected to have a marginally favourable impact on cost-effectiveness.

Economic analysis of other interventions in osteoporosis are less meaningful due to the poor quality of existing evidence. HRT is commonly prescribed for primary prevention of osteoporosis, and has found to be most effective in fracture prevention if taken immediately after the menopause for a period of at least ten years. Fracture protection exists whilst HRT is taken, but effect wanes when therapy is withdrawn. The majority of hip fractures occur at around 80 years, at which time any effect from HRT taken at the menopause will be negligible. The risk of breast cancer associated with HRT becomes significant after more than 10 years of treatment (Persson et al., 1997) and continued use is thought an unrealistic scenario in the UK. For this reason we have not attempted to compare alendronate with HRT. A recent study in the US found a decrease in hip fractures in women over 65 years who were current users of HRT and had been taking HRT for an average of 20 years (Cauley et al., 1995).

Our model provides an estimation of cost-effectiveness and cost-utility of alendronate in fracture prevention applicable to Scotland. Three years of alendronate prescribed to women at high risk of fracture (incidence of 1.3 per cent) will improve quality of life at a cost that may be affordable. If fracture protection is maintained after treatment is discontinued, prescribing to younger women for a short period of time may also be cost-effective. It is hoped the evidence-based conclusions from this paper will assist decision-making by health care commissioners.

References

Aitken, J.M. (1984), 'Relevance of Osteoporosis in Women with Fracture of the Femoral Neck', *British Medical Journal*, 288, pp. 597-601.

Black, D.M., Cummings, S.R., Karpf, D.B. et al. (1996), 'Randomised Trial of Effect of Alendronate on Risk of Fracture in Women With Existing Vertebral Fractures: The Fracture Intervention Trial', *Lancet*, 348, pp. 1535–41.

Cauley, J.A., Seeley, D.G., Enstrud, K., Ettinger, B., Black, D. and Cummings, S.R. (1995), 'Estrogen Replacement Therapy and Fractures in Older Women', *Annals of Internal Medicine*, 122, pp. 9–16.

Cummings, S.R., Black, D.M., Nevitt, M.C. et al. (1993), 'Bone Density at Various Sites for Prediction of Hip Fractures', *Lancet*, 341, pp. 72–5.

Cummings, S.R., Kelsy, J.L., Nevitt, M.C. and O'Dowd, J.J. (1985), 'Epidemiology of Osteoporosis and Osteoporotic Hip Fractures', *Epidemiologic Reviews*, 7, pp. 178–208.

Department of Health (1994), *Advisory Group on Osteoporosis*, Department of Health, London.

Donaldson, L.J., Cook, A. and Thomson, R.G. (1990), 'Incidence of Fractures in a Geographically Defined Population', *Journal of Epidemiology and Community Health*, 44, pp. 241–5.

Effective Health Care Bulletin (1992), *Screening for Osteoporosis to Prevent Fractures*, Vol. 1 (1).

French, F.H., Torgerson, D.J. and Porter, R.W. (1995), 'Cost Analysis of Fracture of the Neck of Femur', *Age and Ageing*, 24, pp. 185–9.

Gillespie, W.J., Henry, D.A., O'Connell, D.L. and Robertson, J. (1997), 'Vitamin D and Vitamin D Analogues in the Prevention of Fractures in Involutional and Postmenopausal Osteoporosis' in W.J. Gillespie, R. Madhok, G.D. Murray, C.M. Robinson, M.F. Swiontkowski (eds), *Musculoskeletal Injuries Module of The Cochrane Database of*

Systematic Reviews. The Cochrane Library. The Cochrane Collaboration; issue 4, Update Software, Oxford.

Harris, A. and Scully, B. (1997), 'Economic Analysis of Treatments for Established Osteoporosis', *Australian Prescriber*, 20 (Supp. 3), pp. 53–7.

Harris, S.T., Watts, N.B., Jackson, R.D. et al. (1993), 'Four-Year Study of Intermittent Cyclical Etidronate Treatment of Postmenopausal Osteoporosis: Three Years of Blinded Treatment Followed by One Year of Open Therapy', *American Journal of Medicine*, 95 (6), pp. 557–67.

Hillner, B.E., Hollenberg, J.P. and Pauker, S.G. (1986), 'Postmenopausal Estrogens in Prevention of Osteoporosis. Benefit Virtually Without Risk if Cardiovascular Effects are Considered', *The American Journal of Medicine*, 80, pp. 1115–27.

Hollingworth, W., Todd, C.J. and Parker, M.J. (1995), 'The Cost of Treating Hip Fractures in the Twenty-first Century', *Journal of Public Health Medicine*, 17, pp. 269–76.

Information & Statistics Division (1996a), *Scottish Health Service Costs: Year Ended 31st March 1996*, ISD, Edinburgh.

Information & Statistics Division (1996b), *Scottish Health Statistics 1996*, ISD, Edinburgh.

Jönsson, B., Christiansen, C., Johnell, O. and Hedbrandt, J. (1995), 'Cost-effectiveness of Fracture Prevention in Established Osteoporosis', *Osteoporosis International*, 5, pp. 136–42.

Kotowicz, M.A., Melton, L.J., Cooper, C., Atkinson, E.J., O'Fallon, W.M. and Riggs, B.L. (1994), 'Risk of Hip Fracture in Women with Vertebral Fracture', *Journal of Bone and Mineral Research*, 9 (5), pp. 599–605.

Lauritzen, J.B., Schwarz, P., McNair, P., Lund, B. and Transbřl, I. (1993), 'Radial and Humeral Fractures as Predictors of Subsequent Hip, Radial or Humeral Fractures in Women, and their Seasonal Variation', *Osteoporosis International*, 3, pp. 133–7.

Lufkin, E.G., Wahner, H.W. and O'Fallon, W.M. et al. (1992), 'Treatment of Postmenopausal Osteoporosis with Transdermal Estrogen', *Annals of Internal Medicine*, 117, pp. 1–9.

Mallmin, H., Ljunghall, S., Persson, I., Naessén, T., Krusemo, U. and Bergström, R. (1993), 'Fracture of the Distal Forearm as a Forecaster of Subsequent Hip Fracture: A Population-Based Cohort Study with 24 Years of Follow-Up', *Calcified Tissue International*, 52, pp. 269–72.

Mountain, J. and Curry, C. (1997), *Scottish Hip Fracture Audit*, 3rd Report to CRAG, CRAG, Edinburgh.

Netten, A. and Dennett, J. (1997), *Unit Costs of Health & Social Care*, PSSRU, University of Kent, Canterbury.

Persson, I., Thurfjell, E., Bergström, R. and Holmberg, L. (1997), 'Hormone Replacement Therapy and the Risk of Breast Cancer. Nested Case-Control Study in a Cohort of Swedish Women Attending Mammography Screening', *International Journal of Cancer*, 72 (5), pp. 758–61.

Torgerson, D. (1996), *The Economics of Bone Density Screening and the Subsequent Use of Hormone Replacement Therapy*, unpublished PhD thesis, University of Aberdeen.

Torgerson, D.J. and Reid, D.M. (1997), 'The Economics of Osteoporosis and its Prevention', *Pharmacoeconomics*, 11 (2), pp. 126–38.

Watts, N.P., Harris, S.T., Genant, H.K. et al. (1990), 'Intermittent Cyclical Etidronate Treatment of Postmenopausal Osteoporosis', *New England Journal of Medicine*, 323, pp. 73–9.

11 Economic Analyses Relating to the Use of Neurological Magnetic Resonance Imaging (MRI)

MICHAEL CLARK,[1] ALA SZCZEPURA,[1] JOHN HUTTON[2] AND JOY FLETCHER[1]

1   *Centre for Health Services Studies, Warwick Business School, University of Warwick*

2   *MEDTAP International*

Introduction

MRI is a 'big ticket' health technology (Lazaro and Fitch, 1995), requiring considerable capital expenditure with associated long-term revenue costs. Assessment of whether expenditure on the provision of MRI is cost-effective is therefore necessary. This chapter reviews a large subsection of economic literature on MRI – relating to the use of MRI for neurological applications. The review provides an indication of the quality of the economic information available to policy makers should they need to assess whether the use or increased use of MRI upon neurological applications is cost-effective.

Initially MRI was mainly used for neurological imaging, and it is still most often used for such patients. Therefore if the literature relating to the use of MRI for neurological applications is inadequate, the evidence base required to assess the case for or against acquisition of MRI more generally is also likely to be inadequate. This subset of the literature was also selected because some of the authors of this chapter undertook a health technology assessment (which included a cost-effectiveness analysis) of the UK's first purely service MRI installation (used for neurological applications) (Szczepura et al., 1990).

Controlling Costs: Strategic Issues in Health Care Management, H.T.O. Davies, M. Tavakoli, M. Malek, A. R. Neilson (eds), Ashgate Publishing Ltd, 1999.

We can thus expand upon the practical and methodological problems which often militate against the provision of good information relating to the cost-effectiveness of MRI.

A Systematic Review of the Economic Literature Relating to the Use of MRI for Neurological Applications

A systematic review of neurological MRI literature with economic content was undertaken. Searches were conducted using the keyword MRI in conjunction with the keyword cost(s) using MEDLINE, INSPEC, and BIDS. Searches were performed for 1990–98, together with hand searching of key journals (*Health Economics*, and the *International Journal of Technology Assessment in Health Care*). Other relevant citations were followed up in order to identify any additional 'grey' literature. The inclusion criteria for the systematic review were as follows;

a) papers should relate to a specific neurological application of MRI;

b) papers must either refer to the cost-effectiveness, cost-benefits, or costs and efficacy of MRI or relate either MRI costs to MRI effectiveness, MRI costs to MRI efficacy, or MRI costs to MRI benefits.

Overall 31 analyses met the inclusion criteria for the review. Studies were evaluated using criteria indicative of the quality of the economic content of the literature. The criteria used for evaluation were derived from criteria previously specified by other authors (Drummond et al., 1987; Udvarheyli et al., 1992; Coyle and Davies, 1996; Drummond and Jefferson, 1996).

Criteria Used for the Review and Findings

The criteria used are detailed below, and numbers of papers fulfilling each of the criteria are indicated.

1   *Whether a clear statement of study perspective and design was provided.*

Possible perspectives of analysis include a health care sector perspective/ hospital perspective, a societal perspective, or a third-party payer's perspective.

Ideally a paper should include an explicit statement of the perspective of the economic analysis. However, very few papers actually met this criterion, so we decided that if the perspective of the analysis could be gleaned from the selection of costs included within an analysis we would allow a paper to meet this criterion. Papers therefore tended to fail this criterion either if the perspective adopted was unclear from the selection of costs, or if the papers did not involve a formal economic analysis. Overall, 20/31 papers fulfilled this criterion.

2   *Whether an adequate range of comparators was included within the study, and whether a comparative economic assessment was conducted.*

We required that analyses have at least one comparator, thereby at least providing a measure of the cost-effectiveness of using MRI for diagnosis, relative to another diagnostic option. Overall, 22/31 papers fulfilled this criterion.

3   *Whether benefits/effects were apparent.*

If a measure of benefits/effects was specified or was apparent analyses fulfilled this criterion. Studies failing to meet this criterion usually did so because a measure of benefits/effects was not included, or because it was unclear which measures of outcome the analysis was concerned with. Overall, 22/31 papers fulfilled this criterion.

4   *Whether adequate cost information was provided, and whether it was suitably identified and valued.*

Cost information was deemed to be adequate even if the inclusion of additional cost data might have improved the analysis, as long as sufficient cost information was included to evaluate cost-effectiveness within the terms of reference of the analysis.

For most studies it was difficult to establish whether costing had been undertaken properly. Thus only if costs appeared unrealistic, or if it was apparent that a misguided methodology had been used for costing, was it concluded that costs were inappropriately valued. Overall, 23/31 papers met this criterion.

5 *Are statistical tests and confidence intervals for stochastic data appropriately applied?*

Only 3/31 analyses contained statistical tests and confidence intervals. In each case the actual statistical tests and confidence intervals were appropriately applied.

6 *Whether discounting was applied when appropriate.*

We thought it reasonable to require that future health benefits and health costs be discounted. However the vast majority of analyses did not consider future health benefits and costs because they typically related short-term diagnostic performance to diagnostic costs, thus the majority of analyses (29/31) passed this criterion by default.

7 *Was sensitivity analysis of key assumptions applied?*

We required that key assumptions should be subject to sensitivity analysis. Papers failing this criterion usually did so because they did not contain a sensitivity analysis. Only 8/31 analyses fulfilled this criterion.

8 *Whether a summary measure of incremental or marginal cost-effectiveness/ cost-benefits was included.*

Such measures enable the reader to ascertain what the economic implications of using MRI are at the margin; 12/31 analyses contained such a summary measure.

9 *Whether a suitable measure of subsequent health outcome was included.*

We had in mind measures of health outcome such as life years or QALYs. Good cost-effectiveness analyses may fail to fulfil this criterion, simply because subsequent health implications are not within the terms of reference of the study. Such measures are nevertheless useful in order to establish whether diagnostic information translates into health benefits, and hence whether diagnostic interventions are justified because of health benefits generated. Only 4/31 analyses met this criterion.

Table 11.1 Findings from a systematic review

Number of criteria met	Number of papers achieving this score	Number of papers achieving this score or better
9 / 9	0	0
8 / 9	4	4
7 / 9	4	8
6 / 9	2	10
5 / 9	5	15
4 / 9	5	20
3 / 9	5	25
2 / 9	5	30
1 / 9	1	31

Analysis of Findings

The number of papers meeting each of the aforementioned criteria is detailed in Table 11.1. It is apparent from the table that the median score is around 5/9 and relatively few papers (15/31) scored 5/9 or above, implying that the literature is not generally of high quality. A large proportion of the papers failed to fulfil important criteria. For example, only 3/31 papers met criterion number 5 which requires that statistical tests and confidence intervals are appropriately applied and detailed. The failure to undertake such tests is of particular concern if analyses also failed to include an adequate sensitivity or threshold analysis. Appropriate use of sensitivity/threshold analysis might allow us to establish whether the conclusions analyses reached would apply if effectiveness or costs differed from reported levels. However, only 8/31 papers contained any sensitivity/threshold analysis. Failure to undertake a sensitivity analysis may also result in conclusions which are less transferable to other contexts (for example other hospitals, or another country where levels of effectiveness/relative costs differ).

Furthermore, only 12/31 papers contained a summary measure of incremental or marginal cost-effectiveness (or a cost-benefit ratio), and an even smaller proportion (4/31) related costs to a summary measure of health outcomes.

Short-list of Potentially Robust Studies using Review Criteria and Qualitative Assessment

We considered that analyses must at the very least fulfil criteria 1–4, 6, and 7, for there to be any real prospect that they will report robust findings. Furthermore, if criterion number 5 is not met we concluded that it is essential that an adequate sensitivity analysis is conducted (criterion number 7). Overall, 8/31 papers fulfilled these criteria (Szczepura et al., 1990; Fletcher et al., 1997; Mushlin et al., 1997; Mooney et al., 1990; Bance et al., 1994; Jordan et al., 1995; Simon and Lubin et al., 1985; King et al., 1997).

However, additional qualitative assessment is required to determine whether the conclusions that authors reach are robust. The first two papers listed (Szczepura et al., 1990; Fletcher et al., 1997) both relate to a health technology assessment conducted by some of the authors of this chapter, of an MRI installed at the Walsgrave hospital in Coventry. The findings of the first analysis (Szczepura et al., 1990) suggested that use of MRI for neurological applications generally increased diagnostic costs. MRI was used largely as a diagnostic 'add-on' and not as a substitute for other expensive diagnostic techniques (e.g. myelography). Furthermore, the benefits that MRI conferred were considered insufficient to justify the expenditure on MRI from a health care sector perspective. These findings were both reasonable and applicable when the analysis was conducted but no longer apply. Recently the use of myelography has declined dramatically, MRI is now more often used as a substitute for myelography (Fletcher et al., 1997). Thus a more recent analysis of the cost-effectiveness of using the same scanner during 1995/96 (ibid.) concluded that it was unclear whether MRI is now cost-effective. However, MRI may well now be cost-effective in neurology because it now averts expenditure on more diagnostic techniques and overnight stays. These new findings are very tentative, reflecting the methodological problems which prevented definitive conclusions being reached.

Two of the papers (Mushlin et al., 1997; Mooney et al., 1990) reported findings from the same basic analysis, which adopts a societal perspective to assess the relative cost-effectiveness of using CT or MRI in patients with equivocal neurological symptoms. Whilst the study is well constructed, no definitive conclusions are reached. Moreover, it is a US analysis, and the finding may not apply to the UK. Another study (Bance et al., 1994) considers the relative cost-effectiveness of using a variety of tests (including audiograms, electronystagmography (ENG), auditory brainstem testing (ABR), and CT and MRI) to diagnose acoustic neuromas from a health care sector perspective.

Once again, though the analysis fails to reach definitive conclusions, and consequently definitive useful findings cannot be generalized from the analysis to the UK. An assessment of the relative cost-effectiveness (from a health care sector perspective) of diagnosing cord compression before and after the introduction of MRI (Jordan et al., 1995) was robust. It concluded that diagnosis was considerably more expensive and less effective prior to the use of MRI than it currently is using MRI. These findings applied throughout the full range of values of the sensitivity analysis. Therefore these US findings are likely to apply in the UK. Another robust analysis (Simon and Lubin, 1985) compared the use of CT and MRI to diagnose dementia, concluding that CT was more cost-effective from a health care sector perspective than MRI. This finding would have been generalizable to a UK setting during the late 1980s; however, the analysis is now so dated that these findings may now no longer apply because of changes in the relative effectiveness and costs of CT and MRI.

A recent analysis (King et al., 1997), which considered the cost-effectiveness from a societal perspective of using expectant management, PRL screening for hormone levels, endocrine screening panels, or MRI to manage incidentally discovered pituitary microadenomas is very robust, and incorporates a thorough sensitivity analysis. It concludes that a single PRL test is both more effective and far less expensive than using MRI follow-up. Due to the huge variation in cost/QALY between the diagnostic options these findings are likely to be generalizable to the UK.

Up-to-date Robust Analyses and Their Generalizability

We conclude that there are 6/31 analyses (detailed in Table 11.2 overleaf) which are sufficiently robust and up-to-date for us to place faith in the conclusions reached (Fletcher et al., 1997; Mooney et al., 1990; Mushlin et al., 1997; Bance et al., 1994; Jordan et al., 1995; King et al., 1997). We also conclude that only half of these analyses reach findings which are likely to apply in the UK (Fletcher et al., 1997; Jordan et al., 1995; King et al., 1997).

Implications of the Findings

The general quality of the literature reviewed was not high. In part this was a by-product of broad inclusion criteria for the systematic review. Had we

Table 11.2 Robust analyses with up-to-date findings

Diagnostic application	Authors	MRI technology	Comparators	Findings	Perspective of analysis	Do findings apply to the UK?
Neurology generally	Fletcher et al., 1997	1.5 T Picker MRI	Before and after the introduction of MRI and the long term impact of gradual diagnostic substitution	*MRI may be cost-effective (tentative conclusion).* This cannot be proven	Health care sector perspective	Yes
Equivocal neurological conditions	Mooney et al., 1990 and Mushlin et al., 1997. Same analysis	1.5 T GE Medical Systems MRI scanner	MRI and CT in patients with suspected Multiple Sclerosis	*MRI may or may not be cost-effective*	Societal perspective	No
Diagnosing acoustic neuromas	Bance et al., 1994	Not clear	Audiograms, electronystagmography, ENG, ABR, CT, and MRI	*MRI may or may not be cost-effective*	Health care sector perspective	No
Diagnosing cord compression	Jordan et al., 1995	Not clear	Before and after the introduction of MRI	*MRI is cost-effective*	Health care sector perspective	Yes
Management of incidentally discovered pituitary microadenomas	King et al., 1997	Not clear	Expectant management, PRL screening for hormone levels, endocrine screening panels, or MRI scanning to manage pituitary microadenomas	*MRI is not cost-effective. A single PRL testing may be the most cost-effective strategy*	Societal perspective	Yes

insisted that analyses must be economic analyses, far fewer papers would have been evaluated, and the median score of papers selected for review would have been higher.

However, we consider the inclusion criteria are appropriate, they allowed us to evaluate literature making unsubstantiated cost-effectiveness claims. We can thus conclude that most literature reaching cost-effectiveness conclusions did so using inadequate supporting analysis (since only 6/31 analyses were sufficiently robust and up-to-date for us to place any confidence in the conclusions reached). If we had used more rigorous inclusion criteria, we would have reached a similar conclusion, namely that only six papers were sufficiently robust and up-to-date for us to place any confidence in the findings, and that only three analyses contained useful and up-to-date findings likely to apply in the UK. In the next section we draw attention to some practical and methodological problems which inhibit the quality of the literature.

The Reasons for Poor Economic Analysis, Including an Overview of Potential Methodological Problems

Many of the studies we reviewed betrayed a general lack of understanding by authors about economic analysis. Often articles were written by people with a medical background lacking a background in health economics. This situation might be improved if those producing economic evaluations of a health technology studied the recommendations made by the BMJ economic methods group (Drummond et al., 1996). If these recommendations are adopted, well constructed and timely analyses can be produced which can subsequently be used to inform the pattern and scale of technology diffusion.

In addition, some key recommendations emerge from our review. Authors should make the perspective of their analysis clear. All too often authors branded a particular technology or application of a technology 'cost-effective' without making it clear to whom these findings might apply. This is important because a technology which is cost-effective from a health care perspective might *not* be cost-effective from a societal perspective, once indirect costs to society have been taken into account, or vice versa. Thus labelling a technology 'cost-effective' is meaningless unless the perspective of the analysis is apparent. Furthermore, cost-effectiveness is a relative concept, hence there is a need to ensure that comparators are identified when cost-effectiveness conclusions are reported.

Researchers also need to select appropriate outcome measures (i.e.

measures of effectiveness/benefits) and should make the choice of outcome measures apparent. Ideally studies should assess the implications of a technology upon health outcomes. To this end outcome measures such as QALYs, or life years could be used. On occasions this may present practical difficulties, for example because the Coventry MRI evaluation (Szczepura et al., 1990; Fletcher et al., 1998) used a heterogeneous sample of patients with neurological conditions a generic outcome measure such as QALYs would have been appropriate. However, a prospective analysis of outcomes would have been difficult because patients would have been too dispersed for good follow-up, and such an analysis might also have been prohibitively expensive.

In such circumstances a modelling approach may provide a solution (Buxton et al., 1997). A model could be developed to isolate the actual impact of an MRI scan upon changes in patient management, and then upon subsequent final health outcomes. Costs can also be modelled taking into account both diagnostic costs and downstream costs arising as a result of changes in patient management.

However because the Coventry MRI research received limited funding (Szczepura et al., 1990; Fletcher et al., 1998) even this did not prove possible, because some of the key information required to place a value upon parameters of the model was not readily available. Intermediate outcome measures were thus used, to indicate the impact upon patient management. This approach thankfully does not discount the possibility that this data on intermediate effectiveness could be used to inform the development of a model at a later date. A model could extrapolate the impact upon health outcomes and downstream costs of using MRI for a wide range of neurological conditions, partly by using information from robust clinical literature.

Adopting such a modelling approach also serves to make explicit the importance of using diagnostic MRI in order to choose between clinical management plans which are demonstrably effective. If the treatment is effective then robust evidence of therapeutic impact of MRI is all that is then needed, to demonstrate the positive impact of MRI upon health outcomes.

Conversely, if the clinical evidence about treatments is weak, then measuring outcomes in a diagnostic trial may not provide the best way to make good the deficiencies of clinical research. Moreover, the basis for using MRI at all is undermined if there is no evidence that treatment is of benefit. Thus using a modelling approach which is informed by data from robust literature provides a means of highlighting those applications of MRI which are not demonstrably cost-effective, as well as those which are cost-effective. For similar reasons use of modelling to evaluate the cost-effectiveness of other diagnostic technologies may prove appropriate.

When evaluating diagnostic technologies, the value that individuals place upon diagnostic information irrespective of its possible implications for clinical management ought also to be considered (Szczepura, 1992; Mushlin et al., 1995). Some of the analyses we reviewed (Mushlin et al., 1997; King et al., 1997) can be commended for the way in which the impact upon patient anxiety (arising as a result of diagnostic uncertainty) was evaluated as a dimension of health outcomes using QALYs.

Outcome measures should also be explicitly presented within a cost-effectiveness, cost-utility, or cost-benefit ratio. Ideally a stochastic approach ought to be adopted to establish whether the ratio is within confidence limits (Drummond et al., 1996). A variety of approaches have been suggested in order to facilitate this (Van Hout et al., 1994; Wakker and Klassen, 1995; Plosky et al., 1997; Laska et al., 1997). Moreover it is also important to select a sufficiently large sample to identify any difference between comparators adequately. Ideally, researchers should test for the statistical significance and report confidence intervals for reported findings; however, on occasion this may prove to be difficult. For example, for some diagnostic applications it may be difficult to recruit sufficient numbers of patients for confidence intervals to be attached to results. This no doubt accounts for the absence of statistical analysis in some of the papers we evaluated. In these circumstances pooling effectiveness data from a variety of centres may provide an appropriate means of obtaining a sufficiently large sample. In other circumstances it may be inappropriate to use conventional statistical techniques, for example if the sample is non-random and hence potentially biased. This was a problem faced by researchers evaluating the Coventry MRI scanner (Szczepura et al., 1990). The problem arose because it was considered unethical to randomize patients to MRI, because this might unfairly deny patients access to MRI.

Authors should report the methodology used to derive costs, and need to ensure that all costs relevant to the perspective of the analysis (including depreciated costs of capital) are considered. If future benefits or costs are considered it is appropriate to discount them (Krahn and Gafni, 1993) and the time scale of reported costs and benefits and details of the discount rate applied should be stated. Clearly discounting (other than for capital costs) may not be necessary if the time scale of the analysis is very short. The time scale of the analysis is also important and should be made explicit as it can make a great deal of difference to reported findings. This is apparent from the evaluation of the Coventry MRI scanner (Szczepura et al., 1990). At the time of the evaluation it was thought that a two year time scale was sufficiently long to allow for an accurate assessment of the costs and benefits of using MRI. However, subsequent events, most notably a heavy fall in the use of myelography, revealed that the original analysis underestimated the extent to which MRI would displace other diagnostic techniques. Early analysis may therefore overestimate the long term net additional cost of introducing MRI into the diagnostic pathway. Therefore researchers must ensure that the duration of an analysis is appropriate, and long enough to capture the impact of any slowly evolving diagnostic substitution. Inevitably, however, because of pressure to produce results promptly to inform policy making and technology diffusion, it is not always possible to have a long evaluation period. Such problems are confounded by pressure upon researchers to contain costs by containing the timespan of analyses.

Evaluations should also include sensitivity analyses (or threshold analysis). Parameters which might potentially vary ought to be identified, and then appropriate upper and lower limits for these parameters ought to be established and used for the sensitivity analysis. If the uncertain parameters are independent of each other, then a one-way sensitivity analysis may be adequate, but if not, then a multi-way sensitivity analysis is required (Briggs et al., 1994). It is, of course, particularly important to include a sensitivity analysis if some of the parameter estimates are potentially biased (for example if a non-random sample has to be used to derive effectiveness information). In such cases sensitivity analysis ought to be used to assess the implications of changes in the value of potentially biased effectiveness estimates upon conclusions.

If a thorough sensitivity analysis is conducted around the relative costs and effectiveness of comparators, then findings may be more transferable to other contexts where baseline levels of relative cost and relative effectiveness differ. Findings are also likely to be more transferable if they relate to a fairly typical setting for the technology. Thus, wherever possible, economic analysis of health technologies should be undertaken in a routine service setting, rather than in atypical environments, for example within teaching hospitals (unless of course the technology is likely to be used mainly in a teaching hospital context as with some neurological applications of MRI).

Comparison of our Findings with those from Other Systematic Reviews

Other authors who conducted reviews of the economic literature relating to health technologies have similarly concluded that there is scope for improvement in relation to the quality of analysis. For example a review of

114 economic analyses relating to vaccination against hepatitis B (Jefferson and Demichelli, 1994) concluded that as a result of 'uncertain or unclear methodology, few studies reach valid conclusions'. Another paper, which systematically reviewed 16 cost-effectiveness analyses relating to breast cancer screening (Brown and Fintor, 1993), indicated that in order to reach firmer conclusions 'much more reliable data on downstream treatment costs and savings and on the frequency and costs of assessment and biopsy procedures would be useful'. A paper which reviewed around 14 economic analyses of smoking cessation therapy (Cohen and Fowler, 1993) referred to the 'limitations and weakness of most of the studies reviewed'. A review of 77 economic analyses in the medical literature (i.e. not necessarily relating to health technology) concluded that conclusions are often 'not based on the use of appropriate analytic techniques' (Udvaheyli et al., 1992). Thus the evidence base on whether or not the use of a health technology is cost-effective is likely to be misleading and inadequate. This inevitably inhibits the ability of NHS managers strategically to plan the diffusion and distribution of health technologies within the NHS efficiently.

Implications of these Findings for Strategic Planning of the Distribution and Diffusion of Health Technologies

In order to plan a health technology strategically, an assessment of provision required is necessary. Unfortunately, though, because there is a paucity of data in relation to the cost-effectiveness of using many health technologies, health service managers are usually ill-equipped to assess this. Thus there is a need to ensure that the NHS has a health technology assessment programme which is adequately resourced and sufficiently focused to inform health service management decisions. This is especially necessary because of the election in 1997 of a Labour government with a new emphasis upon strategically planning the introduction of health technologies within the NHS (NHS Executive, 1997).

When an 'internal market' was introduced in the NHS by the previous government, there was a shift away from using statements of need as the basis for decisions about the allocation of capital resources for 'big ticket' health technologies. Instead, hospital trusts were encouraged to produce business cases (NHS Executive, 1994) to justify the acquisition of expensive health technology. This approach placed emphasis upon establishing whether or not the acquisition of capital equipment improved the financial viability of trusts. The NHS business cases guidelines (ibid.) also encouraged trusts to acquire capital resources to enhance their competitive position. Thus on occasions the business case guidelines encouraged a trend whereby trusts competed with each other to acquire health technology to enhance their competitive position, at the expense of the pursuit of other objectives (for example ensuring that the use of a health technology was cost-effective). Furthermore, the business case guidelines encouraged trusts to disregard any negative impact introduction of a 'big ticket' health technology might have upon neighbouring NHS trusts (for example whether it undermined the financial viability of existing MRI provision).

With the election of a new government the emphasis changed such that 'The days of NHS trusts acting alone without regard for others are over' (NHS Executive, 1997). A new emphasis upon strategic planning has emerged and investment decisions, for example to acquire MRI now need to be consistent with local health improvement programmes (ibid.). This is a welcome development because it may help to reduce the waste and inefficiency associated with the unplanned diffusion of health technologies. Strategic planning can also serve to reduce disparities in access to health technology. Inequality of access will arise if there are wide variations in waiting times for health technologies as a result of disparities in the nationwide distribution of the technology; they also arise if some patients are forced to travel considerable distances in order to benefit from a health technology.

However, for strategic planning to be successful, it is essential that health service managers develop an informed approach to strategic management of health technologies. Unless health service managers can obtain adequate data relating to the cost-effectiveness of health technologies, there is a danger that an information vacuum might encourage a return to the kind of planned approach which existed prior to the internal market. Such an approach sometimes had the disadvantage that decisions relating to capital investment were often 'politically' driven (Mayston, 1990), rather than based upon more rational planning norms.

It is therefore essential to ensure that high quality focused economic evaluations are conducted. Evidence presented in this chapter demonstrates a shortage of such evaluation for expensive health technologies such as MRI. The NHS health technology assessment programme thus needs to be harnessed to undertake such assessments and disseminate the findings appropriately throughout the NHS.

References

Papers meeting the inclusion criteria for the systematic review:

Bance, M.L, Hyde, M.L. and Malizia, K. (1994), 'Decision and Cost Analysis in Acoustic Neuroma Diagnosis', *The Journal of Otolaryngology*, 23 (2), pp. 109–20.

Black, W.C. (1994), 'High-dose MR in the Evaluation of Brain Metastases: Will increased detection decrease costs?', *American Journal of Neuroradiology*, 15, pp. 1062–4.

Bronen, R.A., Fulbright, R.K., Spencer, D.D. et al. (1996), 'Refractory Epilepsy: Comparison of MR Imaging, CT, and Histopathologic findings in 117 patients', *Radiology*, 201 (1), pp. 97–105.

Carrier, D.A. and Arriaga, M.A. (1997), 'Cost-effective Evaluation of Asymmetric Sensorineural Hearing Loss with Focused Magnetic Resonance Imaging', *Otolaryngology-Head and Neck Surgery*, 116, pp. 567–74.

Du Boulay, G.H., Hawkes, F., Lee, C. et al. (1990), 'Comparing the Cost of Spinal MR with Conventional Myelography and Radiculography', *Neuroradiology*, 32, pp. 124–36.

Durand-Zaleski, I., Reizine, D., Puzin, D. et al. (1993), 'Economic Assessment of Magnetic Resonance Imaging for Inpatients: Is it still too early?', *International Journal of Technology Assessment in Health Care*, 9 (2), pp. 263–73.

Fletcher, J., Clark, M. and Sutton, F. (1997), 'Costs and Cost-effectiveness of MRI in the Neurosciences: Change in practice and cost, 1988–96', report for the Walsgrave NHS Trust, by the Centre for Health Service Studies, Warwick Business School, University of Warwick, Coventry, UK.

Jordan, J.E., Donaldson, S.S. and Enzmann, D.R. (1995), 'Cost-effectiveness and Outcome Assessment of Magnetic Resonance Imaging in Diagnosing Cord Compression', *Cancer*, 75 (10), pp. 2579–86.

Khangure, M.S. and Ives, F.J. (1995), 'Cost versus Efficacy of Magnetic Resonance Imaging', *Australian Family Physician*, 24 (4), pp. 538–45.

King, J.T., Justice, A.C. and Aron, D.C. (1997), 'Management of Incidental Pituitary Microadenomas: A cost-effectiveness analysis', *Journal of Clinical Endocrinology and Metabolism*, 82 (11), pp. 3625–32.

Linker, S.P., Ruckenstein, M.J., Acker, J. and Gardner, G. (1997), 'An Accurate, Cost-effective Approach for Diagnosing Retrocochlear Lesions utilising the T2-weighted, Fast-spin Echo Magnetic Resonance Imaging Scan', *The Laryngoscope*, 107, pp. 1525–9.

Mayr, N.A., Yuh, W.T., Muhonen, M.G. et al. (1994), 'Cost-effectiveness of High-dose MR Contrast Studies in the Evaluation of Brain Metastases', *American Journal of Neuroradiology*, 15 (6), pp. 1053–61.

Moffat, D.A. and Hardy, D.G. (1989), 'Early Diagnosis and Surgical Management of Acoustic Neuroma: Is it cost effective?', *Journal of the Royal Society of Medicine*, 82, pp. 329–32.

Moffat, D.A., Hardy, D.G. and Baguley, D.M. (1989), 'Strategy and benefits of acoustic neuroma searching', *Journal of Laryngology Otology*, 103, pp. 51–9.

Mooney, C., Mushlin, A.I. and Phelps, C.E. (1990), 'Targeting Assessments of Magnetic Resonance Imaging in Suspected Multiple Sclerosis', *Medical Decision Making*, 10 (2), pp. 77–94.

Mushlin, A.I., Mooney, C., Holloway, R.G. et al. (1997), 'The Cost-effectiveness of Magnetic Resonance Imaging for Patients with Equivocal Neurological Symptoms', *International Journal of Technology Assessment in Health Care*, 13 (1), pp. 21–34.

Podd, T.J. and Walkden, S.E. (1992), 'The Use of MRI in the Investigation of Spinal Cord Compression', *The British Journal of Radiology*, 65, pp. 187–8.

Raber, E., Dort, J.C., Sevick, R. and Winkelaar, R. (1997), 'Asymmetric Hearing Loss: Toward cost-effective diagnosis', *The Journal of Otolaryngology*, 26 (2), pp. 88–91.

Ravi, K.V. and Wells, S.C. (1996), 'A Cost Effective Screening Protocol for Vestibular Schwannoma in the late 90s', *The Journal of Laryngology and Otology*, 110, pp. 1129–32.

Reese, L. (1990), 'Magnetic Resonance Imaging in Canada', *Dimensions*, pp. 10–14.

Renowden, S.A. and Anslow, P. (1993), 'The Effective Use of Magnetic Resonance Imaging in the Diagnosis of Acoustic Neuromas', *Clinical Radiology*, 48, pp. 25–8.

Robson, A.K., Leighton, S.E.J., Anslow, P. and Milford, C.A. (1993), 'MRI as a Single Screening Procedure for Acoustic Neuroma: A cost effective protocol', *Journal of the Royal Society of Medicine*, 86, pp. 455–7.

Saaed, S.R., Woolford, T.J., Ramsden, R.T. and Lye, R.H. (1995), 'Magnetic Resonance Imaging: A cost-effective first line investigation in the detection of vestibular schwannomas', *British Journal of Neurosurgery*, 9 (4), pp. 497–503.

Seidenwurm, D., Russel, E.J. and Hambly, M. (1994), 'Diagnostic Accuracy, Patient Outcome, and Economic Factors in Lumbar Radiculopathy', *Radiology*, 190 (1), pp. 21–5.

Shah, V.C. and Surya, N. (1996), 'Cost-Effectiveness of Magnetic Resonance Imaging in Specific Situations in India', *Academy Radiology*, 3 Suppl 1, S113–S115.

Shelton, C., Harnsberger, R. and Allen, R. (1996), 'Fast Spin Echo Magnetic Resonance Imaging: Clinical application in screening for acoustic neuroma', *Otolaryngology-Head and Neck Surgery*, 114 (1), pp. 71–6.

Simon, D.G. and Lubin, M.F. (1985), 'Cost-effectiveness of Computerized Tomography and Magnetic Resonance Imaging in Dementia', *Medical Decision Making*, 5 (3), pp. 335–54.

Szczepura, A.K., Fletcher, J. and Fitz-Patrick, D. (1990), 'An Evaluation of the Introduction of Magnetic Resonance Imaging (MRI) in a UK Service Setting', Occasional Paper No. 1, Health Services Research Unit, Warwick Business School, University of Warwick, Coventry, UK.

Thornbury, J.R., Fryback, D.G., Turski, P.A. et al. (1993), 'Disk-caused Nerve Compression in Patients with Acute Low-back Pain: Diagnosis with MR, CT Myelography, and plain CT', *Radiology*, 186, pp. 731–8.

Watson, C., Clifford, R.F. and Cendes, F. (1997), 'Volumetric Magnetic Resonance Imaging: Clinical Applications and Contributions to the Understanding of Temporal Lobe Epilepsy', *Archives of Neurology*, 54, pp. 1521–31.

Welling, D.B., Glassock, M.E., Woods, C.I. and Jackson, C.G. (1990), 'Acoustic Neuroma: A cost-effective approach', *Otolaryngology-Head Neck Surgery*, 103 (3), pp. 364–70.

Other references:

Briggs, A., Sculpher, M. and Buxton, M. (1994), 'Uncertainty in the Economic Evaluation of Health Care Technologies: The role of sensitivity analysis', *Health Economics*, 3, pp. 95–104.

Brown, M.L. and Fintor, L. (1993), 'Cost-effectiveness of Breast Cancer Screening: Preliminary results of a systematic review of the literature', *Breast Cancer Research and Treatment*, 25, pp. 113–18.

Buxton, M. (1987), 'Problems in the Economic Appraisal of New Health Technology' in *Economic Appraisal of Health Technology in the European Community*, Oxford University Press, Oxford.

Buxton, M.J., Drummond, M.F., Van Hout, B.A. et al. (1997), 'Modelling in Economic Evaluation: A unavoidable fact of life', *Health Economics*, 6 (3), pp. 217–27.

Cohen, D.R. and Fowler, G.H. (1993), 'Economic Implications of Smoking Cessation Therapies: A review of economic appraisals', *Pharmacoeconomics*, 4 (5), pp. 331–44.

Coyle, D. and Davies, L. (1996), 'How to Assess Cost-effectiveness: Elements of a sound economic evaluation' in M.F. Drummond and A. Maynard (eds), *Purchasing and Providing Cost-effective Health Care*, Churchill Livingstone, London.

Drummond, M.F. and Jefferson, T.O. (1996), 'Guidelines for Authors and Peer Reviewers of Economic Submissions to the BMJ', *British Medical Journal*, 313, pp. 275–83.

Drummond, M.F., Stoddart, G.L. and Torrance, G.W. (1987), *Methods for the Economic Evaluation of Health Care Programmes*, Oxford University Press, Oxford.

Jefferson, T. and Demicheli, V. (1994), 'Is Vaccination Against Hepatitis B Efficient? A review of the world literature', *Health Economics*, 3, pp. 25–37.

Jefferson, T. and Demichelli, V. (1995), 'Are Guidelines for Peer-reviewing Economic Evaluations Necessary? A survey of current editorial practice', *Health Economics*, 4, pp. 383–8.

Krahn, M. and Gafni, A. (1993), 'Discounting in the Economic Evaluation of Health Care Interventions', *Medical Care*, 31 (5), pp. 403–18.

Laska, E.M., Meisner, M. and Siegel, C. (1997), 'Statistical Inference for Cost-effectiveness Ratios', *Health Economics*, 6, pp. 229–42.

Lazaro, P. and Fitch, K. (1995), 'The Distribution of "Big Ticket" Medical Technologies in OECD Countries', *International Journal of Technology Assessment in Health Care*, 11 (3), pp. 552–70.

Mayston, D. (1990), 'Managing Capital Resources in the NHS' in A.J. Culyer, A.K. Maynard and J.W. Posnett (eds), *Competition in Health Care: Reforming the NHS*, Macmillan, Basingstoke.

Mushlin, A.I., Mooney, C., Grow, V. and Phelps, C.E. (1994), 'The Value of Diagnostic Information to Patients with Suspected Multiple Sclerosis', *Archives of Neurology*, 51, pp. 67–72.

NHS Executive (1994), 'Business Case Guide', *Capital Investment Manual*, HMSO, London.

NHS Executive (1997), *The New NHS: Modern, dependable*, HMSO, London.

Polsky, D., Glick, H.A., Willke, R. and Schulman, K. (1997), 'Confidence Intervals for Cost-Effectiveness Ratios: A comparison of four methods', *Health Economics*, 6 (3), pp. 243–52.

Szczepura, A.K. (1992), 'Routine Low Cost Pathology Tests; Measuring the value-in-use of bacteriology tests in hospitals and primary care', *Health Services Management Research*, 5, pp. 225–37.

Udvaheyli, S., Graham, A., Colditz, P.H. et al. (1992), 'Cost-Effectiveness and Cost-Benefit Analyses in the Medical Literature: Are the Methods Being Used Correctly?', *Annals of Internal Medicine*, 116, pp. 238–44.

Van-Hout, B.A., Miawenn, J., Gilad, S. and Rutten, F.F.H. (1994), 'Costs, Effects, and C/E ratios alongside a clinical trial', *Health Economics*, 3, pp. 309–19.

Wakker, P. and Klaasen, M.P. (1995), 'Confidence Intervals for Cost/effectiveness Ratios', *Health Economics*, 4, pp. 373–81.

12 Evaluating Telemedicine Support of Chronic Disease Management

DEREK G. CRAMP, ALASTAIR MORGAN, ABDUL V. ROUDSARI
AND EWART R. CARSON
Centre for Measurement and Information in Medicine, City University

Introduction

Across Europe there are moves to improve the delivery and quality of care but at the same time to try and contain the escalating costs of delivering these services by removing the many barriers that exist between the provision of institutional health care, care in the community and primary care. Present structures are seen not only to be inefficient but also not to provide seamless care. Movement of health care delivery towards the primary sector and the home setting can result in substantial benefits in terms of health outcome, social provision, cost-effectiveness and resource utilization, particularly in relation to the management of chronic disease. However, it is widely recognized that achievement of such a system of care is highly dependent on telematics (information and communications technologies) for the optimal transfer of clinical, demographic and administrative information between the different providers of services in the health sector. It is in this context that there is a growing interest in telemedicine; an interest arising partly because of technological push and driven by advances in telecommunications. But telemedicine is now emerging from its research and demonstration stage and as it matures is providing ways in which it could be an important adjunct in the future for improved access to care in the community, particularly in relation to the management of chronic disease. The 'hospital without walls' concept could thus be realized.

Controlling Costs: Strategic Issues in Health Care Management, H.T.O. Davies, M. Tavakoli, M. Malek, A. R. Neilson (eds), Ashgate Publishing Ltd, 1999.

However, the proponents of adopting a new technology, such as a telemedicine based service, all too often pay little attention to the real world context and ignore the multidimensional and multi-attribute nature of the problems and associated costs of introducing a new technology. In order to design, implement and subsequently assess and evaluate the benefits and disbenefits of delivering such a service, it is necessary to ensure that there is a full and proper understanding of all the technical and logistic dimensions, clinical activities and human concerns that are involved. It is for such situations that the integrative discipline of systems science and its modelling methodology is well suited.

In this chapter, the design and evaluation of decision support systems, including those incorporating a telematic component, are considered. It is argued that effective design and evaluation are dependent upon the adoption of appropriate methodology set firmly within a systemic framework. Systems modelling is proposed as an approach to system design, with evaluation adopting an approach incorporating evaluability analysis and formative and summative evaluation, including the use of stakeholder matrix analysis.

This systems modelling approach has been developed and used not only for the specification of a telemedicine system for the domiciliary management of maintenance haemodialysis of patients with end-stage renal disease, but also for building a model for the evaluation of its efficacy, cost-effectiveness and its fit into effective day-to-day clinical practice. The model paradigms described are of a generic nature and suitable for general application in health technology assessment.

Systems Methodology

To obtain a good understanding of the delivery of health care for chronic disease is very much a case of coming to terms with complexity. It is for such situations that systems science has evolved to facilitate analysis and hence aid understanding. Within this integrative and holistic discipline a wide range of methodologies has been devised for the necessary systemic analysis, spanning a broad spectrum of 'hard' and 'soft' approaches including the viable systems model (Beer, 1984) and the soft systems methodology (Checkland, 1981). Summary accounts of these and other methodologies can be found in the introductory text of Flood and Carson (1993). The methodology described here is part of an ongoing project to develop systems models using multi-attribute utility theory and more specifically multidimensional value criteria models. This approach is based on the pioneering work of M'Pherson (1980 and 1981) who originally developed and implemented the methodology for technology assessment in industry and has progressively refined it to take account of subjective values and intangibles when assessing the value of information (1994).

Systems Modelling

As implied above, the complexity associated with the clinical management of a chronic disease, such as diabetes or end-stage renal disease, needs an appropriate model-based systems analysis to be undertaken in order to clearly identify the ways in which it may be possible for information technology to be used for supporting its management (Carson et al., 1997a).

One approach that has been found to be helpful, and that is becoming widely adopted, is to develop models which depict the processes of health care delivery and management in terms of feedback systems (Cramp and Carson, 1994 and 1995). In its simplest representation, the process of health care delivery can be viewed as comprising four elements that together make up a cybernetic loop (see Figure 12.1). These elements correspond to decision-maker, effector, controlled system and information system. For example, the clinical decision-maker determines what treatment should be effected with the consequent impact on patient state and health outcome being monitored to enable information to be fed back to the decision-maker. This basic model can be modified, for instance through loop extensions or by the incorporation of multiple loops. In this way health care delivery can be analysed at different levels of scrutiny. Equally it is possible to take a view beyond the specific, but restrictive, perspective of the clinical activities loop to embrace broader issues such as patient preference and health outcome as well as taking full account of resources and other dimensions of the management process (see Figure 12.2). This modelling approach can provide clear representations of distributed modes of health care delivery such as, for example, would be implied by the adoption of a telemedicine framework.

Evaluation

An evaluation phase is a cardinal feature of systems methodology, and it is becoming an important issue in telemedicine as it matures (Field, 1996; Hailey and Jacobs, 1997) but there is not as yet a formalized methodology. One view, and adopted by us, is that it is comprised of three consecutive stages namely,

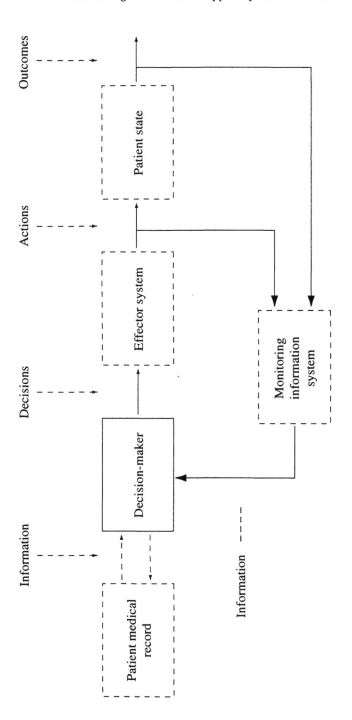

Figure 12.1 Generic decision-making model formulated in terms of the four components of clinical decision-maker, affecting the clinical process or activity, the patient state as the system being controlled and an information system constituting the feedback loop

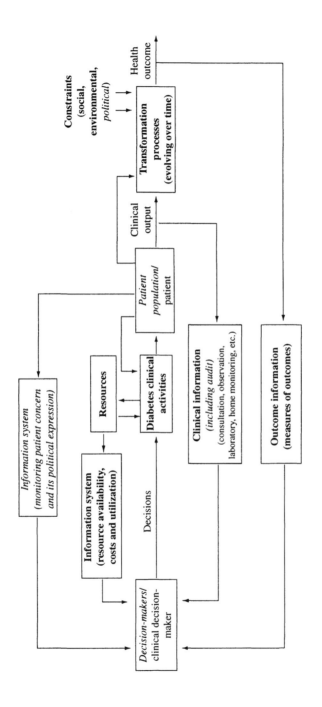

Figure 12.2 An overall model of the decision-making process depicted in terms of multiple feedback loops

Note: the model incorporates health outcome in addition to clinical output. Two levels of resolution are shown: health policy (in italics) and clinical practice as it relates to the individual patient. Entities and processes common to both levels of resolution are shown in bold type.

Source: Adapted from Cramp and Carson, 1995.

evaluability assessment, formative evaluation and summative evaluation (Bashshur, 1995).

Evaluability assessment provides an operational definition of the system in which information technology is being included (whether as telemedicine or with clinical decision-making without the added component of remote care delivery). This definition relates to specific attributes, characteristics and configurations together with a specification for problems and issues to be evaluated (inputs and outputs and their interactions). A range of evaluation criteria can be provided, which are specified in terms of the main stakeholders of the system in question, with expected benefits and costs quantified as far as possible from their different perspectives. Typically a stakeholder analysis matrix would be established with the two dimensions corresponding respectively to stakeholders and evaluation criteria. The particular stakeholders will vary dependent on the particular chronic disease in question and the mode of health care delivery, but might typically include: patient, family/carer, members of the primary care clinical team, members of the hospital clinical team, managers, technical staff, together with those responsible for the payment of the health care in question. Relevant criteria could typically include system availability, accessibility, quality of care delivered, cost-effectiveness and acceptability.

Formative evaluation focuses on the description of the system design and implementation and, in particular, on the assessment of its intermediate or short term effects on the process of health care delivery and consequent influence on the various stakeholders. Summative evaluation seeks to determine the ultimate impact of the system on health outcomes and, relating to a longer time scale, this stage can be expected to support recommendations for modifying the process of health care delivery in the light of the impact of the information technology. At this stage the stakeholder analysis matrix would normally provide the basis for data collection from the various stakeholders arising from interviews and the subsequent analysis of the data that they yield.

Any cost-effectiveness analysis requires a full definition of effectiveness, and the means by which it may be measured, in quantitative terms wherever possible. This raises issues concerned with fixed and variable costs, direct and indirect costs, and marginal and average costs. Other dimensions include: medically, examining the impact of the IT system on the effectiveness and efficiency of health care delivery; examining the system from an economic view point, including both capital and running costs; examining the full functioning of the system from a technical perspective; examining the impact on organizational features; and examining behavioural changes arising from the introduction of information technology. All these are relevant whether the technology be that of telemedicine or clinical decision support.

Telemedicine and Clinical Decision Support

Clinical decision support can be modelled as an extension of the feedback loop configuration referred to above, where in the case of chronic disease the decision-maker may be a hospital, general practice or community-based clinician or the patient themselves in their home setting. The clinical decision support facility may be regarded as an overlayering of the health care delivery loop so that in effect there is a further feedback interaction between the decision support function and the decision-maker. Figure 12.3 depicts this interaction of the decision support function with the decision-maker and the several sources of feedback information. The various types of decision support functionality are also indicated.

This layout is extended in the case of telemedicine. Consider a typical configuration of the home setting, the hospital or other clinical centre, with the two being linked by appropriate telecommunications networks. This communication link permits telemonitoring of the patient, a two way exchange of data messages and an interaction facilitating the provision of telecare. In both home and clinical settings the patient and clinician will typically interact with patient assistant and clinical assistant respectively which can be regarded as the decision support facility in each case.

Preliminary studies, where the ingredients of good systems practice, telemedicine and decision support have been applied to chronic disease management, are described for diabetes (Andreassen et al., 1997) and end-stage renal disease (Carson et al., 1997b). It is this latter management situation that will be described in greater detail below.

Home Maintenance Haemodialysis

The management of end-stage renal disease is a major clinical challenge. Home haemodialysis could offer the patient with this disease the convenience of home treatment, the potential for enhanced rehabilitation in a familiar environment and the possibility of decreased cost over time. Currently, however, its take-up across Europe is limited and indeed has decreased over recent years. Problems have included a lack of support of the patient in the

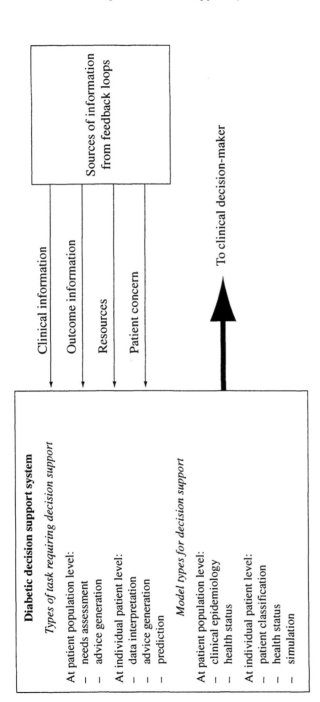

Diabetic decision support system

Types of task requiring decision support

At patient population level:
– needs assessment
– advice generation

At individual patient level:
– data interpretation
– advice generation
– prediction

Model types for decision support

At patient population level:
– clinical epidemiology
– health status

At individual patient level:
– patient classification
– health status
– simulation

Clinical information

Outcome information

Resources

Patient concern

Sources of information from feedback loops

To clinical decision-maker

Figure 12.3 The decision support function, with input from the several feedback loops and interacting with the clinical decision-maker

Note: the range of model functionality is depicted dependent upon the nature of the type of decision requiring support.

Source: Adapted from Carson, 1998.

home setting and difficulties concerning provision of resources at home. One way of overcoming such problems is by the addition of a telemedicine dimension to home dialysis. This involves complementing the traditional home haemodialysis with a telematic link (video, voice, data and text) between the patient's home and the hospital control centre with its clinical expertise. Such provision has the potential to increase the use of home haemodialysis and hence improve the rehabilitation of the dialysis patient.

Some of the methodological issues arising in the development of such a service have been addressed in the European funded HOMER-D project and have been described (Carson et al., 1997b). In essence the functionality of an existing dialysis machine is being enhanced by including state of the art, advanced multimedia and networking technology. In this way support for the patient is offered by the provision of monitoring services through bidirectional communication links between the hospital-based central control station and a remote terminal unit in the patient's home or other satellite location.

Modelling the System

In developing this telematic system, extensive use has been made of the modelling approach adopted by Cramp and Carson (1994 and 1995) in order to ensure proper system specification. Modelling has been carried out at successively fine levels of resolution and in this way a conceptual model of the required telemedicine information and control architecture can be arrived at. This leads directly to the specification of hardware and software for system realization, with the approach to evaluation being as described above.

Figure 12.4 provides an overview of this modelling approach. The principal components of the clinical management process, including those which relate specifically to the haemodialysis treatment cycle are shown within the circle. For simplicity longer term concerns, such as those relating to patient rehabilitation, are not depicted since they do not immediately impact upon the design of the telematic home haemodialysis system. The generic decision-making model, as was shown in Figure 12.1, is then applied to each of these treatment cycle components of clinical management in turn. The result of its application to the haemodialysis treatment session is depicted in Figure 12.5. Progression through this modelling activity leads to the representation of the telematic treatment session given in Figure 12.6.

In progressing from the conceptual model, the information gathering stage begins by taking the patient profile from the patient's medical record. Instructions are then given to the patient by the clinical link. Once this is

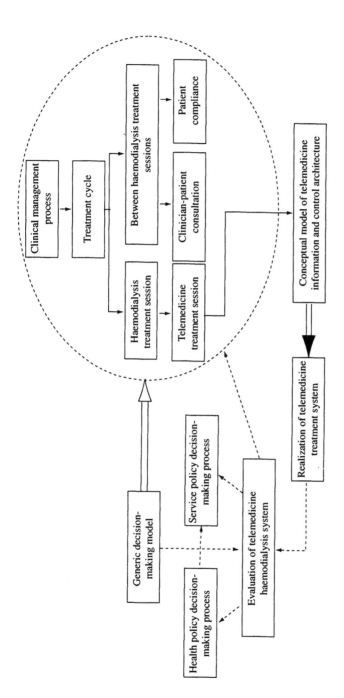

Figure 12.4 A model-based framework for the design, realization and evaluation of a telematic home haemodialysis service

Note: the generic decision-making model is applied, at a range of levels, to the components of the clinical process in order to arrive at a conceptual model for the telematic information and control architecture. The telemedicine treatment system can then be realized and evaluated in an iterative manner as shown.

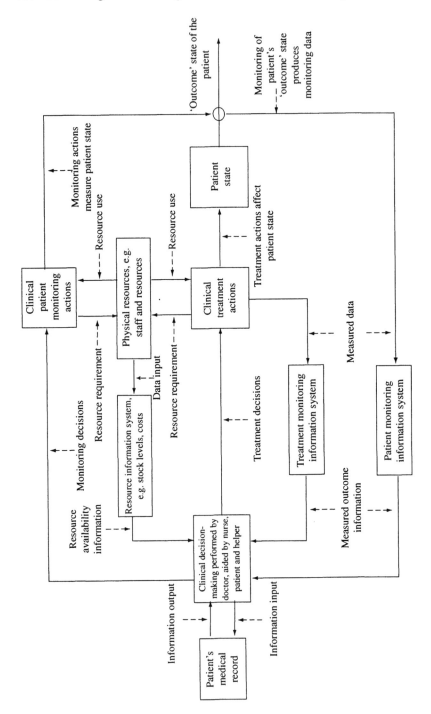

Figure 12.5 Conceptual model of the haemodialysis treatment session

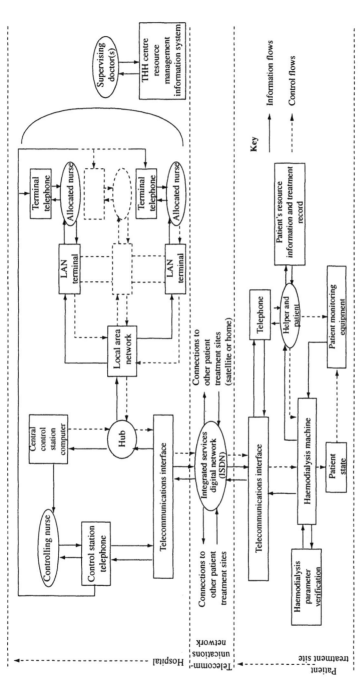

Figure 12.6 Conceptual model of the telematic information and control architecture for hardware/software realization

Source: Adapted from Carson et al., 1997b.

done, certain monitoring actions are performed by the patient, such as measurement of blood pressure and weight. These data are then fed back to the hospital centre. Unless there is contraindication of the monitoring actions, the haemodialysis treatment is then initiated. From this point in the procedure, information generated by the haemodialysis machine, e.g. blood flow rate, is monitored and fed back to the hospital. Normally, monitored information will only be acted upon when an alarm condition occurs. Where appropriate, any such alarm states detected during the monitoring process can be recorded in the patient's medical record by the clinical staff. At the conclusion of the treatment session, further monitoring actions are undertaken and the corresponding data are recorded in the patient's medical record.

It is the progression through increasingly fine levels of resolution of the modelling approach that yields the conceptual model of the required telemedicine information and control architecture that is shown in Figure 12.6. This conceptual representation of the architecture leads directly to the specification of the hardware and software to be adopted in the telemedicine system. The prototype developed in this way for the HOMER-D project has first been demonstrated at the Aretaieon Hospital in Athens. Initial test data for assessment and evaluation of this telemedicine system have been collected there, and currently arrangements are being made to evaluate the system at further locations in two other European countries.

Evaluation

The integral nature of the evaluation process in relation to a telematic system for health care delivery has been clearly shown in the schema of Figure 12.4. It is within this framework that the three stage process of evaluability analysis, formative evaluation and summative evaluation as already described should be applied.

Using the stakeholder analysis as part of the second and third stages offers considerable insight into the nature of evaluation, where the problem is essentially one that is multidimensional, multi-variable and multi-attribute. A candidate stakeholder matrix is shown in Figure 12.7. The stakeholders are grouped under four aggregated headings of patient, together with family and / or carers; clinical staff; technical staff; and those concerned with paying for health care or occupying related management functions. These broad categories are clearly capable of further disaggregation. For instance the category of clinical staff embraces medical and nursing personnel in both primary care and hospital centre, and in parts of the evaluation process there would clearly

Criteria Stake- holders	Safety	Reliability	Accept- ability	Ergonomic design	Effective- ness	Efficiency	Cost
Patient/ family/ carer							
Clinical staff centre/ satellite							
Technical staff							
Health care payment							

Figure 12.7 Stakeholder matrix for the evaluation of a telemedicine system, applicable to the HOMER-D configuration

Note: the matrix can be partitioned into the necessary precursor requirements of safety, reliability, acceptability and ergonomic design, with system worth then being evaluated in terms of effectiveness, efficiency and cost.

be the need to take into account the views of each of these sub-categories individually.

Seven criteria are presented in the matrix as constituting dimensions of the evaluation process. However, these seven can effectively be divided into two distinct clusters. Those of safety, reliability, acceptability and ergonomic design can be considered to represent a filter through which it is necessary for the proposed telematic system to pass if it is to remain a candidate for further evaluation. It is interesting to examine these criteria from the perspective shown in Figure 12.8. Here the variables are considered from the standpoint of the five dimensions of variable type that constitute the quantitative and qualitative data being collected as the evidence to be assessed and evaluated. It is to be noted that no economic variables are included in this necessary, preliminary filtering process. Equally noteworthy is the fact that technical measures play no further part (at least in a direct sense) in the evaluation process beyond their function in relation to this filter.

The technical data will all be quantitative in nature. Observational data will be a mix with rather more being quantitative than qualitative. The reverse will be true in the case of questionnaire data, where the qualitative component will dominate. Having satisfied the filtering assessment, the worth of the HOMER-D system can then be considered. This measure is a function of the three remaining criteria, namely effectiveness, efficiency and cost, where by costs we mean real or absolute cost. This function should be determined using a model which takes fully into account the multi-attribute utilities that will apply, where the types of variable and parameter that make up these three criteria are as depicted in Figure 12.8.

Criteria \ Variables	Safety	Reliability	Accept-ability	Ergonomic design	Effective-ness	Efficiency	Cost
Medical	✓	✓			✓	✓	
Economic	░	░	░	░			✓
Technical	✓	✓	✓	✓	░	░	░
Organiza-tional	✓	✓	✓			✓	
Social			✓		✓		

Figure 12.8 Relationship between evaluation criteria and the types of variable being included in the formulation of those criteria

This is the methodological framework which is now being further developed and refined for adoption in the HOMER-D project. However, it is apparent that this framework should have wider applicability in the process of evaluating telemedicine systems in general, not just those confined to the clinical domains of chronic disease.

In one sense the stakeholder matrix can be regarded as a device to aid cost-effectiveness analysis. Adopting the matrix as part of a properly systemic evaluation means that for each of the matrix cells, measures can be devised that include as many as are appropriate of the medical, economic, technical, behavioural and social dimensions of the specific criterion. Although quantitative measures should be adopted wherever practicable, qualitative measures will clearly dominate in those cells reflect principally the impact of social and behavioural variables.

The general form of the stakeholder matrix will apply in relation to the full range of decision support systems, whether local or involving telemedicine provision, but some variation in the definition of evaluation criteria can be permitted to reflect particular issues or concerns.

Summary

This chapter has highlighted the need for adopting a sound systems methodology if information and telecommunications technology is to be applied to best effect in the management of chronic disease. This is true whether IT takes the form of local clinical decision support or a wider telemedicine configuration. Modelling activity is essential if designs are to be achieved that take full account of all the user requirements. Evaluation must form an integral part of the systems methodology, rather than being merely an additional *post hoc* activity after system implementation. These issues have been illustrated in the context of the home management of end-stage renal failure, though they have general applicability across the spectrum of chronic disease management and beyond.[1]

Note

1   The authors gratefully acknowledge the support and contributions of their colleagues in the HOMER-D project, and the funding provided to the Health Care Telematics Project HC-1022 (HOMER-D) by the Commission of the European Union.

References

Andreassen, S., Carson, E.R., Cashman, S.J., Engelbrecht, R., Fletcher, L.R., Harvey, M., Hejlesen, O.K., Massi Benedetti, M., Piwernetz, K., Sönksen, P.H. and Vaughan, N.J.A. (1997), 'A Methodology for Assessing Information Technology Systems in Diabetes Care', *Diabetes, Nutrition and Metabolism*, 10, pp. 255–64.
Bashshur, R.L. (1995), 'On the Definition and Evaluation of Telemedicine', *Telemedicine Journal*, 1 (1), pp. 19–30.

Beer, S. (1984), 'The Viable Systems Model: Its provenance, development, methodology and pathology', *Journal of the Operational Research Society*, 35, pp. 7–25.

Carson, E.R. (1998), 'Decision Support Systems in Diabetes: A systems perspective', *Computer Methods and Programs in Biomedicine*, 56, pp. 77–91.

Carson, E.R., Cramp, D.G., Morgan, A. and Roudsari, A.V. (1997a), 'Systems Methodology, Telemedicine and Clinical Decision Support: Their role in the management of chronic disease', in *Proceedings of the IEEE/EMBS International Conference on Information Technology Applications in Biomedicine – ITAB '97*, V. Eck and I. Krekule, eds, IEEE Piscataway, NJ, pp. 7–10.

Carson, E.R., Cramp, D.G., Darnige, A., Koutsikos, D., Murley, D., Morgan, A. and Vavatsikos, T. (1997b), 'A Systems Methodology for the Development and Evaluation of a Telemedicine Home Haemodialysis Service' in *Proceedings of the 19th Annual International Conference of the IEEE EMBS – Magnificent Milestones and Emerging Opportunities in Medical Engineering*, IEEE, Piscataway, NJ (CD-ROM).

Checkland, P.B. (1981), *Systems Thinking, Systems Practice*, John Wiley, New York.

Cramp, D.G. and Carson, E.R. (1994), 'Health Care Planning and Priority Setting – A Modelling Approach' in M. Malek (ed.), *Setting Priorities in Health Care*, John Wiley & Sons, Chichester.

Cramp, D.G. and Carson, E.R. (1995), 'Assessing Health Policy Strategies: A model-based approach to decision support' in *Intelligent Systems for the 21st Century. Proceedings of the 1995 IEEE Conference on Systems, Man and Cybernetics*, IEEE, Piscataway, NJ.

Field, M.J. (ed.) (1996), *Telemedicine: A Guide to Assessing Telecommunications in Health Care*, National Academy Press, Washington, DC.

Flood, R.L. and Carson, E.R. (1993), *Dealing with Complexity: an Introduction to the Theory and Application of Systems Science*, 2nd edn, Plenum Press, New York.

Hailey, D. and Jacobs, P. (1997), 'Assessment of Telehealth Applications' (a draft discussion paper for comment), Alberta Heritage Foundation for Medical Research, Edmonton.

M'Pherson, P.K. (1980), 'Systems Engineering: An approach to whole-system design', *The Radio and Electronic Engineer*, 50 (11/12), pp. 545–58.

M'Pherson, P.K. (1981), 'A Framework for Systems Engineering Design', *The Radio and Electronic Engineer*, 51 (2), pp. 59–93.

M'Pherson, P.K. (1994), 'Accounting for the Value of Information', *ASLIB Proceedings*, 46 (9), pp. 203–15.

13 The Cost-effectiveness of Economic Evaluations

ELISABETH BROCK AND MO MALEK
Department of Management, University of St Andrews

Introduction

Health economics is a discipline which seeks to compare the relative costs and outcomes of various health care interventions in order to give recommendations concerning the most cost-effective use of scarce resources in the provision of health care. It can be argued that a discipline which places such demands on the provision of health care should itself also be subject to evaluation along the same rigorous set of criteria. Had the discipline of health economics itself been subjected to such assessment, the effectiveness of present day health economics in reaching its self-set targets of changing practice might have been called into question. It will be shown that in order to increase the impact of health economics on real-world health care decisions, it is not only necessary to make changes to the demand but also to the supply of economic evidence. Concentrating only on educating decision-makers in the techniques and appropriate usage of existing economic evaluations may not be the most efficient way of achieving the objective of making economic evaluations an indispensable part of health care decision-making. We live in an environment where public services look increasingly towards the adoption of routine private sector business practices in order to improve their performance. The fundamental difference between the two sectors is the private sector's ability to satisfy customer needs. One of the main reasons for this is that in the private sector customers make their demand known directly and without any third party involvement. Elementary marketing theory tells us that a product can only be successful if it addresses a real or perceived need of the customer. The customers of economic evaluations are the decision-makers in the public

Controlling Costs: Strategic Issues in Health Care Management, H.T.O. Davies, M. Tavakoli, M. Malek, A. R. Neilson (eds), Ashgate Publishing Ltd, 1999.

or private sectors. They need information which is both timely and relevant to assist the decision-making process. Based on the available evidence, it seems that presently health economics is not meeting these demands as well as it perhaps could. Health economists seem to be caught in a mindset of trying to sell health economics to decision-makers, not recognizing that their product may not necessarily address the decision-maker's need.

This chapter will first examine the context within which health policy decisions are taken. By examining this context, it is possible to see how the present toolbox of economic evaluation techniques may not always address the decision-maker's need for relevant and timely information. One way of satisfying these demands would be to develop techniques which rely on readily-available or quick-to-collect data. This chapter then suggests a method of evaluating different health care interventions which uses readily-available data and attempts to give an estimate of the unknown variables by using 'implied values'.

The Context of Health Care Policy Decision-making

It is important to recognize that the resources available to the NHS are limited. One way of ensuring that the best use is made of them is based on the concept of evidence-based medicine. This means that people should only be given medical treatment which has been shown in the medical literature to have a positive impact on people's health.

The recommendations we should give to public policy makers concerning the relative merits of different health care interventions would thus be determined solely by their proven clinical effectiveness in the first place. This is a necessary but not sufficient condition.

It can be argued that in order to be effective, policy recommendations should also take into account the prevailing climate of public policy. A different way of expressing this is that not only should we take the technical environment into account when formulating policy recommendations but also the political, economic, legal and social environment if we want research to have a direct impact on decision-making. A survey of the by no means abundant literature of the factors determining the impact of economic evaluations on decision-making suggests that a study only has a chance of influencing decision-making if the content of the study fits the decision-making environment present at the time.

... the usefulness of a piece of research is not a normative concept derived from the findings themselves but a descriptive one contingent on the disposition of the policy makers and the pressures bearing on them (Klein, 1990, p. 504).

Wildavsky and Tenenbaum (1981) expressed this simply as '... politics drive data: values need corroborating facts'.

The conclusion reached by the majority of research into whether an economic evaluation has any impact, direct or indirect, on decision-making, is rather bleak. Coyle (1993, p. 31) concluded that the 'greatest determinant of the level of impact made by studies is not the actions of decision-makers but the actions of the researchers'. The factors most frequently identified across the literature as determining the level of impact of a study on decision-making are the following. Most important are logistical problems such as obtaining relevant and timely information. Problems also arise in the dissemination of the research evidence. The results need to be communicated to the decision-makers in such a form as to enable them to understand the study's relevance and to interpret its results. Another major factor influencing the level of impact of a study on decision-making is the methodology of the study itself. Coyle concluded from his research that increasing the academic standards of evaluations does not necessarily lead to an increase in the influence evaluations have on decision-making. An evaluation of rather 'poor' quality may well be the most appropriate to influence policy.

We have seen that the environment in which health care decisions are taken is characterized by imperfect information, communication problems across specialties and perpetual budgetary and time pressures. There is a need for health economics as a discipline to change in response to the environmental conditions it faces. The onus is now on health economics to provide decision-makers with information which they can recognize as being relevant to the decision they need to take. This information needs to be available to them at the time when the decision is to be taken. The existing toolkit of health economics may not always be able to deliver all of these. New techniques of economic evaluation which may serve as either supplements or alternatives to the existing toolkit are needed. One way of addressing the cost and the time issue at the same time would be to make increased use of existing or routinely collected data.

In the following section, a method is suggested for evaluating different health care interventions which uses readily-available data and attempts to give an estimate of the unknown variables by using 'implied values'.

Exploration of Method

We assume that we have to make a decision between health care intervention programmes A and B. The central idea of the approach is that health care intervention A can be considered economically viable compared to health care intervention B if the costs of A are less than the sum of the costs of B and the effects on utility attained by the patient as a result of effects of intervention B on his/her quality of life and mortality. We can represent this in the following way:

$$
\begin{array}{ccccc}
\text{costs of} & & U_B & & \text{costs of} \\
\text{intervention} & + & \text{(utility change due to} & > & \text{intervention} \\
\text{B} & & \text{changes in quality of} & & \text{A} \\
& & \text{life and mortality} & & \\
& & \text{associated with B)} & &
\end{array}
$$

To find the costs of the two different health care intervention programmes is probably one of the easier tasks associated with economic evaluations. The methodology which is employed for this depends on the quality of the cost information which is already available and the timeframe within which a decision between A and B needs to be taken. The relative merits of the various methods of costing have been discussed at length in the literature on cost-of-illness studies already. Therefore the validity of this method should not be questioned because of weaknesses in costing since this is a problem which this method shares with all other forms of economic evaluation.

The utility effects associated with programme B are estimated by solving the identity for U_B.

$$
\begin{array}{ccccc}
& & \text{costs of} & & \text{costs of} \\
U_B & > & \text{intervention} & - & \text{intervention} \\
& & \text{A} & & \text{B}
\end{array}
$$

We thus avoid directly measuring utility effects. The monetary value associated with these utility effects is 'implied' from the difference in costs between programme A and B.

Case Study

The proposed method is now applied to a practical example. We will compare a programme of treating osteoporosis with a programme of preventing osteoporosis. The prevention programme can be considered economically viable if the sum of the treatment costs and the utility effects due to the loss of quality of life and increased mortality as a result of osteoporosis is greater or equal than the costs of preventing it. Prevention may also be viable even if the two are only equal because in the absence of serious adverse effects on utility associated with the prevention programme, prevention is seen to be better than treatment.

$$\text{treatment costs} \; + \; \begin{array}{c}\text{utility deficit due to}\\ \text{loss of QoL and}\\ \text{increased mortality}\end{array} \; \begin{array}{c}>\\ =\end{array} \; \begin{array}{c}\text{prevention}\\ \text{costs}\end{array}$$

This equation would enable us to calculate how much the loss of quality of life due to osteoporotic fractures would have to be worth in monetary terms per person, or per incident, for a particular prevention programme to be economically worthwhile.

Osteoporosis is a condition in which bone mineral content declines progressively. As a result, bones are more susceptible to fracture. The most common fractures are fractures of the hip, spine and wrist. In the UK, it has been estimated that there are 60,000 hip fractures, 50,000 wrist fractures and 40,000 clinically diagnosed spinal fractures per year in postmenopausal women. In the UK, 22.5 per cent of white women over 50 have low bone density which is the major risk factor for developing fractures. In the US, the lifetime risk of having a hip, wrist or vertebral fracture is almost 40 per cent in white women and 13 per cent in white men from age 50. The cost of hip fracture ranges from slightly over £2,000 to slightly over £6,000. In Britain, the total quantifiable costs of osteoporosis are estimated to be £ 640 million per year. Of this, £411 million is attributable to direct medical costs (Priorities for Prevention, 1994). The quality of life after hip fracture is hardly examined at all but is generally acknowledged to be poor. One survey found that less than half of hip fracture patients who had been living in their own homes before the fracture had been able to return there. Between 12 and 40 per cent of hip fracture patients die within one year of the fracture. Most of them die within the first six months after the fracture. Of the survivors, over 50 per cent still suffer pain after six months. Only about a third had regained full mobility after six months. About 17 per cent of them had also suffered significant complications, such a wound infections (Cooney and Marottoli, 1993). Vertebral fractures can cause considerable pain, disability and inconvenience. The most common symptoms of vertebral fractures are back pain and pain and shortness of breath on exertion, a loss of height and curving of the spine and reduced rib cage and vertebral movement which causes poor respiratory function (Cook, Gordon et al. 1993).

Despite this there is very little literature which attempts to measure quality of life in osteoporosis patients in such a way that this might be incorporated into an economic evaluation. An alternative way of dealing with this lack of data, especially given the decision-making environment described before, might be to employ the method which was described above.

The prevention programme considered here is based on evidence from a randomized controlled trial. This showed that alendronate reduced the absolute risk of hip fracture by 1.1 per cent in postmenopausal women with osteoporosis and previous vertebral fractures (Black, Cummings, Karpf et al., 1996).

To demonstrate the proposed method, data is taken from a cost-utility study of alendronate for fracture prevention in 70 year-old women with a previous fracture history (Jones and Scott, 1998).

Jones and Scott constructed a model of 1,000 women aged 70 years with a previous fracture history. This model allows them to make a comparison between the outcome achieved after intervention with alendronate and no intervention. The target population of the proposed prevention programme is 1,000. The length of the prevention programme was assumed to be three years. The treatment costs were calculated as the sum of inpatient hospital costs, rehabilitation, physiotherapy and district nurse costs. The average cost per hip fracture was £4,757, which is similar to other studies' results. This was multiplied by the percentage of absolute hip fracture reduction, 1.1 per cent, to give the undiscounted treatment costs of £52,327. This is the cost the NHS would have to incur if no prevention programme was instituted.

This figure is then discounted by 5 per cent to give us the total discounted treatment costs of £44,864.[1] The third number we need to plug into our identity is the prevention costs. These are calculated as the annual drug and drug-related costs of £367 multiplied by the number of years for which the they are incurred, in this case three years, and multiplied by the target population. Thus the prevention costs associated with this particular prevention programme based on alendronate are £1,101,000. This is discounted by 5 per cent to allow for the differential timing of the cash flow. It is assumed that the prevention costs are incurred in equal parts over the course of the three years. This gives us the discounted prevention costs of the programme, £1,049,404. We can now plug these numbers into the identity to find out how much the loss of quality of life and mortality associated with hip fracture would have to be worth to each woman of the target population to make this prevention programme economically viable.

$$\text{treatment costs} \quad + \quad U_B \quad \overset{>}{=} \quad \text{prevention costs}$$

where U_B = implied monetary value associated with loss of quality of life and mortality associated with the disease the prevention programme is trying to prevent.

Thus:

$$£44,864 \quad + \quad U_B \quad \overset{>}{=} \quad £1,101,000$$

$$U_B \quad \overset{>}{=} \quad £1,101,000 - £44,864$$

This gives us a value for U_B of at least £1,004,540 over the course of the three year prevention programme. The discounted value of U_B is then at least £861,267.[2] This translates into a value for U_B of at least £ 0.79 per woman of the target population per day over the three year duration of the prevention programme. This means that the loss of utility as a result of the loss of quality of life and mortality associated with hip fracture would have to be worth at least £0.79 to each of the 1000 women who are participating per day over the course of the three year programme in order for this prevention programme to be economically worthwhile. It is now possible to compare different programmes for the same disease or different diseases on the basis of this.

Further application of this method to establish its validity for different types of diseases and different types of health care interventions is indicated before any policy recommendations can be reliably based on it.

This crude method would allow us at least a preliminary assessment of the benefits side of any given illness for which the costs have already been estimated. If it becomes clear by using this method, that the case is not clear-cut or fraught with political sensibilities, it may then be advisable to undertake a full traditional quality of life assessment.

Compared to calculating traditional cost-outcomes ratios, the 'implied values method' has the advantage of requiring less and also less-costly information. In order to calculate cost-outcomes ratios for programmes A and B, one needs to know the cost of programme A and the costs of programme B. It is also necessary to provide a measure of the outcomes of the two programmes. This is information which is not routinely available for the majority of illnesses. It may also be difficult to collect, depending on the particular illness in question. The measurement of outcomes is a time-consuming process because today's measurements require data to be collected by questionnaire, which is costly because it requires manpower both in collecting the information and for analysing it. Outcomes measurement is also an area of health economic investigation which is fraught with methodological dispute. In addition, the interpretation of most existing outcomes measurements may not be self-evident to a decision-maker who has only had the most rudimentary training in health economics. In contrast, the proposed method of 'implied values' only requires us to know the costs of the two programmes which are to be compared. This itself is not always easy but this is something the method has in common with all other forms of economic evaluation.

To summarize: crude as it may be, this method has the advantage of being cheap, quick and easy to use, as well as being easy to understand for the decision-maker without specialist health-economics knowledge. It may thus address some of the problems which were found to hinder the use of economic analyses in real-life decision-making.

Conclusion

The aim of the discipline of health economics is to inform the health care policy debate and help to produce better decisions over health care resource allocation. The existing literature leaves doubts over whether the present strategy of educating decision-makers in the techniques of economic evaluations is the most effective and efficient way of achieving this goal. The needs of the decision-maker are for relevant and timely information. By taking these needs into account, the existing techniques of economic evaluation may be improved and supplemented by new techniques. This chapter has developed one such technique and explored it with a practical example. If the discipline of health economics manages to incorporate the needs of its customers further, it may be better placed to achieve its aim of helping to improve resource allocation in the health care sector and improve the cost-effectiveness of economic evaluations.

Notes

1 The formula used for this is Present Value = cost of treatment * (1-discount rate) $^{\text{no. of years}}$.
2 The concept of 'time preference' does not only apply to financial matters but also to outcomes. The debate over whether discounting future health outcomes is likely to bias decisions against prevention programmes has not been solved satisfactorily yet. However, Drummond et al. (1997) conclude that the weight of the argument is in favour of discounting future health effects. They also suggest discounting effects and costs at the same rate.

References

Black, D.M., Cummings, S.R., Karpf, D.B. et al. (1996), 'Randomised Trial of Effect of Alendronate on Risk of Fracture in Women With Existing Vertebral Fractures: The Fracture Intervention Trial', *The Lancet*, 348, pp. 1535–41.

Cook, D., Gordon, H. et al. (1993), 'Quality of Life Issues in Women With Vertebral Fractures Due to Osteoporosis', *Arthritis and Rheumatism*, Vol. 36, No. 6, pp. 750–6.

Cooney, L.M. and Marottoli, R.A. (1993), 'Functional Decline Following Hip Fracture' in C. Christiansen (ed.), *Osteoporosis 1993*, proceedings of 4th International Symposium on Osteoporosis and Consensus Development, Riis B. Rodovre, Denmark.

Coyle, D. (1993), 'Increasing the Impact of Economic Evaluations on Health Care Decision-Making', discussion paper 108, Centre for Health Economics, University of York.

Drummond, M.F., O'Brien, B., Stoddart, G.L. and Torrance, G.W. (1997), *Methods for the Economic Evaluation of Health Care Programmes*, 2nd edn, Oxford University Press.

Klein, R. (1990), 'Research, Policy, and the National Health Service', *Journal of Health Politics, Policy and Law*, Vol. 15, No. 13.

Jones, J. and Scott, D.A. (1998), 'Cost-effectiveness of Alendronate for Fracture Prevention in Postmenopausal Women', paper presented at the Strategic Issues in Health Care Management: Managing Quality and Controlling Cost, Third International Conference, University of St Andrews, 2–4 April.

Priorities for Prevention (1994), *Osteoporosis – a Decision-making Document for Diagnosis and Prevention*, National Osteoporosis Society, Bath.

Wildavsky, A. and Tenenbaum, E. (1981), *The Politics of Mistrust*, Sage, Beverley Hills.

14 Decision Analysis: Purpose, Pitfalls and Potential

MANOUCHE TAVAKOLI,[1] HUW T.O. DAVIES[1] AND
RICHARD THOMSON[2]

1   Department of Management, St Andrews University
2   Department of Epidemiology and Public Health, School of Health Sciences,
     Medical School, Newcastle upon Tyne

Introduction

Decision-taking occurs at all levels within health systems: from macro decisions about health policy (such as organizing the financing and provision of care) through resource allocation to regional and local services, right down to decisions over specific interventions for individual patients. At whatever level decisions are taken, the decision-taker is rarely, if ever, in full possession of all the facts. Most decisions are taken against a background of incomplete and imperfect information compounded by uncertainty. Rapid escalation of technological sophistication and increased organizational complexity further complicate decision-taking in modern health services.

For some straightforward medical problems any well-trained doctor can take an appropriate decision – when the options are limited and the costs and the benefits are clear-cut. However, more frequently the correct course of action is not clear. The relationships between actions taken and desired (or unwanted) outcomes are unclear and uncertain. Indeed, even the full range of options (from which a specific course of action must be selected) may be poorly specified. Therefore, without help, doctors and patients may make poor decisions. They may be blind to certain options; may fail to attach the correct probabilities to possible events; or may fail to recognize the range of patients' concerns and weight them accordingly. Further, the rapid accumulation of medical information over recent decades may tend to obscure rather than to illuminate. The question is whether a more structured approach to decision-taking can help to overcome these problems.

Controlling Costs: Strategic Issues in Health Care Management, H.T.O. Davies, M. Tavakoli, M. Malek, A. R. Neilson (eds), Ashgate Publishing Ltd, 1999.

There is now a growing literature on improving decision-making in health care and there are several good introductions to decision analysis (Weinstein and Fineberg, 1980; Weinstein, 1981; Warner and Luce, 1982; Sox et al., 1988; Drummond et al., 1994; Clemen, 1996; Detsky et al., 1997a and 1997b; Krahn et al., 1997; Naglie et al., 1997; Naimark et al., 1997).

This chapter reviews some of the difficulties of taking appropriate clinical decisions. It then explains and examines the increasing use of decision analysis (DA) as a means of structuring complex problems. Decision-analytic techniques can be used to guide the management of individual patients or can be used to address policy questions about the use of treatment for groups of patients, for example using DA to underpin health policy and guidelines (Ginsberg and Lev, 1997; Lilford et al., 1998). This chapter is primarily concerned with the latter, i.e. the focus is on decisions aggregated across patient groups. The aim is therefore threefold:

i) to identify the potential of DA to underpin health policy and treatment guidelines;

ii) to discuss unresolved issues inherent in structuring clinical decisions using DA;

iii) to examine ways in which research evidence might help in providing the information for decision analysis.

Background

Difficulties Arising in Clinical Decision-making

In general, clinical decisions are problematic because they involve a) integration of complex information from a variety of sources; b) imperfect or incomplete information; c) the presence of uncertainty, and d) a complex interaction between the clinician and the patient, each of whom may bring widely different values to the decision. Many clinical decisions are not supported by clear evidence but nonetheless decisions have to be made even in the absence of robust information (Detsky et al., 1997a/b). These difficulties are explained below.

Complexity Technological and pharmacological progress present clinicians with a far greater range of treatment options than hitherto. Decisions may involve choosing between broad approaches (e.g. surgical or pharmacological) or deciding on the specific details of therapy (e.g. specific drug, dose, route of administration, duration and use of adjuvant therapy). In many therapeutic areas the range of choices is bewildering, involving not just branching (making choices between alternative therapies e.g. whether to treat patients with hypertension with b-blockers or diuretics) but also looping (involving revision and review of treatment in the light of patient's heath status e.g. whether to continue treatment with warfarin after a minor bleed). Crucially, the pathways between actions and outcomes are often unclear. Thus not only may the problem itself be unstructured, but any individual stakeholder may possess only an incomplete picture. Even if all the necessary information is available upon which to make a valid decision, the human mind may lack the ability to integrate effectively such complex information.

Imperfect knowledge Furthermore, rapid change in the knowledge base and the simple volume of information limit the capacity of individual clinicians to maintain and develop their skills. Thus decisions are often made with incomplete or imperfect knowledge. Clinicians may be unsure of the full impact of interventions (e.g. their side effects), the likelihood of specific outcomes, or the valuations placed by patients on those outcomes. The contextualized nature of some of the information (e.g. patient valuations of different outcome states) means that perfect information is in practice frequently unattainable.

Uncertainty Even when the problem is well understood and clearly articulated there remains the play of chance to complicate matters. The relationships between actions and outcomes are more usually probabilistic rather than deterministic. Medicine is a stochastic art. Thus chance alone can turn a good decision into a poor outcome (or vice versa). Hence the attitude of the clinician and patient (and perhaps relatives and carers) to risk will also have some bearing on what constitutes a good decision.

Trading-off different outcomes Interventions rarely have simple and purely beneficial outcomes. The choice between different interventions may be between, for example, a better chance of longevity versus increased quality of life (e.g. whether to choose radiotherapy or surgery for throat cancer). Thus one problem that clinicians and patients may face is to achieve a balance between potential treatment outcomes. Side effects not only vary from one treatment to another, but will also be tolerated differently by different individuals. Individuals may have divergent preferences in how they trade off gains in one outcome versus losses in another.

Rise in consumerism Recent years have seen a sharp rise in patient participation in the decision-making process. Patients now are much more informed, demand greater information on the benefits and risks of interventions, and expect to participate more fully in decision-making (Farrell, 1996). These shifts in patient attitudes present greater demands on clinicians when exploring treatment options.

One way of dealing with the difficulties described above is formal problem structuring and analysis using decision analysis.

The Rise of Decision Analysis (DA)

Poor information about the effectiveness of interventions can lead clinicians to base decisions on what *might* be of benefit – with little assessment of the likely magnitude of that benefit, the potential for harm, or the costs incurred. Decision analysis (DA) attempts to overcome these limitations by a clear structuring of the problem and a formal analysis of the implications of different decisions. DA is based on expected utility theory, first described by Von Neumann in the 1920s, and by the late 1940s its application in economics was widespread (Von Neumann and Morgenstern, 1947). As early as 1959, Ledley and Lusted (1959) described the intellectual basis for the application of decision analysis to medical problems, but it was not until 1967 that a published application of decision analysis for a specific clinical problem appeared (Henschke and Flehinger, 1967), using decision analysis to address the question of whether radical neck dissection was beneficial in patients with oral cancer but no tangible neck tumour. Decision analysis was used for economic and clinical evaluations through the 1970s, and in 1981 *Medical Decision Making*, a journal focused on decision analysis, began publication (Petitti, 1994).

Nature of Decision Analysis

In essence, there are five steps to a decision analysis, which are outlined below.

Step 1: Identifying and bounding the problem The first step in any decision analysis is to identify and bound the problem. This process begins with a precise identification of the main issue: what is the core decision or set of decisions that are unclear? DA then involves breaking down the problem into its component parts, the first of which is the identification of the major alternative courses of action. Other components of the problem are then identified. These are usually events that follow the first course of action and its alternative(s). The final component of the decision problem is identification of the full range of possible outcomes. Note that careful consideration of all aspects of the problem, including aims and objectives, can lead to the discovery of alternatives that were not obvious at the outset.

Step 2: Structuring the problem Much of the decision analysis is about decomposing problems in order to understand their structures, identify areas of uncertainty, and pinpoint the outcomes of value. Decomposition is the key to decision analysis: the approach is 'divide and conquer' (Clemen, 1996). The first level of decomposition is therefore to simplify the structure by breaking down the problem into clearer and smaller pieces. Subsequent decomposition (structuring) will involve careful consideration of elements of uncertainty in different parts of the problem.

Decomposition and modelling the problem are carried out through the use of influence diagrams (Nease and Owens, 1997; Owens et al., 1997), and decision trees (see Figure 14.1) as methods for building models of decision problems (Detsky et al., 1997a/b) (see case study). These are complementary graphical modelling tools. An example of a decision tree is shown in Figure 14.2.

Decision trees are built from left to right. When time is an issue, earlier events and choices are depicted on the left and later ones on the right. Trees consist of nodes, branches and outcomes.

Nodes represent points where patients can take different pathways. There are two kinds of nodes: the *decision node* represented by a square, and a *chance node* represented by a circle. Decision nodes identify points where the alternative actions are under the control of the decision-maker; chance nodes represent alternative outcomes which occur probabilistically. At any given chance node there are probabilities associated with each possible event, the sum of these probabilities of the events must equal one. Thus any chance node defines events that are mutually exclusive and jointly exhaustive.

The decision tree is completed by *branches* that emerge from nodes and define the routes that patients may take to reach specific *outcomes*.

Figure 14.1 Developing a decision tree

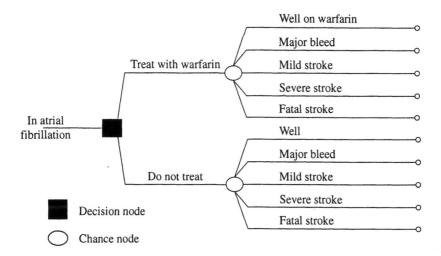

Figure 14.2 Basic decision model

Note: the treatment decision was modelled as a Markov process with duration set equal to life expectancy. This figure shows the initial treatment decision and the possible outcomes for the first year only.

Step 3: Adding information The use of decision trees creates a representation or model of the decision problem. Probability estimates are then used to reflect the uncertainty inherent in the problem. In addition, values (i.e. patient perceived utility) are attached to the various possible outcomes in order to model the way in which stakeholders may value and trade off different outcomes. Thus, the value (utility) of each outcome and the probability that each consequence will occur must be assessed in order to make the model analyzable. Such information may come from a variety of sources, e.g. randomized controlled trials, observational studies, meta-analyses and reviews, primary data collection and/or expert consensus.

Step 4: Analysis Analysis is conducted to determine the most desirable options at each of the decision nodes (e.g. best outcome, cost minimization or best cost-utility ratio depending on the objectives of the study). This is done by a method of 'folding back and averaging'. That is, the 'expected value' of each decision choice is calculated from the probabilities assigned to given routes and the utilities attached to the outcomes reached by those routes.

Case study in decision analysis

Stroke prevention in patients with atrial fibrillation

Patients with atrial fibrillation are at greatly increased risk of developing stroke, and this can be prevented by treatment with warfarin, an anticoagulant. Despite this, treatment uptake has been slow, with a demand for guidelines to support clinical decision-making. In view of this, we sought to develop 'evaluative guidelines' using decision analysis (DA) on the use of anticoagulants in patients with atrial fibrillation. Estimates of the effectiveness of anticoagulants, and of the risk of stroke and of adverse bleeding events, were derived by systematic literature review, appraisal and synthesis. Estimates of the quality of life (utility) that patients attached to the various outcomes, including stroke and the utility of being on warfarin treatment, were derived from a study of patients using the standard gamble method. The treatment decision was modelled as a Markov process.

The use of this model meant that we were able to estimate the threshold stroke risk above which patients of different ages would benefit from anticoagulation by applying the median utility values derived. However, utilities varied considerably between patients and a sensitivity analysis demonstrated that treatment decisions were very sensitive to changes in these values, particularly the patient utility of being on warfarin. Thus, patients with identical clinical characteristics would gain or lose from warfarin therapy according to their own utility for being on treatment.

Thus, guidelines based on decision analysis could aid identification of patients who would benefit from anticoagulation. A population based approach, for example using median utilities, could provide an overall population benefit, but would entail treating some patients who might have a marked disutility for treatment by warfarin, and thus who would not be optimally treated at an individual level. Thus, given the variation in patients' utilities, explicit assessment of each patient's values would ideally be required.

Step 5: Sensitivity analysis Given that most decision trees are complex, small shifts in the individual probability estimates, or in the values applied to outcomes, may lead to large changes in the likely optimal decision. Sensitivity analysis aims to address this and is used for two main reasons. First, it is a way of making the uncertainty explicit (the uncertainty associated with the analytical results), and second it is a useful method of debugging or correcting errors in the model (both structural and programming errors) (Krahn et al., 1997). Sensitivity analysis is the process of repeatedly folding back the tree using different values for probability and utility variables. It assesses the stability of any conclusion reached by the model to the assumptions made in the modelling process. The analyst looks at the robustness (or otherwise) of decision rules to variations in key model parameters. Sensitivity analysis can also identify crucial areas of information deficiency which may guide further research, and pinpoint the exact information of greatest importance in the decision-making process.

Thus decision analysis provides structure, guidance and analytical tools for thinking systematically about difficult and complex decisions. It incorporates and helps identify sources of uncertainty, presents this uncertainty in a quantitative way, and relates decision pathways to outcomes in an explicit manner.

Advantages and Potential of Decision Analysis

DA offers a number of advantages over more informal and intuitive attempts to aggregate and synthesize information relating to complex decisions. It is, however, simply an *aid* to decision-making, not a substitute for human judgment. Clinical practice remains both an art and a science.

Clarification

There will be many occasions when previous experience, training and expert opinion will be sufficient to ensure a 'good' decision, or where the consequences of alternative decisions are such that they merit a trial of therapy with subsequent patient review. However, many other clinical decisions are so complex that an explicit, systematic and quantitative approach to decisionmaking becomes an attractive option. Decision analysis offers such an approach. It does this through a thorough and logical evaluation of alternative strategies to determine the 'best' available strategy dependent on the objective of the decision-maker.

As indicated above, the linkages between actions and outcomes may not always be clear. For example, in some randomized trials the optimal decision remains uncertain because there may be several outcomes – thus the intervention may alleviate the risk of one event whilst increasing the risk of another. This may be reflected in the dropout of patients from trials because of side effects. Thus, one of the advantages of a decision analysis is that it can incorporate these various outcomes with different possible levels of risk taking account of patient characteristics (Naglie and Detsky, 1992; Lilford et al., 1998).

Quantification

Decision analysis is a quantitative approach that estimates the relative net value of different decision options. This information can then be used either to inform individual patients of the clinical decisions or to formulate policy recommendations about groups of (similar) patients. It is the explicit quantitative aggregation of data on probabilities and utilities that provides a more systematic approach to information synthesis.

Incorporation of Patient Preferences

Because each possible health outcome can be given a value, this (in theory) allows patient preferences to be built into the model. Although not without problems (see later) the DA approach can move beyond clinical outcomes to incorporate and analyze the valuation placed on those outcomes by individual patients.

Exploration

Once a DA model has been developed in executable form (usually operationalized using specialist software) the analyst can use the model to explore the decision process. This may take the form of asking a series of contingency (*'What if...?'*) questions to allow a deeper understanding of the interconnectedness of decisions and outcomes. Thus the analyst may be interested in using the model for far more than just calculation of the expected values from different choices. For example, the model may be used to promote insight into the key factors influencing decisions and thus help to inform the need for new primary research or a more elaborate DA model.

Credibility

The robustness of the model's conclusions to variations in the underlying assumptions can be assessed using sensitivity analysis. If the main decisions suggested by the model are stable in the face of variations in the underlying assumptions then the credibility of the decisions and the model is enhanced.

Explicit

DA involves an explicit problem definition that may allow open interrogation or challenge by stakeholders or third parties. Thus critics can identify parts of the model or underlying assumptions with which they disagree. The import of these can then be tested with further sensitivity analyses or model restructuring. This openness fosters clear communication and rational debate as to the model validity and utility. This in turn should lead to clearer conceptualizations, better models and, ultimately, better decision-making.

Problems with the Use of Decision Analysis

So far we have focused on the potential benefits of decision analysis. However, decision analysis is not without problems. The major concerns are outlined below.

Too Narrow a Definition of the Problem

It has been argued that the problems decision analysis attempts to solve are defined too narrowly, do not account for all possible choices or outcomes, and therefore do not reflect actual clinical practice. This is, of course, true. However, decision analysis attempts to identify the most important factors concerned with the problem, not necessarily every possibility. It helps focus the problem. The question then is not whether any particular DA is complete in the true sense, but whether its coverage makes it appropriate for the decision under examination.

Black Box Approach

Decision analysis can be very time-consuming and complex, especially in gathering the necessary data to structure the tree and perform the analysis. Despite the positive benefits of the explicitness of the approach, if clinicians are not involved in the creation and analysis of the DA model, they may be unable to comprehend the approach and may be uncomfortable with the mathematical complexities. As a result, they may distrust the outputs of a decision analysis, even if they can see the inputs. Thus the model itself may be seen as less than transparent (a black box). To a clinician the workings may be, for all practical purposes, opaque.

This is a problem similarly shared by the guidelines movement. However, in evidence-based guidelines, different recommendations can be tagged with a label indicating the strength of evidence that underlies them (e.g. meta-analysis, RCTs, observational data or expert opinion). No such ready tagging exists for DA, and therefore the recommendations that arise from DA models may appear uncertainly supported (unless one is prepared to investigate the details of the model).

The development of sophisticated and user-friendly computer software packages has simplified the process of decision analysis substantially. Also the development of computer-assisted decision-making and computer literacy amongst clinicians has increased, including the increasing use of desktop computer in general practice. Primary care computer systems may enhance the application of DA, but much has to be done before DA can become an integral part of the clinical practice of even the most devoted enthusiast.

Replacing Judgment and Dehumanizing Care

Doubts about the validity or quality of research evidence used to guide practice, compounded by concerns about the appropriateness of probabilities derived from published literature or clinician 'guesstimates', raise concerns about the application of decision analysis to an individual practice or patient. Clinicians seeking guidance on clinical decisions are concerned with whether the guidance provided by DA is robust and appropriate. Thus, it is legitimate to ask whether the implied displacement of clinical judgment by decision aids (derived from DAs) is a good thing. For example, decision analysis may be seen to dehumanize patient care by placing numerical values on health states that are essentially qualitative. Although it would be possible to tailor a DA model to an individual using their own personal preferences, in practice this is somewhat difficult, requiring separate elicitation of patient values on each clinical occasion. Thus, patient preferences included in the model are usually only included in aggregate. However, this has its own problems. It has been suggested that, in seeking the greatest good for a population, decision analysis may expose patients to treatment who were destined to do well without any medical intervention, or that some patients will inevitably be exposed to greater loss so that others may benefit from the intervention (Brett, 1982; Deber and Goel, 1990). Thus, aggregation may involve both winners and losers at both extremes of the spectrum. This is because decision models yield an average value for a cohort of like individuals, and therefore this expected value could be the result of say a small gain for everyone or a mixture of large gains for some and losses for others.

This raises ethical problems about the population based approach to guidance derived from decision analysis (although these concerns also apply to any application of population based measures of risk and benefit to individual clinical decisions). Furthermore, there is a concern that guidance emerging from DAs may be too prescriptive with the implication that to some degree clinical freedom could be played down verging on 'cookbook' medicine, a charge that has also been applied to the use of clinical guidelines.

Assumptions Regarding Composition of Utilities

In many instances the benefits associated with an outcome will be intangible, e.g. relief of pain. Even if a method for assessing such utilities is determined (which is both valid and reliable), the important question of 'whose preferences?' remains – should they be derived from doctors, patients or society? Although various methods have been proposed and used to measure utility, none is established as a gold standard. The major problem is that various techniques can give wide and at times conflicting results, due to methodological reasons. The most popular methods of measuring utility are standard gamble (SG) (Torrance, 1986 and 1987; Feeny and Torrance, 1989), health utility index (HUI) (Boyle et al., 1995; Torrance et al., 1996), and time-trade-off (TTO) (Torrance et al., 1972; Torrance, 1987). Unfortunately, different indices may give different conclusions, with different policy implications. Finally, individual preferences may vary with time or experience, which may not be reflected in the analysis (Krahn et al., 1994). However, the standard gamble technique is generally considered to be the most reliable method of utility measurement (Torrance, 1986 and 1987; Feeny and Torrance, 1989). It is based on expected utility theory, and it is the only method with an underlying theoretical base and hence could be argued that it should be the gold standard in the setting of DA.

Neglect of Process Utility

DA models examine the expected pay-off from choosing one treatment avenue rather than another. However, there may be important asymmetry between the routes being compared. For example, choosing to put a patient on a drug therapy is a decision that can be kept under constant review and rescinded if changes in the patient's health status warrant. However, a decision to proceed with surgery offers no possibilities of going back. Thus there may be process utility to both patient and doctor in keeping their options open. DAs that focus on net expected values ignore the utility gained from options retained. Decision models may therefore fail to capture factors that matter to patients. Thus, there are concerns that patients preferences do not always adhere to expected utility theory, which underlies DA, when choosing between risky options (Ubel and Loewenstein, 1997).

Improving the Link between Primary Research and DA

One of the major difficulties in developing DA models is in identifying high quality (reliable and valid) data to include in the model (Detsky et al., 1997a/b). A clearer understanding of data issues by those developing and funding primary clinical research may help to develop better data resources for DA. Several types of research-derived data are needed.

- *Epidemiological data:* data are needed on the risk of subsequent outcomes in the natural history of disease. For example, we need to know the absolute risk of stroke in patients who have atrial fibrillation if they are untreated to compare to the outcomes with patients who are treated with warfarin to prevent stroke. Ideally this data should come, not from trial control groups, but from general population inception cohort studies. Such absolute risk data is sparse in the epidemiological literature, which tends to concentrate on aetiological studies primarily concerned with relative risks. Inception cohorts of patients under routine treatment are also necessary to assess the likely risk of adverse events in routine practice, for example for bleeding risks with warfarin anticoagulation therapy.
- *Effectiveness data:* these are essential to estimate putative treatment benefits and so provide the probabilities of certain outcomes given specific decisions over therapeutic interventions. Ideally, such information on effectiveness would come from high quality RCTs and meta-analyses, preferably with pre-defined subgroups to allow the effectiveness in different groups to be assessed to support targeting of treatment to those most likely to benefit. Access to these studies is improving, although some concerns remain over the highly selected nature of trial participants and the applicability of trial circumstances to routine practice.
- *Health state valuation data:* estimating the utilities that patients attach to specific outcomes is problematic and contentious (whose values? what method of elicitation?). There remains a lack of good studies in this area and those that do exist are usually small-scale (tens of patients compared to the thousands that may feature in RCTs or meta-analyses). Better patient preference studies may help provide a firmer basis for the utilities used in DA models.

Risk and benefit estimates from epidemiological studies and clinical trials are of necessity probabilistic in nature. That is, they must be derived by aggregating across patient groups. In contrast, patient preferences are individualistic and patient-specific. Using aggregates of these may be inappropriate.

Clear conceptualizations of problematic decisions using a DA approach may help clarify the data required from primary research. If such data needs are clearly articulated, this in turn may feed into future study design. Unfortunately, such integration of primary research and DA is not at present usual – although the potential is clear.

Concluding Remarks

DA is useful in structuring and simplifying complex problems into smaller and more manageable pieces facilitating quantitative analysis. It is only an aid to solve complex problems in a systematic way with risk incorporated in the decision-making process under the background of imperfect information and uncertainty; it is not designed to replace the decision-maker's judgment. Its potential lies with its explicitness, and the ease with which it can be used to integrate complex data. It allows incorporation of patients' preferences, and of outcomes with different levels of risk, and promotes insight into the key factors influencing decisions. Consequently, it may also inform the need for new primary research or for construction of a more advanced DA model. The integration of primary research and DA has a large potential for enriching the applications of DA and better identification of research needs.

However, certain problems remain to be overcome. There is the issue of whether to use DA to create better informed guidelines for populations of patients (Lilford et al., 1998), or to derive means of eliciting and incorporating individual patient values, either explicitly or implicitly (Dowie, 1996; Dowie, 1997). Furthermore, the acceptability and the wider application of DAs will largely depend on the view taken by the clinicians of their use in medical practice. This may require direct participation of clinicians at the start of developing decision trees in order to increase understanding and transparency of both the problem and the process leading to the final outcome, and to ensure that decision models reflect the realities of clinical practice. Lessons from the guidelines movement should tell us that, if DAs are to gain wider credibility and use, potential users will need closer involvement in their development, and ways will need to be found to express both the uncertainty embodied in their construction and the quality of the evidence incorporated.[1]

Note

1   The authors wish to thank David Parkin, Angela Robinson, Mark Sudlow, and Martin Eccles for permission to use the case study on warfarin and for their contributions in discussing the issues around DA that have helped with the preparation of this paper.

References

Analytica. Lumina Decision Systems, Inc., 4984 El Camino Real, Suit 105, Los Altos, CA 94022.

Boyle, M.H., Furlong, W., Feeny, D., Torrance, G.W. and Hatcher, J. (1995), 'Reliability of the Health Utilities Index – Mark III used in the 1991 cycle 6 Canadian General Social Survey Health Questionnaire', *Quality of Life Research*, 4, pp. 249–57.

Brett, A.S. (1982), 'Hidden Ethical Issues in Clinical Decision Analysis', *New England Journal of Medicine*, 305, pp. 1150–2.

Clemen, R.T. (1996), *Making Hard Decisions: An Introduction to Decision Analysis*, Duxbury Press, London.

DATA: Decision Analysis by TreeAge. TreeAge Software, Inc., P.O. Box 329, Boston, MA 02199.

Deber, R. and Goel, V. (1990), 'Using Explicit Decision Rules to Manage Issues of Justice, Risk, and Ethics in Decision Analysis: When is it not rational to maximize expected utility?', *Medical Decision Making*, 10, pp. 181–94.

Detsky, A.S., Naglie, G., Krahn, M.D., Naimark, D. and Redelmeier, D.A. (1997), 'Primer on Medical Decision Analysis: Part 1 – Getting Started', *Medical Decision Making*, 17, pp. 123–5.

Detsky, A.S., Naglie, G., Krahn, M.D., Naimark, D. and Redelmeier, D.A. (1997), Primer on Medical Decision Analysis: Part 2 – Building a Tree, *Medical Decision Making*, 17, pp. 126–35.

Dowie, J. (1996), 'Evidence Based, Cost-effective and Preference-driven Medicine: Decision analysis based medical decision making is the pre-requisite', *Journal of Health Services Research and Policy*, 1, pp. 104–13.

Dowie, J. (1997), 'Decision Analysis in Guideline Development and Clinical Practice: The "Clinical Guidance Tree"' in: H. Selbman (ed.), *Guidelines for Guidelines in Health Care: Papers and Reports of the WHO Conference on Guidelines in Health Care Practice*, Nomos-Verlag, Baden-Baden.

DPL: Decision Programming Language. Applied Decision Analysis, Inc., 2710 Sand Hill Road, Menlo Park, CA 94025.

Drummond, M.F., Stoddart, G.L. and Torrance, G.W. (1994), *Methods for the Economic Evaluation of Health Care Programmes*, Oxford University Press, Oxford.

Farrell, C. (1996), *Health Care Partnerships: Debates and strategies for increasing patient involvement in health care and health services*, King's Fund, London.

Feeny, D.H. and Torrance, G.W. (1989), 'Incorporating Utility-based Quality-of-life Assessment Measures in Clinical Trials. Two Examples', *Medical Care*, 27, pp. S190–204.

Ginsberg, G.M. and Lev, B. (1997), 'Cost-Benefit Analysis of Riluzole for the Treatment of Amyotrophic Lateral Sclerosis', *Pharmacoeconomics*, 12, pp. 578–84.

Henschke, U.K. and Flehinger, B.J. (1967), 'Decision Theory in Cancer Therapy', *Cancer*, 20, pp. 1819–26.

Krahn, M.D., Mahoney, J.E., Eckman, M.H. et al. (1994), 'Screening for Prostate Cancer: A decision analytic view', *Journal of American Medical Association*, 272, pp. 781–6.

Krahn, M.D., Naglie, G., Naimark, D., Redelmeier, D.A. and Detsky, A.S. (1997), 'Primer on Medical Decision Analysis: Part 4 – Analyzing the Model and Interpreting the Results', *Medical Decision Making*, 17, pp. 142–51.

Ledley, R.S. and Lusted, L.B. (1959), 'Reasoning Foundations of Medical Diagnosis: Symbolic logic, probability, and value theory aid our understanding of how physicians reason', *Science*, 130, pp. 9–21.

Lilford, R.J., Pauker, S.G., Braunholtz, D.A. and Chard, J. (1998), 'Getting Research Findings into Practice: Decision analysis and the implementation of research findings', *British Medical Journal*, 317, pp. 405–9.

Naglie, G., Krahn, M.D., Naimark, D., Redelmeier, D.A. and Detsky, A.S. (1997), 'Primer on Medical Decision Analysis: Part 3 – Estimating Probabilities and Utilities', *Medical Decision Making*, 17, pp. 136–41.

Naglie, I.G. and Detsky, A.S. (1992), 'Treatment of Chronic Nonvalvular Atrial Fibrillation in the Elderly: A decision analysis', *Medical Decision Making*, 12, pp. 239–49.

Naimark, D., Krahn, M.D., Naglie, G., Redelmeier, D.A. and Detsky, A.S. (1997), 'Primer on Medical Decision Analysis: Part 5 – Working with Markov Processes', *Medical Decision Making*, 17, pp. 152–9.

Nease, R.F. and Owens, D.K. (1997), 'Use of Influence Diagrams to Structure Medical Decisions', *Medical Decision Making*, 17, pp. 263–75.

Owens, D.K., Shachter, R.D. and Nease, R.F. (1997), 'Representation and Analysis of Medical Decision Problems with Influence Diagrams', *Medical Decision Making*, 17, pp. 241–62.

Petitti, D. (1994), *Meta-Analysis, Decision Analysis, and Cost-Effectiveness Analysis: Methods for Quantitative Synthesis in Medicine*, Oxford University Press, Oxford.

Precision Tree. Palisade Corporation, 31 Decker Road, Newfield, NY 14867.

Sox, H.C., Blatt, M.A., Higgins, M.C. and Marton, K.I. (1988), *Medical Decision Making*, Butterworh Publishers, Stoneham, Maryland.

Torrance, G.W. (1986), 'Measurement of Health State Utilities for Economic Appraisal: A review, *Journal of Health Economics*, 5, pp. 1–30.

Torrance, G.W. (1987), 'Utility Approach to Measuring Health-related Quality of Life', *Journal of Chronic Disease*, 40, pp. 593–603.

Torrance, G.W., Feeny, D.H., Furlong, W.J., Barr, R.D., Zhang, Y. and Wang, Q. (1996), 'Multiattribute Utility Function for a Comprehensive Health Status Classification System. Health Utilities Index Mark 2', *Medical Care*, 34, pp. 702–22.

Torrance, G.W., Thomas, W.H. and Sackett, D.L. (1972), 'A Utility Maximization Model for Evaluation of Health Care Programs', *Health Services Research*, 7, pp. 118–33.

Ubel, P.A. and Loewenstein, G. (1997), 'The Role of Decision Analysis in Informed Consent: Choosing between intuition and systematically', *Social Science & Medicine*, 44, pp. 647–56.

Von Neumann, J. and Morgenstern, O. (1947), *Theory of Games and Economic Theory*, Wiley, New York.

Warner, K.E. and Luce, B.R. (1982), *Cost-benefit and Cost-effectiveness in Health Care: Principles, practice and potential*, Health Administration Press, Ann Arbor, Michigan.

Weinstein, M.C. (1981), 'Economic Assessment of Medical Practices and Technologies', *Medical Decision Making*, 1, pp. 309–30.

Weinstein, M.C. and Fineberg, H.V. (1980), *Clinical Decision Analysis*, W.B. Saunders Company, Harcourt Brace Jovanovich, Inc., Philadelphia.

CONCLUDING REMARKS

15 Strategic Issues in Health Care Management – Future Challenges

CHARLES NORMAND

Department of Public Health and Policy, London School of Hygiene and Tropical Medicine

Improving Quality and Controlling Costs

Health care systems around the world are struggling to find the best combination of outcomes, quality of care, efficiency, and cost. The current debate in the USA about managed care offers many interesting insights into the issues. Between 1992 and 1997 the proportion of employees insured under managed care plans rose from 36 per cent to 85 per cent, and there have recently been signs of a backlash against the associated (visible) constraints on access to care (Timmins 1998). The early signs are that the temporary success in controlling costs has ended. Demands for choice of provider, direct access to specialist services and better experience of health care for patients are generating pressures for increased expenditure. This is in addition to other pressures for increased costs, such as the ageing population and increasing capacity to benefit from interventions. Governments and employers are expressing increasing concern about the effects of spending on health care programmes on economic growth and competitiveness.

The major challenges for management in the health sector are to understand these issues, distinguish between the real and imagined problems, have insight into the measurement and definitional questions and be able to identify which of the issues are tractable. It is not possible in this chapter to deal with all of the important questions, and instead the focus will be on a few areas where it may be useful to concentrate. In particular the discussion will concentrate on

Controlling Costs: Strategic Issues in Health Care Management, H.T.O. Davies, M. Tavakoli, M. Malek, A. R. Neilson (eds), Ashgate Publishing Ltd, 1999.

quality of care, public participation in health care decision making, ageing, incentives, patient choice and control of costs.

Making Sense of the Quality Debate

It is self-evident that quality of health care has many dimensions, and measurement of quality many pitfalls. In the health sector in the 1990s a movement has emerged of policy makers and researchers concerned with outcomes. Quality is increasingly being defined in terms of success in achieving health gain. There are good reasons to support this clear focus on what is achieved in health care. For many treatments it is possible to tell a plausible story about significant health gain, but the realized benefits may be of quite limited value. Similarly, new approaches (such as minimally invasive surgery) seem to be less risky than conventional operations, but may in fact be associated with higher risks. Moving from measurement of inputs and process to outcomes replaces conjecture about effectiveness with data on what is achieved. While there are reasons to encourage this change of focus, it is important not to lose sight of the importance of the quality of the processes of care. The majority of patients treated in most health systems are elderly, and in many cases the period of treatment is long. Better quality of life associated with the period of treatment can be important in such circumstances. In some instance there may be a trade-off between better processes and better final outcomes, especially in cancer treatments, where some of the more effective drugs are not well tolerated by patients. The main point is that we should really measure quality over the whole period in which health and quality of life are affected, and not simply focus on the final outcome of treatment.

The measurement of quality of care has both conceptual and practical problems. When comparisons are being made it is important, but very difficult to control for differences in case mix. A recent study of neonatal care found that there were incompatible systems of measurement of case severity (Mugford et al., 1998), and that these were not applied consistently. Particular problems arise when indicators used to measure quality are open to different interpretations. For example poor quality of services may lead to readmission of the patient to hospital. It is therefore a plausible quality indicator. However, it is desirable to discharge patients as early as possible to minimize infection risk, even if this means that a larger number will have to be readmitted. Thus high readmission rates may be associated with high quality of care. In order for readmission rates to be a useful indicator of quality it is crucial to know who is readmitted, and whether it would be feasible and desirable to prevent the readmission.

Another common difficulty is that indicators used for measurement of quality can easily be manipulated. There is a social science law, normally credited to Charles Goodhart, that any observed relationship used for policy purposes breaks down. If a quality indicator is derived from (for example) the observation that low infection rates are associated with short stays in hospital, then short length of stay might be chosen as a quality indicator. However, there is then the risk that managers and clinicians can change the length of stay, but not achieve any change in the infection rate.

The implication of this general difficulty is that measuring quality of care, as with many other similar tasks, must be understood as a constantly evolving process. Tools for measurement have a life cycle. First they are identified, developed and used, and then they decay and should be allowed to die. Development of measures is a continuous rather than discreet process, with new tools needed as old ones lose their usefulness. This has the major drawback that it can be difficult to monitor quality changes over time, since methods of assessment change, and may not allow trends to be identified. But little can be done to avoid the need frequently to change the measurement tools. A good analogy is the use of waiting lists to measure excess demand for health services. As has often been pointed out, the length of a waiting list reflects policy to put patients on as well as to take them off. Any competent manager can choose (within limits) the length of the list.

A further and sometimes (associated) difficulty is to ensure that it is understood that the purpose of quality measurement is to improve services. There is a danger that the agenda becomes taken over by the quality measurement technicians. Quality assurance has become an industry, with many people having vested interest in processes and approaches. There are good reasons for using well established and tested tools, but this also means that it is common for tools to be used even when they are not well suited to the tasks. There are obvious dangers that the agenda ceases to be driven by the need to improve quality of care. There is also the danger that clinicians and managers, who should be the users of quality measurements become alienated from the process, and do not use the results, however robust they may be.

There is always a trade-off between some dimensions of quality of care and the volume of services that can be provided within any given resources. A frequent problem in managing the development of quality is when this trade-off is ignored or denied. The issue is conceptually simple. Optimal quality of care will seldom be care of the maximum possible quality, but will be the level at which the additional gains in welfare from higher quality exactly offset the losses from any reduction in quantity. In other words, at the margin resources provide equal benefits whether for increased quantity or quality of care. Once again there are formidable difficulties in measurement here.

This point is difficult to sell in any public debate. The point is that while it is possible to do more to improve quality but it is not, overall, desirable to do so. Many of those who work in quality assurance start from the idea that the aim is continuous improvements, and that the aim is to maximize rather than optimize the quality. This point will be developed further in the discussion of cost control.

Public Participation in Decision-making

Experience of public participation in setting priorities in health care can be frightening (Bowling et al., 1993). Problems exist both in what processes should be used and in ensuring some consistency of the results.

It is very difficult to carry on a debate about health care priorities when little is known by the public (and sometimes professionals) about the effectiveness of much of the care provided. It is also difficult to discuss rationing with people who deny the existence of or need for rationing. It remains respectable in many countries to claim that all interventions and care that improve health or quality of life for patients should be available, regardless of cost. Of course, when presented with *reductio ad absurdum* cases of very high costs and only very small benefits few would choose to make a service available, but the general failure of the political and public debate to engage on the existence (and desirability) of rationing is a hindrance. The result is normally to encourage linguistic contortions in any discussion of scarcity and setting priorities in access to care.

A problem is how best to educate those involved in decision making. On one hand it is clearly necessary for people involved in setting priorities to have some understanding of illness, treatment and outcomes if they are to participate usefully. However, information is not neutral, and it is common for people who are well informed to 'go native', that is to take on the views of experts and managers. Thus the informed participant ceases to represent the public view.

A particular problem is how best to achieve the use of clear principles and consistency in the choices made. Certain public prejudices are well known – people generally favours services for children, those that use exciting technology and those that extend life, and do not consider services for those with HIV and preventive services to be a high priority. Of course in some cases this might lead to choices that maximize health improvements, but research evidence shows that there are normally quite marginal gains in health from many uses of complex technologies.

A further difficulty in achieving useful public participation is the probabilistic nature of many health benefits, and the difficulty most people have in using such data. Most people would agree to deny treatment that generates with certainty a very short extension of life at very high cost. But when the same (small) average gain is made up of some people with no gain and a few people whose benefits will be very large, it is more difficult to gain a consensus to deny access to care.

Really the lesson from attempts to involve the public in decision making is that it is not easy to achieve, the results may not be consistent, and the views expressed may not be those that would achieve objectives of longer life and better health. Some measures to increase consistency, such as providing information and guidance may reduce the public belief that real participation is involved.

Population Ageing and the Quantity and Quality of Care

The demand for control of costs of health care comes in part from concern about the growth of demand for care. Two sources of cost increases are normally cited – the development of new care technologies (with the associated possibility of providing effective care where this was not previously possible) and the effects of ageing. It is important for managers to be clear about these two sets of issues. Technical developments *per se* cannot increase and should decrease the cost of care (Normand, 1998). For example, as technology allows shorter stays in hospital, this leads to lower costs. There is now some emerging evidence that the unit costs of acute health care are indeed falling – mainly from shorter patients stays in hospital and more day procedures. The problems of rising costs spring not from the higher cost of existing services, but from doing more. Whether or not this is desirable depends on the cost and effectiveness of the additional services. It is important to see technical change as an opportunity, but not in itself as a cost. Expansion of services without evaluation of costs and benefits may lead to unjustified additional costs. There are some occasions when a new technology offers no improvement in the service, but increases costs. For example, a new X-ray machine may offer the possibility of more complex images, but if the need is for simple ones it may simply raise costs. Under these (probably quite common) circumstances the source of the higher cost is the use of over-specified equipment.

The effects of ageing are interesting and often misunderstood. It is important to understand two points that are well supported by the data (Mendelson and Schwartz, 1993; Barer et al., 1995; Busse and Schwartz, 1996). First, proximity to death is a much more significant factor in acute health care costs than age. Second, after controlling for cause of death, the additional health care costs associated with the last year of life fall with age. The intuition behind this is simple – more effort is made to cure disease in younger people, and for older people the management tends to be more conservative, and may be mainly palliative. There may also be systematic discrimination on age for some treatments. Although the need for long term care, and management of some chronic conditions is likely to rise, there is no reason to be very worried about ageing *per se* as a source of higher costs, and there may be some reduction at least in acute care costs.

What is clear from studies is that the growth of costs of care for elderly people is mainly caused by more services per person, and only to a lesser extent from growing numbers of people receiving services (Barer et al., 1995). It may be that advances in medicine offer disproportionate opportunities to treat conditions common in old age (and this would not be surprising given the concentration of morbidity in this population), but growing costs are not simply a passive response to a growing number of elderly people in the population. It is not clear what is the typical effect of ageing is on use of long term nursing home and social care, and in most countries the overall burden is rising, but again it is difficult to identify the effects of the growing elderly population separate from the effects of different decisions about what is appropriate care.

The overall conclusions from analysis of the data on ageing are that age itself is not of great importance, and that the direct effects on costs of ageing are likely to be gradual. In the case of some acute services the effect will be to reduce costs. It is likely that attitudes to providing services for elderly people will change, but the main source of rising costs are decisions to provide treatment not the changes in numbers of people needing them.

Appropriate Incentives and Control of Costs

One of the great challenges for health services managers is to combine development of measures to build quality and legitimacy with keeping costs under control. The need to control costs comes both from the an objective of avoiding the macroeconomic consequences of high health care costs, and the fact that the various types of market failure in health care tend to mean normal market mechanisms cannot control costs adequately.

As argued above, there is a trade-off between some features of quality and cost. While no-one would argue against cost-less improvements in quality, it is important to consider improvements in the processes and outcomes of care against the effect on cost, and therefore the volume of care that can be provided at any level of resources. A serious risk is that too much focus on the quality of care might weaken the determination and incentives to control costs.

Experience of different approaches to the control of cost shows that methods that limit the overall budget, and have a 'single pipe' through which resources must flow, tend to be most effective. Other systems to control cost through more micro approaches are generally less successful. However, some features of good cost control may conflict with some of quality of care. Systems that are cash constrained often do their rationing in ways that produce visible excess demand for care People can afford the price of services (since they are free or nearly free), and are eligible for care, but wait a long time or fail to gain access. Other systems of rationing make it clearer who does and who does to have the right to receive care. There is also a tendency for systems that are very cash constrained to ignore process quality, since this can be more easily sacrificed than volume or final outcome.

One aspect of quality that is difficult to develop in cash constrained systems is patient choice. Again this is not a simple concept. Is it choice that is desired, or do people just want to get their own way? Reforms in central and eastern Europe have put great emphasis on more choice, but it is not clear that people really wanted more choice – many probably just want better services. Given what we know about problems of information asymmetry, and other aspects of market failure, we need to be careful to ensure that development of choice is in aspects of care where the patient can make a useful contribution, and where the patient values this role. If what is wanted is better treatment, and being treated in a more humane way, patient choice as normally described my be of limited relevance.

Some Conclusions

The chapters in this volume and the companion volume (Davies et al., 1999) cover a wide range of approaches to improving the management and delivery of care. The aims are to look at the challenges facing the planners and managers of services, and to see how better quality and more acceptable care can be provided. This is generally an important aim. However, it is the purpose of this chapter to emphasize that many issues in health care are highly complex, that paradoxical findings are common, and that a very good understanding of the health care environment is needed if we are to be sure that the measures and approaches taken have a good chance of making care more appropriate, of better quality and likely to produce better outcomes, while allowing the system to remain financially sustainable in the face of some growing challenges.

References

Barer, M.L., Evans, R.G. and Hertzman, C. (1995), 'Avalanche or Glacier?: Health Care and the Demographic Rhetoric', *Canadian Journal on Aging*, 14, 2, pp. 193–224.

Bowling, A., Jacobson, B. and Southgate, L. (1993), 'Health Service Priorities: Explorations in consultation of the public and health professional on priority setting in an inner London health district', *Social Science and Medicine*, 37, 7, pp. 851–7.

Busse, R. and Schwartz, F.W. (1997), 'Hospital Utilisation Per Year of Life is not Increasing with Higher Life Expectancy: Results from a 7 year cohort study in Germany' in R. Busse and F.W. Schwartz, *Leistungen und Kosten der medizinischen Versorgung im letzten Lebensjahr*, final project report for the German Ministry of Education, Science, Research and Technology, pp. 8–20, Medizinische Hochschule Hannover.

Davies, H.T.O., Malek, M., Neilson, A.R. and Tavakoli, M. (1999), *Managing Quality: Strategic Issues in Health Care Management*, Ashgate Publishing Ltd., Aldershot.

Mendelson, D.N. and Schwartz, W.B. (1993), 'Effects of Aging and Population Growth on Health Care Costs', *Health Affairs*, 12, 1, pp. 119–25.

Mugford, M., Howard, S., O'Neill, C., Dunn, A., Zelisko, M., Normand, C., Malek, M., Hey, E., Halliday, H. and Tarnow-Mordi, W. (1998), 'Limited Comparability of Classifications of Levels of Neonatal Care in UK Units', *Archives of Disease in Childhood*, 78, 3, SISI F179–F184.

Normand, C. (1998), 'Ten Popular Health Economic Fallacies', *Journal of Public Health Medicine*, 20, 2, pp. 129–32.

Timmins, N. (1998), 'The US Model: System heads back into crisis', *Financial Times*, 2 July.

List of Contributors

Ron Akehurst

Trent Institute for Health Services Research – Sheffield Unit, School of Health and Related Research, Sheffield University

Steve Beard

Trent Institute for Health Services Research – Sheffield Unit, School of Health and Related Research, Sheffield University

Dick Beath

Avon Health Authority, Bristol

Alan Brennan

Trent Institute for Health Services Research – Sheffield Unit, School of Health and Related Research, Sheffield University

Elisabeth Brock

Department of Management, University of St Andrews

Neill Calvert

Trent Institute for Health Services Research – Sheffield Unit, School of Health and Related Research, Sheffield University

Yéroboye Camara

Ministry of Health, Conakry, Guinea

Ewart R. Carson

Centre for Measurement and Information in Medicine, City University, London

---

Controlling Costs: Strategic Issues in Health Care Management, H.T.O. Davies, M. Tavakoli, M. Malek, A. R. Neilson (eds), Ashgate Publishing Ltd, 1999.

Jim Chilcott — *Trent Institute for Health Services Research – Sheffield Unit, School of Health and Related Research, Sheffield University*

Nesrin E. Çilingiroglu — *Department of Public Health, School of Medicine, Hacettepe University, Ankara*

Michael Clark — *Centre for Health Services Studies, Warwick Business School, University of Warwick, Coventry*

John E. Clarke — *Scottish Homes, Edinburgh*

Sékou Condé — *Ministry of Health, Conakry, Guinea*

Derek G. Cramp — *Centre for Measurement and Information in Medicine, City University, London*

Bart Criel — *Department of Public Health, Institute of Tropical Medicine, Antwerp, Belgium*

Huw T.O. Davies — *Department of Management, University of St Andrews*

Xavier de Béthune — *Department of Public Health, Institute of Tropical Medicine, Antwerp, Belgium*

Sheila Ellwood — *Aston Business School, Aston University*

Moira Fischbacher — *Department of Management Studies, University of Glasgow Business School*

Joy Fletcher — *Centre for Health Services Studies, Warwick Business School, University of Warwick, Coventry*

Arthur Francis — *University of Bradford Management Centre*

Michel Gody	*Ministry of Health, Conakry, Guinea*
Jackie Green	*Avon Health Authority, Bristol*
Xiao-Ming Huang	*GE Capital Global Consumer Finance Ltd, Leeds*
John Hutton	*MEDTAP International, London*
Jan Jones	*Scottish Health Purchasing Information Centre, Aberdeen*
Mo Malek	*Department of Management, University of St Andrews*
Alan Maynard	*York Health Policy Group, University of York*
Chris McCabe	*Trent Institute for Health Services Research – Sheffield Unit, School of Health and Related Research, Sheffield University*
Siobhan E. McClelland	*School of Health Science, University of Wales Swansea*
Alastair Morgan	*Centre for Measurement and Information in Medicine, City University, London*
Aileen R. Neilson	*Department of Management, University of St Andrews*
Charles Normand	*Department of Public Health and Policy, London School of Hygiene and Tropical Medicine*
Suzy Paisley	*Trent Institute for Health Services Research – Sheffield Unit, School of Health and Related Research, Sheffield University*

Nick Payne   *Trent Institute for Health Services Research – Sheffield Unit, School of Health and Related Research, Sheffield University*

Ceri J. Phillips   *School of Health Science, University of Wales Swansea*

Abdul V. Roudsari   *Centre for Measurement and Information in Medicine, City University, London*

David A. Scott   *Scottish Health Purchasing Information Centre, Aberdeen*

Moussa Sylla   *PRIMA (Projet de recherche sur le Partage des Risques-Maladie), Medicus Mundi Belgium, Kissidougou, Guinea*

Ala Szczepura   *Centre for Health Services Studies, Warwick Business School, University of Warwick, Coventry*

Manouche Tavakoli   *Department of Management, St Andrews University*

Richard Thomson   *Department of Epidemiology and Public Health, School of Health Sciences, Medical School, University of Newcastle*

Sue Ward   *Trent Institute for Health Services Research – Sheffield Unit, School of Health and Related Research, Sheffield University*

Mohammed Lamine Yansané   *PSR (Projet Santé Rurale), GTZ (Gesellschaft fûr Technische Zusammenarbeit) and Ministry of Health, Conakry, Guinea*

Printed and bound by CPI Group (UK) Ltd, Croydon, CR0 4YY

21/10/2024

01777082-0004